CW00666721

Routledge Philosophy GuideBook to

Merleau-Ponty and *Phenomenology of Perception*

Maurice Merleau-Ponty is hailed as one of the key philosophers of the twentieth century. *Phenomenology of Perception* is his most famous and influential work and an essential text for anyone seeking to understand phenomenology. In this GuideBook Komarine Romdenh-Romluc introduces and assesses:

- Merleau-Ponty's life and the background to his philosophy
- the key themes and arguments of *Phenomenology of Perception*
- the continuing importance of Merleau-Ponty's work to philosophy

Merleau-Ponty and Phenomenology of Perception is an ideal starting point for anyone coming to his great work for the first time. It is essential reading for students of Merleau-Ponty, phenomenology and related subjects such as art and cultural studies.

Komarine Romdenh-Romluc is a lecturer in the Department of Philosophy at the University of Nottingham.

ROUTLEDGE PHILOSOPHY GUIDEBOOKS

Edited by Tim Crane and Jonathan Wolff,
University of Cambridge and University College London

Routledge Philosophy GuideBook to

Merleau-Ponty and *Phenomenology of Perception*

Komarine
Romdenh-Romluc

Routledge
Taylor & Francis Group

LONDON AND NEW YORK

First published 2011
by Routledge
2 Park Square, Milton Park, Abingdon, Oxon OX14 4RN

Simultaneously published in the USA and Canada
by Routledge
711 Third Avenue, New York, NY 10017 (8th Floor)

Routledge is an imprint of the Taylor & Francis Group, an informa business

Typeset in Garamond by Taylor & Francis Books
Printed and bound in Great Britain by TJ International Ltd, Padstow,
Cornwall

British Library Cataloguing in Publication Data
A catalogue record for this book is available from the British Library

Library of Congress Cataloging in Publication Data
Romdenh-Romluc, Komarine.
Routledge philosophy guidebook to Merleau-Ponty and Phenomenology of
Perception by Komarine Romdenh-Romluc.
p. cm. – (Routledge philosophy guidebooks)
Includes bibliographical references (p.) and index.
1. Merleau-Ponty, Maurice, 1908–1961. Phénoménologie de la perception.
2. Perception (Philosophy) 3. Phenomenology. I. Title.
B2430.M3763P47365 2010
142'.7–dc22
2010008205

ISBN13: 978-0-415-34314-5 (hbk)
ISBN13: 978-0-415-34315-2 (pbk)
ISBN13: 978-0-203-48289-6 (ebk)

For my parents

CONTENTS

ACKNOWLEDGEMENTS

Many people have taught me about Merleau-Ponty's philosophy, and helped me to understand his *Phenomenology of Perception*. My greatest debt is to two teachers: David Bell, whose lectures on Husserl first piqued my interest in Merleau-Ponty, and Bert Dreyfus, whose work on Merleau-Ponty first enabled me to find a way into his thought. I have also greatly benefited from discussion with Taylor Carman, Bert Dreyfus, Sean Kelly, Matthew Kennedy, B. Scot Rousse, Charles Siewert, Jonathan Tallant, Dan Watts and Mark Wrathall. I would like to thank all of them for their comments and advice. In addition, I am grateful to audiences at Barnard College and the universities of Hull, Lancaster, Nottingham and Warwick for helpful discussions of the material contained herein. I completed this GuideBook during a period of research leave, which was jointly funded by the University of Nottingham and the Mind Association. I am grateful to both institutions for their support.

INTRODUCTION

Maurice Merleau-Ponty was born on 14 May 1908 in Rochefort-sur-Mer, a town on the west coast of France. His father was killed early in the First World War, whilst serving as an artillery officer. Merleau-Ponty's mother then moved the family to Paris, where she raised him, along with his sister and brother. Merleau-Ponty attended school at the Lycée Janson-de-Sailly and the Lycée Louis-le-Grand, before attending the École Normale Supérieure (ENS) from 1926 until 1930, where he obtained his Agrégation de Philosophie. Upon graduating from the ENS, he completed a year of military service, before taking up a teaching post at the Lycée de Beauvais for two years until 1933. From 1933 until 1934, Merleau-Ponty was the recipient of a bursary from the Centre National de la Recherche Scientifique, which allowed him to pursue his research on perception. He then returned to teaching, and held positions at the Lycée de Chartres, the ENS and the Lycée Condorcet. Merleau-Ponty served in the infantry during the Second World War until the French forces were defeated by the Nazis and he was demobilised. He was then involved in setting up a small intellectual Resistance group with Sartre, called Socialisme et Liberté, which was somewhat ineffective, as Sartre himself admitted. Merleau-Ponty obtained his Docteur ès lettres in 1945 on the basis of two dissertations: *La Structure du Comportement* (*The Structure of Behaviour*) (1942), and *Phénoménologie de la Perception* (*Phenomenology of Perception*) (1945). It was also in 1945 that Merleau-Ponty, Sartre and de Beauvoir founded the literary and political journal, *Les Temps Modernes*. Merleau-Ponty played an important role in the journal, but did not wish to publicise his involvement. He was named as a member of the editorial board, but he did not sign his name to the many editorials that he wrote. Between 1946 and 1949, he taught at the University of Lyon and ENS. In 1949 he was appointed to the Chair of Child Psychology at the Sorbonne. In 1952 he took up the Chair of Philosophy at Collège de France. He was the youngest person to have been appointed to the position, which he held until his death. Around the time of this appointment, Merleau-Ponty fell out with Sartre and de Beauvoir over their increasingly divergent political views and resigned from *Les Temps Modernes*. There was some reconciliation between them before his death. Merleau-Ponty died of a heart attack on 3 May 1961 in Paris. He was aged 53.

Merleau-Ponty's philosophy is concerned with the nature of consciousness, the world and their relation. He holds that our current conceptions of these things are flawed. His aim in the *Phenomenology of Perception* is to show us this and provide new ways of thinking about them. Merleau-Ponty identifies two opposing notions of consciousness that characterise our thinking about it. One construes consciousness as radically different from the world. Merleau-Ponty sees both the Cartesian soul and the Kantian Transcendental Ego as instances of this conception of consciousness. The other view identifies consciousness with some lump of physical matter such as the brain, the nervous system or the body. It holds that the doings of consciousness can be fully explained by appealing to causal laws. This conception is found in much scientific thinking about subjectivity. Merleau-Ponty rejects both notions. He argues that what we ordinarily think of as mental states and activities are constituted by *bodily* engagement with the world. The subject of these states and activities is thus essentially embodied. But, to understand this form of bodily subjectivity, we need to reject the traditional idea of the body as a mere object, a piece of biological mechanism, which somehow contains consciousness within it. Instead, we need to recognise that the body *is* a form of consciousness. Moreover, since it is the body's interactions with the world that constitute mental states and activities, consciousness is not separate from its environment. It is essentially embedded within it. Merleau-Ponty argues that the two flawed conceptions of consciousness go hand-in-hand with two notions of the world. One takes the world to be constituted by the subject. Merleau-Ponty sees the transcendental idealism of Kant and the early Husserl as exemplifying this position. The other construes the world as existing independently of consciousness, which is just one of many things within it. This view is endorsed by the natural sciences. Merleau-Ponty rejects both conceptions. Instead, he argues that the world and consciousness are mutually dependent parts of one whole. Neither can exist without standing in this relation to the other.

In the course of his investigations, Merleau-Ponty covers a vast amount of ground. His work examines perception, hallucination, action, the emotions, thought, language, the nature of dreaming and madness, space, time, natural objects, the cultural world, the nature of our relations with others, human freedom, painting, mathematics, truth and politics. His studies are informed not only by his knowledge of many philosophical thinkers, but also by his detailed understanding of the psychology literature. It would be impossible to do justice to such a rich text in just one volume. Thus my aim in this GuideBook has been to set out the central strands of Merleau-Ponty's position, and explain how he argues for them. My hope is that this will provide the reader with a framework, which will aid in understanding the rest of the text.

1

MERLEAU-PONTY'S PHENOMENOLOGY

What is phenomenology? Since *Phenomenology of Perception* (PhP) (Merleau-Ponty 1962) is, as the name suggests, a work of phenomenology, it is sensible to begin, as the text does, by addressing this question. But, as Merleau-Ponty notes, this is not an easy question to answer. Different phenomenologists conceive of phenomenology differently, and it is not always easy to decide who falls into this category in the first place. One might minimally characterise phenomenology as philosophy that investigates experience from a first-person point of view, that is, as it is presented to the subject. But this minimal definition is not very informative, and is also open to misunderstandings. To grasp Merleau-Ponty's philosophical project, we need to understand *his* conception of phenomenology. This will be the focus of the present chapter.

Merleau-Ponty puts forward his conception of phenomenology in the preface to PhP. A figure who features prominently in the preface is Edmund Husserl. Merleau-Ponty's influences are many and various. They include Henri Bergson, Simone de Beauvoir,

René Descartes, the Gestalt psychologists, Martin Heidegger, Immanuel Kant, Claude Lévi-Strauss, Jean-Paul Sartre, Ferdinand de Saussure and Edith Stein, amongst many others. But his most important influence is undoubtedly Husserl. Edmund Husserl is widely thought of as the founder of phenomenology – although Husserl himself talks of having discovered an idea that is inherent, but not fully realised, in the work of previous philosophers. Merleau-Ponty considers himself to be merely bringing Husserl's philosophical project to fruition. Whether or not Merleau-Ponty was correct about this matter is debated, and I will say more about their relation later. But it is clear that a grasp of Merleau-Ponty's philosophical project requires an understanding of Husserl's. Different conceptions of phenomenology can be found in Husserl's work. The extent of the continuity between them is debated. We can identify two stages in Husserl's work that are important for understanding Merleau-Ponty and his relation to Husserl: the first is found in *Cartesian Meditations* (Husserl 1988); the second is that which he offers in *Crisis of the European Sciences and Transcendental Phenomenology* (Husserl 1970).

HUSSERL AND *CARTESIAN MEDITATIONS* (CM)

In CM, Husserl is concerned with what he sees as the sorry state of human knowledge. Philosophy is no longer a unified discipline, which for Husserl shows that philosophers are no longer working together to produce 'objectively valid results' (1988: 4–5). The natural and human sciences are also beset by a significant problem: they are incomplete. Of course, there is an obvious sense in which science is incomplete. Scientists have not yet discovered everything there is to know about the world. Any of our current scientific hypotheses might turn out to be incorrect in the light of new evidence. Scientific investigation is not yet finished. But it is not this that bothers Husserl. He identifies a further sense in which science is incomplete, which begins from the thought that motivated Descartes: I can be certain about the content of my own experiences but I cannot be sure about the existence and nature of the external world. This is because the content of my own experiences is *given* to me. It is presented to me in such a way that I can know it immediately, without making any inferences or relying on any presuppositions. The external world, in contrast, is not given to me. Experience *may* provide me with knowledge of it, but only if I assume that the world I experience really exists. Scientific investigation begins with observation – i.e. experience. The idea that observation yields knowledge of the world thus presupposes that the world that seems to confront us in experience actually exists. The whole of science therefore rests on an assumption which has yet to be justified. Science lacks a foundation. It is this that troubles Husserl. He aims to reinvigorate philosophy by setting philosophers a new goal. Philosophy's task will be to explicate the existence of the world, thus providing science with a foundation. The new philosophy is phenomenology.

Husserl intends phenomenology to be a science. By this he means that it will be a systematic inquiry that yields objective truths. It will not proceed in a haphazard fashion, but will follow methods that we have reason to believe will produce accurate results. Insofar as all sciences are like this, phenomenology will be continuous with the natural and human sciences. However, there is a very important sense in which phenomenology will differ from science. The natural and human sciences are naturalistic. They take the world they investigate to be one that obeys the laws of nature. These laws are discovered through scientific inquiry. The results of scientific investigations are explanations of the natural world that appeal to such laws. As we have seen, science presupposes the existence of the world. All of its results depend on this presupposition. Since Husserl's aim is to explicate the existence of the world, thus providing a foundation for science, he cannot make use of any results that depend on this presupposition. It follows that he cannot appeal to the laws of nature and his inquiry cannot yield causal explanations of what he studies. Husserl's investigation, in other words, cannot be naturalistic. A non-naturalistic inquiry which seeks to provide a foundation for ordinary human knowledge is classed as a *transcendental* inquiry.

The natural and human sciences lack a foundation because they presuppose that the world exists. To provide them with a foundation, Husserl's inquiry should not depend on any presuppositions – or else his system will itself need a foundation – and it must yield results that are absolutely certain. Since phenomenology will produce results that are presuppositionless and indubitable, Husserl calls it a *rigorous* science. To be rigorous, phenomenology must appeal only to what is given – the content of one's own experiences. Moreover, Husserl claims that it must be restricted to *describing* what is given, rather than explaining it. This is because explanations go beyond what is given. They involve making inferences from generalisations, appealing to hypotheses, conjecturing, and so on. Husserl takes descriptions, on the other hand, to merely capture what is given. The phenomenologist must thus proceed by describing their own experiences. One may be puzzled at this point. Phenomenology is supposed to be producing results that are objectively valid, and which are capable of providing a foundation for the natural and human sciences. But it's not very clear how describing one's own experiences will satisfy these aims. To see how this is supposed to work, we need to know more about how one should do phenomenology.

There are different ways to describe one's experiences. Suppose that I get lost on the way to my friend's house. I phone my friend for directions, and he asks me to describe what I can see. I tell him that I can see a church to my left, a pub to my right, and a fork in the road ahead. I have described my current experience, but my description is of no use to the phenomenologist. My friend and I both assume that the things I seem to see actually exist – it is only if we assume this that it makes sense for me to describe what I see as a way of locating where I am. But the phenomenologist cannot assume the existence of the world that seems to confront him or her. Before describing this experience, the phenomenologist must thus perform what Husserl calls the 'Transcendental-Phenomenological Reduction'. The purpose of the Reduction is to 'bracket' what Husserl refers to as our 'natural attitude': the assumption that the world exists. This does not involve doubting the existence of the world. Instead, one simply suspends belief in it. One puts aside the belief that the world exists. Since all scientific theories depend on this assumption, they must also be bracketed when one performs the Transcendental-Phenomenological Reduction. Some of these scientific theories concern consciousness, for example, scientists view it as part of the causal order, dependent on the brain, and so on. Thus suspending the natural attitude also involves putting aside scientific theories about consciousness. Husserl claims that after performing the Transcendental-Phenomenological Reduction, the qualitative character of experience is left untouched. But rather than considering the things one seems to see as independently existing worldly entities, one should consider them as ways that experience is structured. Consciousness is conceived as the Transcendental Ego – subjectivity that is not part of the causal order or dependent on any aspect of the world.

After performing the Transcendental-Phenomenological Reduction, the phenomenologist is able to discover the structures of consciousness. However, at this stage, this involves merely dealing with the way that their own experiences are structured. The phenomenologist must do more to obtain the universal results that Husserl is after. Husserl holds that the phenomenologist must move beyond the particular form of their own experiences to discover the structures of experience in general. They must investigate the *essential* structures of consciousness. To do this, they must perform what Husserl calls the 'Eidetic Reduction', which brackets the particular and contingent features of an experience to reveal its essence. I might experience a dog, for example, as medium-sized, black with white paws, amber eyes and so on. But not all dog-experiences share these features. They are not part of the essence of dog-experiences. The essential structure of dog-experiences will comprise those features that a dog-experience must exhibit in order to qualify as such. The Eidetic Reduction involves engaging in a process which Husserl calls 'Eidetic Variation'. One imagines the thing one experiences as having different features to find out whether changing a particular property destroys its identity as a thing of that type. If it does not, then that particular property is not essential to it. If it does, then that particular feature *is* part of the thing's essence. Thus I imagine the dog I experience as being brown instead of black. The difference in colour does not change its identity as a dog, thus I can conclude that being black is not essential to being a dog-experience. But if I imagine it having hooves, it no longer qualifies as a dog-experience. I can therefore conclude that being presented as having paws *is* essential to being a dog-experience.

A very important essential structure of consciousness is intentionality. All consciousness is of or about something. A central task of Husserl's phenomenology is to provide an account of intentionality. He attempts to do this without reference to an independently existing world. A second essential structure of consciousness is temporality: conscious events and activities are ordered in time. Husserl also aims to develop an account of temporality. Again, his goal is to do this without appealing to an external world.

The position that Husserl reaches as a result of his investigations is a form of transcendental idealism. He holds that the ordinary world that confronts us in our day-to-day lives is constituted by the Transcendental Ego – consciousness which lies outside the causal order of the natural world and is wholly different from it. In CM, he seems to view transcendental idealism as a direct result of performing the Transcendental-Phenomenological Reduction. This procedure reveals the given – what can be known for certain. For Husserl, this is the content of one's own experiences – the mental acts of one's Transcendental Ego. Importantly, the qualitative character of experience remains exactly the same. There is no change whatsoever to the world that seems to confront one in experience. It follows that the Transcendental Ego's mental acts – which are all that remain after the Transcendental-Phenomenological Reduction has been performed – must be sufficient for the existence of the world. In other words, the world is constituted in experience. On its own, this is not an adequate argument for transcendental idealism. Husserl's reasoning here is supplemented by arguments he offers in previous works. These need not concern us here.[1]

The tenor of Husserl's project so far is thoroughly Cartesian, although the position he ultimately reaches has more in common with Kant's transcendental idealism. However, the Cartesian framework that Husserl adopts in CM is somewhat disrupted by the claims he makes in the Fifth Meditation. The aim of Husserl's investigation is to account for the existence of the everyday world in terms of the phenomenologist's own experiences. An important feature of this world is that it is one that each of us shares with other people. I experience things in the world as capable of being experienced by others, and my experience presents me with other consciousnesses. For Husserl's account to be complete, he must thus explain how I can experience another consciousness. If he cannot do this, then the world that his phenomenology explicates will be solipsistic. It will be a world that belongs to only one subject: the phenomenologist. The Fifth Meditation deals with this issue.

It is clear that one cannot have direct, introspective access to another's mental life. If another person is to feature in one's experience, it can only be via perception of his or her body. But on the Cartesian picture, the body is an object that belongs in the external world. It is not essentially related to consciousness. The perception of a body is at the very most *evidence* for the existence of another; it is not possible to directly perceive that person. There are well-known difficulties with this picture, and Husserl rejects it.

He develops his alternative model by considering the experience he has of his body, noting that it is very different from his experience of other objects. He points out four important ways in which it differs. It immediately and spontaneously expresses his emotions – if he is embarrassed, it blushes; if he is happy, he spontaneously walks around smiling with a spring in his step; if he is miserable, his body walks around with its shoulders hunched, dragging its feet. His body is sensitive – he can touch things with parts of his body and feel sensations in them; his body feels pain; it feels sensations of heat and cold; its parts sometimes itch, and so on. His body immediately responds to his will – if he decides to pick up a glass of water and drink from it, his body immediately performs this action. Finally, it is the centre of his egocentric space. Perception is always perspectival – it presents the world from a particular point of view in space. The perceiver experiences themselves as located at the place from which they see. Husserl notices that this is where he experiences his body as being. Husserl thus concludes that his own body is not presented as an object, but as a living conscious being which is not separate from his mind. It is a physical manifestation of his consciousness. If the body is an external object with no essential connection to the consciousness it houses, then others will never be directly perceivable. But if the body is instead a living subject, and other minds are embodied beings, then they will be perceivable elements in the world. Husserl accounts for the experience of others in this way. The details of his account are not important here. What is significant is the conception of the body that he reaches through doing phenomenology. His description of bodily experience puts pressure on the notion of a subject who lies outside the world and can be considered in isolation from it. Husserl's Cartesian framework is under threat.

HUSSERL AND *CRISIS OF EUROPEAN SCIENCES AND TRANSCENDENTAL PHENOMENOLOGY* (CES)

The conception of phenomenology that can be found in Husserl's last writings, particularly those published posthumously as CES, is different from the one he put forward in CM. The basic form of phenomenology is the same. It can be summarised by the following three claims:

(1) Human knowledge is in decline and will be saved by philosophy.
(2) Philosophy must proceed by describing experience as it is lived, that is, what it is like from the perspective of the experiencing subject.
(3) To do this, one must perform the Transcendental-Phenomenological Reduction, which involves suspending our natural or commonsense view of the world and consciousness.

But Husserl's understanding of these claims alters.

Husserl sees human knowledge as being in crisis. The problem is that the Galilean conception of science has been identified with *the* rational form of inquiry, so that anything that cannot be investigated in these terms cannot be investigated rationally. The Galilean conception of science investigates what can be precisely measured. Only those properties and events that are determinately measurable are deemed to be real. It follows that any inquiry into what cannot be precisely measured is irrational on this picture. This includes all questions of value – for example, ethics, aesthetics and so on. But it is these questions of value that are most pressing for us. We need to know how to live ethical lives, how to build a society that allows us to flourish, and so on. The elevation of Galilean science to *the* rational form of inquiry thus means that the issues that have most significance for us cannot be rationally investigated. Husserl finds this unacceptable. The goal of philosophy – i.e. phenomenology – is to resolve these difficulties. It will do this by establishing that there is no justification for taking Galilean science to be the only rational form of inquiry. The resulting account of Galilean science's proper place will show how inquiries into matters of value can be rational.

Phenomenology must proceed by describing experience as it is presented to the experiencing subject. This task is complicated by the experiencing subject's ordinary way of thinking, which interferes with their capacity to describe their experience as they live it. Thus they must first perform the Transcendental-Phenomenological Reduction, which involves suspending their ordinary way of thinking about the world and consciousness. In CES, the Transcendental-Phenomenological Reduction does not take the phenomenologist from the natural attitude – the assumption that the external world that seems to confront him or her in experience actually exists – to experiential content that exists outside the natural, causal order. Instead Husserl takes our ordinary conception of the world to be that provided by Galilean science. We take it for granted that the only real properties are those that can be precisely measured, and this belief prevents us from noticing certain aspects of our experience. Putting aside this conception of the world allows us to take a fresh look at experience, or, to put the matter more precisely, the world as we experience it. Husserl calls the world as we experience it, the *Lebenswelt* or lived world. It is the everyday world that we – embodied subjects – inhabit.

After performing the Transcendental-Phenomenological Reduction, we discover that the things we encounter in the *Lebenswelt* do not just possess those properties that Galilean science claims are real. They also possess properties that Galilean science claims are merely subjective. If I see someone kicking their dog, I literally perceive this act as morally reprehensible. I do not just judge that the act is wrong; I experience its wrongness. Similarly, a rotting carcass literally looks disgusting. A sunset literally appears beautiful. A kitten is literally perceived as cute. Moreover, we do not perceive the *Lebenswelt* as having the measurable properties that Galilean science takes to be the only real ones. There are, for example, no perfect circles in the *Lebenswelt*. Instead, the determinately measurable properties of Galilean science are idealised abstractions of the properties we actually experience the *Lebenswelt* as containing. Since this is so, there is no justification for taking Galilean science to be the only rational form of inquiry. It is concerned with only one aspect of the *Lebenswelt*, which it investigates in idealised form. Other aspects of the *Lebenswelt* can be investigated rationally too. Phenomenology will investigate all aspects of the *Lebenswelt*, and uncover its essential structures.

Whether or not this new conception of phenomenology constitutes a radical break with Husserl's earlier thought is debated. However, what is important for our purposes is *Merleau-Ponty's* understanding of Husserl's thought. He sees Husserl's philosophy as shifting away from a broadly Cartesian way of thinking, towards a conception of consciousness as historically situated and essentially embodied. Husserl is no longer concerned with obtaining results that are absolutely certain. The subject-matter of phenomenology is not the content of one's own experiences, conceived as independent of an externally existing world and capable of being known with absolute certainty. Instead, phenomenology studies an intersubjective world about which an individual phenomenologist may be mistaken. In CM, Husserl aims to obtain results that are universally true: results that hold for all people in all times in all places. The *Lebenswelt*, however, is culture-relative. Different cultures and societies see the world differently. They have differing conceptions of what is beautiful, what is morally acceptable, and so on. These are bound up with the way that the world appears to them. The woman whom Renaissance people would have seen as beautiful and sexually alluring appears overweight and unattractive to people living in modern Western society. Different societies live in different life-worlds. Finally, Husserl's ideas about the body are at odds with his Cartesian starting-point. Descartes admits that his experience does not present him as being in his body like a pilot is in a ship (Descartes 1996). However, he still conceives of the body as being on the world side of the mind–world divide. It is a part of the external world, and as such its existence can be doubted. It is not essential to consciousness. Husserl realised that this conception of the body was inadequate. The body is instead a living subject. One finds oneself an embodied being inhabiting a world containing others.

MERLEAU-PONTY'S RELATION TO HUSSERL

Merleau-Ponty takes himself to be continuing Husserl's project. To grasp his conception of phenomenology, we must understand how he interprets Husserl. The task of interpreting someone can be guided by different principles. On the one hand, one might simply aim to give an exact account of what the person said. On the other hand, one might aim to interpret that person according to the 'principle of charity',[2] which involves trying to find the most rational, consistent reading, even if this requires one to go beyond the text to reconstruct what the person might have been trying to say. Some might argue that it is impossible to give an exact account of a philosopher's thought, and every interpretation involves an element of the latter approach. A third strategy is the one adopted by Merleau-Ponty. He indicates what he thinks about the relation between himself and Husserl in his essay 'The Philosopher and His Shadow' (Merleau-Ponty 1964a: 159–81). In this essay, Merleau-Ponty quotes Heidegger (1996):

> The greater the work accomplished (and greatness is in no way equivalent to the extent and number of writings) the richer the unthought-of element in that work. That is, the richer is that which,

through this work and through it alone, comes toward us as never yet
thought of.

(Merleau-Ponty 1964a: 160)

Merleau-Ponty claims that what he does with Husserl is evoke
the un-thought-of element in his work. This is apt to sound
puzzling – how can an account of what someone did *not* think
nevertheless be an interpretation of that person's work?

Merleau-Ponty's thought here is this. It is indisputable that a
person's ideas develop over time. Philosophical systems do not
occur to someone all in one go. A philosopher starts with a set of
ideas, and then spends time working them out in finer detail,
thinking through the implications, revising earlier claims as
inconsistencies come to light, and so on. Through this process,
their initial ideas are transformed. The trajectory of the philosopher's thought can be traced from their earlier writings to those
produced later. Heidegger can be understood as claiming that the
greater a thinker, the more their thought could be developed.
These potential developments are what is un-thought in their
work – the thoughts they have not yet had. This suggests a way
to interpret someone. One might take up their train of thought
and continue to develop their thoughts along the same trajectory.
In this way, one will be thinking their un-thought thoughts.
Merleau-Ponty adopts this approach to Husserl. He thinks of
himself as picking up Husserl's train of thought and continuing
to develop his ideas in the way that Husserl would have done if
his work had not been halted by his death. Of course, the strategy
of thinking someone's un-thought thoughts raises all kinds of
questions. Not least the issue of how one decides whether one is
developing someone's work correctly, so that one ends up
with claims that they would have endorsed if they had been
able to continue their work. But all that is important for
our purposes is Merleau-Ponty's conception of his relation to
Husserl.

We have just seen that Husserl's later work transforms his
earlier ideas. Merleau-Ponty's view is that as Husserl carries out
his phenomenological project, he comes to realise that his

Cartesian starting-point is no longer tenable. The structure of his project remains the same. He still thinks that human knowledge is in decline, but can be saved by philosophy. He still thinks that one should do philosophy by describing one's experiences. He still thinks that, to describe experience properly, we need to suspend our natural attitude towards the world. The result of phenomenological investigation is an account of the essential structures of experience. But he moves towards a radically anti-Cartesian conception of his phenomenological project in CES. Merleau-Ponty views himself as continuing to develop these ideas along this trajectory, making the anti-Cartesian conception of phenomenology explicit.

MERLEAU-PONTY'S PHENOMENOLOGY

Merleau-Ponty's phenomenology has the same structure as Husserl's, but, just as the later Husserl reconceived the basic elements of earlier Husserlian phenomenology, so too Merleau-Ponty's understanding of these basic elements is different. He has a broader notion of the problem that phenomenology is designed to solve. He is no longer simply concerned with human knowledge. Instead, the problem is our conceptual framework – in particular, the way we conceive consciousness, the world and their relation. He argues that our current conceptual framework is flawed. It does not accurately reflect the nature of the things it describes, and, moreover, it gives rise to a number of intractable problems. The aim of phenomenology is to develop a new, more accurate conceptual framework, which will dissolve these problems.

Merleau-Ponty calls our everyday conceptual framework, 'Objective Thought'. Different interpretations of Objective Thought are offered in the literature. Gardner (2011), for example, takes it to be a thesis about the character of experience, and so what an account of experience needs to explain. On his reading, it is defined by acceptance of 'a particular, highly abstract, transcendental explanandum, namely the *objectual character* of experience, its articulation into objects and its character as experience, that is, as involving a relation of subjects to objects'.

Hammond et al. take Objective Thought to be a view about what the world is like:

> According to [Objective Thought], the world consists of clearly identi-fiable objects – such as houses, trees, stones, etc. – each of which has a definite location at any given time in a single spatial framework. Every object has a set of determinately specifiable properties – for example, a particular size, shape, weight, colour, and so on – which can be described independently of one another. These objects can interact causally with each other; and all their properties are open, in principle, to a complete description and causal explanation. The world conceived in this way Merleau-Ponty often calls 'the universe'. Broadly speaking, then, Objective Thought characterizes the world in a way that makes it a suitable candidate for scientific treatment. But Objective Thought is indifferent, as such, to the rival philosophical claims of realists and idealists as to whether this world exists 'in its own right' or is somehow constituted by a transcendental subject.
>
> (Hammond et al. 1991: 131–2)

Finally, Priest (2003) takes Objective Thought to be simply the claim that we can come to know the world as it is in-itself. '"Objective Thought" is the thought that what is realistically the case may be accessed by the subject in a way that is unaffected by the interpretations and pragmatic concerns of that subject' (2003: 6). There is something correct about all of these interpretations, but none of them provides a full account of what Merleau-Ponty means by Objective Thought.

Merleau-Ponty holds that Objective Thought has its roots in perception itself. To understand what Objective Thought is, we need to introduce some of his ideas about perception. He claims that the role of perception is to present the perceiver with an intersubjective world of things which have a definite character and a location in that world. However, the perceiver is not pre-sented with this world 'all at once'. Perception, for Merleau-Ponty, is an ongoing process of exploration and discovery, from which the intersubjective world of things gradually emerges for the perceiver, who is first presented with *phenomena*. These are often indeterminate and ambiguous items that have not yet crystallised into definite things, but which nevertheless cannot be identified with 'inner' items such as sense-data. They are 'the cradle of things' (Merleau-Ponty 1945: 71; 1962: 58; 2002: 68). Phenomena are vague something-or-others that invite further exploration. As one explores them, they take shape as things that others could also discover. Imagine, for example, that I am walking in a park. I see something in the distance, but I cannot make out what kind of thing it is. I see that it is near some distant trees, but I am not sure whether it is in front of the trees or level with the trees, etc. In this case, I experience something that is presented as being a part of the world – it appears to be something out there, near the trees – but it is not yet presented as something that has a definite character (I cannot see what kind of thing it is) or a definite location (I cannot see exactly where it is). Suppose then that I walk over to it. As I get closer, it comes into focus. I can see that it is a carved stone with figures of some sort etched in it. I can also see that it is just in front of the trees. If I get closer still, I can see that the figures carved into the stone are animals.

Merleau-Ponty then claims that 'it is the essence of consciousness to forget its own phenomena, thus enabling "things" to be constituted' (1945: 71; 1962: 58; 2002: 67). Consciousness does not focus on phenomena, but passes over them to focus on the things that emerge for the perceiver through the perceptual process. Suppose, for example, that my friend asks me what I saw in the park. It will not occur to me to tell her that I saw a vague shape in the distance. I will say that I saw a stone with animals carved into it. In other words, I naturally focus on the thing that emerged out of the process of perceptual discovery. Merleau-Ponty claims that the reason we are apt to forget phenomena is so that things can emerge for us. We can see from this brief description that Merleau-Ponty conceives of perception as a movement from what is ambiguous and indeterminate to what is determinate, squarely located in the shared world, and so available to others – a process that is aided by consciousness's tendency to forget its own phenomena. But he also claims that complete determinacy is never achieved in perception – what is seen in the distance, for example, will always appear indistinct. He claims that complete objectivity is never fully achieved in perception either – I cannot view the world from nowhere; I always perceive the world from my own particular perspective.

Objective Thought is thought that takes up this impetus and continues the movement towards what is determinate and objective. It is characterised by a view of the world as composed of determinate entities that stand in external relations to one another. A determinate entity is one where there is a fact of the matter about whether or not it exists, and whose properties can be determinately specified. There are different sorts of external relation. The relevant notion here is the relation between the parts of a whole, where that whole is nothing more than the sum of its parts. A full understanding of such a whole can be achieved by first listing its constituents, and then saying how they are related. External relations obtain between a jar and the marbles within it, because the whole is nothing more than the sum of the marbles and the jar. Objective Thought thus conceives of the world as composed of determinate entities which are related in such a way that a reductive analysis of the world and everything in it is possible. The central kind of relation between things in the world is causal. Objective Thought sees the world as causally determined.

Merleau-Ponty also characterises Objective Thought as thinking that is 'prejudiced' in favour of the world (1945: 65; 1962: 53; 2002: 62). It is a tendency, when thinking about experience (and other aspects and activities of consciousness), to focus on its objects, rather than the experience itself. This 'prejudice' develops from consciousness's tendency to forget phenomena and focus on things. It often manifests as a methodological bias, whereby one investigates conscious phenomena by reasoning from claims about its objects. Consider, for example, the theorist who draws conclusions about the field of vision by reasoning about which segment of the world can throw its image on the retina. The theorist's reasoning should lead them to conclude that we 'perceive a segment of the world precisely delimited, surrounded by a zone of blackness, packed full of qualities with no interval between them, held together by definite relationships of size similar to those lying on the retina' (Merleau-Ponty 1945: 11; 1962: 5; 2002: 6). But, of course, visual experience is not like this at all. Merleau-Ponty tells us that the theorist is led astray in attempts to understand visual experience, because, instead of examining visual experience itself, the theorist naturally begins the investigation by thinking about the world of objects presented in such experience. In this way, the theorist's thinking is prejudiced in favour of the world.

Objective Thought gives rise to two seemingly opposed philosophical positions: Empiricism and Intellectualism. Note that Merleau-Ponty does not use 'Empiricism' with its usual meaning – the term has a technical usage in his philosophy. Empiricism and Intellectualism agree on what the world is like but they disagree about its metaphysical status and, correspondingly, the status of consciousness. Empiricism can be loosely identified with a certain kind of scientific realism. It is committed to the following four theses:

E1   The world is composed of determinate entities that stand in external relations to one another and it is causally determined.
E2   This world is the world-in-itself.
E3   We can come to know about the world-in-itself.
E4   Consciousness is just another thing in the world, and so obeys its laws.

Intellectualism is a form of idealism, – particularly the transcendental idealism espoused by Kant, and the earlier Husserl. Merleau-Ponty sees Intellectualism as developing from Empiricism as theorists realise the limitations of, and problems with, the Empiricist position. The central problem is that on the Empiricist view, consciousness is a mere thing in the world, and is thus subject to its laws, including the laws of causation. Merleau-Ponty holds that the doings of consciousness defy causal explanation. The Intellectualist sees this, and so claims that consciousness is *not* a mere part of the world, but is wholly different from it. Merleau-Ponty holds that once this position is taken to its logical conclusion, one has to claim that consciousness constitutes the world. In other words, one has to think of consciousness as the Transcendental Ego. Intellectualism is thus committed to the following four claims:

I1   The world is composed of determinate entities that stand in external relations to one another and it is causally determined.
I2   This world is constituted by consciousness.
I3   We cannot come to know about the world-in-itself.
I4   Consciousness lies outside the world and is wholly different from it.

Merleau-Ponty holds that theories can display Empiricist or Intellectualist tendencies without being fully blown Empiricism or Intellectualism.

Merleau-Ponty's understanding of our ordinary view has similarities with Husserl's conception of it in CES. In his last works, Husserl characterises our ordinary view as the belief that the only rational form of inquiry is Galilean science. A consequence of this is the belief that the only real entities are those that Galilean science studies – entities whose properties and behaviour can be determinately measured. Objective Thought is similar insofar as it conceives of the world along Galilean lines as determinately measurable. But Merleau-Ponty sees this as having further-reaching consequences.

Like Husserl, Merleau-Ponty holds that the phenomenologist must proceed by performing the Transcendental-Phenomenological Reduction, which involves suspending a certain attitude. But we can identify two conceptions of it in his work. In the preface he states that 'The most important lesson which the reduction teaches us is the impossibility of a complete reduction' (Merleau-Ponty 1945: viii; 1962: xiv; 2002: xv). Here, Merleau-Ponty is referring to the earlier Husserl's formulation of the Transcendental-Phenomenological Reduction. The view that is suspended is the natural attitude, the core of which is the unthinking assumption that there is a real world outside of me. The earlier Husserl holds that after performing the Transcendental-Phenomenological Reduction, experience is considered in isolation from its worldly objects. The experiencing subject is conceived as a Transcendental Ego that is not part of the world, and whose doings/states are uncaused. Husserl's earlier conception of phenomenology thus presupposes the Cartesian view of experience as inner representations whose qualities remain the same whether or not they present the world correctly.

Merleau-Ponty sees Husserl as coming to realise that this view of experience is untenable. Experience cannot be considered in isolation from its worldly objects. Nor can the experiencing subject be conceived as lying wholly outside the world. Moreover, he sees Husserl as discovering this as a result of doing phenomenology. Of course, if experience and the subject cannot be viewed in this way, then one cannot suspend the belief that there is an 'external' world. Thus by trying to perform the Transcendental-Phenomenological Reduction, Husserl discovered that its performance is impossible. The second conception of the Transcendental-Phenomenological Reduction that can be found in Merleau-Ponty's work is more akin to the late Husserl's understanding of it. In CES, performing the Transcendental-Phenomenological Reduction involves suspending the view that the only real entities are those whose properties and behaviour can be determinately measured. One must suspend this view to accurately describe the world as it is experienced. In Merleau-Ponty's phenomenology, Objective Thought must be suspended to accurately describe experience. This is the second conception of the Transcendental-Phenomenological Reduction that can be found in his work, and which features most prominently in it.

On the second understanding of the Transcendental-Phenomenological Reduction, suspending it reveals experience as it is lived – that is, how things appear to the subject who experiences them. But as we might expect, Merleau-Ponty's conception of lived experience is radically anti-Cartesian. For him, experience is immediately of the world and cannot be considered in isolation from it. We will examine this thesis in detail in Chapter 6. For now, we can note that suspending Objective Thought leaves what Merleau-Ponty calls the *phenomenal field*: the worldly region that is presented in experience, considered as it appears to the perceiver. This is phenomenology's fundamental object of investigation. The task of the phenomenologist is to describe it and uncover its essential structures.

The phenomenal field is related to Husserl's *Lebenswelt*. Merleau-Ponty holds that the perceived world and the perceiving subject are mutually constituting; perception is this process of constitution. The aim of perception is to constitute a world of definite things that are there for everyone; the process admits of various stages. The end result is the *Lebenswelt*, which is the intersubjective world of more or less determinate things. Prior to the emergence of the *Lebenswelt*, however, there is the phenomenal field. At this stage what is perceived are phenomena. No clear line can be drawn between the phenomenal field and the *Lebenswelt*, which retains elements of ambiguity and indeterminacy. The phenomenal field itself admits of varying stages. Sometimes, Merleau-Ponty's analysis focuses on the *Lebenswelt*, but at other times it focuses on the phenomenal field. It is clear that, for Merleau-Ponty, describing the phenomenal field (or the *Lebenswelt*) is an ontological project. It does not involve describing some inner domain of consciousness that is independent from the external world. To describe the phenomenal field is to describe an experienced region of the world. It involves cataloguing the items contained in the phenomenal field. Although these are experienced items, they are also things that transcend one's experience of them. Thus describing the phenomenal field involves describing worldly entities.

Merleau-Ponty recognises that performing the Transcendental-Phenomenological Reduction to reveal the phenomenal field is not an easy task. He remarks, 'Nothing is more difficult than to know precisely *what we see*' (1945: 71; 1962: 58; 2002: 67). What we see is very familiar and this can make it hard to gain a clear perspective on it. It is not just the familiarity of what we see that makes it hard to know. Merleau-Ponty argues that the assumptions of Objective Thought also make it difficult to know what we see. What we expect to find when we examine lived experience, and so what we look for, is dictated to a large extent by our unthinking acceptance of Objective Thought's perspective. Of course, performing the Transcendental-Phenomenological Reduction involves suspending Objective Thought. One might think that, once this has been suspended, one will be able to know what one sees. However, bracketing Objective Thought is no mean feat. It is not obvious how one can simply suspend one's entire conceptual framework. Finally, it is difficult to know what we see because of consciousness's tendency to forget its own phenomena. Merleau-Ponty describes this as a 'crypto-mechanism' that operates within perception but, nevertheless, he holds that, in spite of this crypto-mechanism, 'consciousness could bring [its phenomena] into its presence' (1945: 71; 1962: 58; 2002: 67–8).

MERLEAU-PONTY'S STRATEGY

Merleau-Ponty adopts an interesting strategy in PhP to overcome these difficulties: he makes extensive use of scientific case studies, many of which are studies of pathologies. It's not immediately obvious how exactly he is using the case studies. But it is important to settle this issue. The scientific work to which Merleau-Ponty refers was conducted in the first half of the twentieth century and earlier, some of it over one hundred years ago. Consequently, some has been superseded by more recent scientific investigation. To give just one example, Merleau-Ponty makes extensive use of the case of Schneider – a man studied by the psychologists Kurt Goldstein and Adler Gelb (1920), whose capacities were severely diminished as a result of a brain injury sustained in the First World War. Merleau-Ponty uses this case to present theses about lived space, action, intentionality and other related ideas. However, it is now generally agreed that Schneider's brain lesions were too large to support the very specific claims about his disabilities that Goldstein and Gelb make, and which Merleau-Ponty appropriates. A possibility is that, where Merleau-Ponty's philosophical ideas depend upon these outdated case studies, they have become correspondingly obsolete. This is bad news for the increasing number of contemporary theorists who look to his work for inspiration. To decide whether or not this is the case, we need to determine the role that the scientific case studies play in his work.

Theorists disagree on this issue. A popular reading is one offered by Hammond et al. (1991), who suggest that Merleau-Ponty uses the scientific case studies as a means of rendering the familiar, unfamiliar. They write, '[t]he pathological case operates as a heuristic device that shocks one into awareness of what is taken for granted. It is a means of gaining distance from the familiar, so that one is better able to explicate it' (1991: 181). 'The familiar' includes one's experience in general. It also includes a more specific aspect of one's experience – the phenomena that one experiences but does not readily notice, due to one's natural focus on the things that develop out of them. It also includes one's ordinary way of thinking – Objective Thought. By comparing familiar experience with a pathological case such as that of Schneider, features of the former are brought to our attention. By choosing cases which conflict with the concepts and assumptions of Objective Thought, these are revealed to us, where before they went unnoticed.

On this interpretation, the scientific case studies discussed by Merleau-Ponty fulfil the same purpose as a certain kind of thought experiment. Consider, for example, the scenario envisaged by Jarvis Thomson (1971), in her defence of abortion. She asks the reader to imagine waking up to find that they have been kidnapped by a society of music lovers and attached to the kidneys of a famous violinist who has a fatal ailment and will otherwise die. To save his life, he must remain attached to their kidneys for nine months. In this thought experiment, Jarvis Thomson takes some essential features of pregnancy (one person's life being sustained by their attachment to another's body for nine months) and embeds them in an unusual scenario. The aim of the thought experiment is to make the situation of pregnancy unfamiliar, thus forcing us to examine it afresh. Furthermore, one of Jarvis Thomson's aims is to get us to question an assumption that is often made in discussions of abortion, namely that if the foetus is a person, then its right to life is absolute and trumps any rights the mother may have over her own body. The violinist's case is designed to be in tension with this assumption – the violinist is a person, but it is not at all clear that his right to life trumps someone else's rights over their own body. By highlighting this routinely made assumption, it can be questioned.

If Hammond et al.'s (1991) reading is correct then it makes little difference to Merleau-Ponty's philosophical claims whether or not the case studies are still (or ever were) valid. Merleau-Ponty could use an entirely fictitious example like Jarvis Thomson does and still fulfil his aim of making the familiar unfamiliar. There is, of course, some rhetorical value in using real life examples. Consider, for example, Oliver Sacks's tale of attempting to awaken patients who had contracted sleeping-sickness, by using the drug L-Dopa (Sacks 1996). If this story were mere fiction, it would not be anything like as unsettling. Similarly, if the Schneider case is real, then it has more impact than a hypothetical one, and as such can be more effective at 'shocking one into awareness of what is taken for granted' (Hammond et al. 1991: 181) than a case such as Jarvis Thomson's. The shock-value is diminished if claims that Merleau-Ponty makes about Schneider's abilities are now held to be false. But, since a fictitious example could fulfil the function of bringing the familiar to our attention, Merleau-Ponty's philosophy remains largely unaffected.

There is some textual support for Hammond et al.'s reading. Merleau-Ponty writes, 'in order to see the world ... we must break with our familiar acceptance of it' (1945: viii; 1962: xiv; 2002: xv). He also says that analysing the pathological cases enables us to better see the familiar one (1945: 127; 1962: 109; 2002: 125). However, it is hard to see why he would analyse the scientific cases in so much detail if he merely uses them to high-light the familiar. In fact, this is only part of the story. To fully understand the role the scientific case studies play in his investigation, we need to know more about the overall shape of his argument in PhP. It is to this that I now turn.

Merleau-Ponty rejects the realist claim that consciousness is a mere part of the world that exists independently of it. He aims to show instead that the world and consciousness are mutually dependent parts of one whole. Merleau-Ponty's philosophy is thus – like Husserl's – transcendental. But, as we will see, he explicitly distances himself from the earlier Husserl's Kantian framework. There is disagreement over how Merleau-Ponty reaches his transcendental position in PhP. To give just three examples, Baldwin (2003) reads PhP as containing *some* argument for its transcendental standpoint, but interprets this argument as being rather weak. The weakness of this argument leads Gardner (2011) to read Merleau-Ponty as providing no proper argument. Instead, he claims, the transcendental position is assumed from the outset. Merleau-Ponty's goal is to radically revise transcendental philosophy, not to argue for the transcendental stance. Hyppolite suggests to Merleau-Ponty in an interview that PhP falls into two unrelated halves – the first is a work of philosophical psychology, whilst the second is a work of metaphysics (Merleau-Ponty 1964b).

The weak argument that Baldwin attributes to Merleau-Ponty is based on various remarks that Merleau-Ponty himself makes in PhP. He rejects the claim that the world exists in-itself. Instead, he claims that the world is dependent on consciousness. In the preface, Merleau-Ponty objects to the scientific point of view, which claims that we know about the world-in-itself, on the following grounds: 'All my knowledge of the world, even my scientific knowledge, is gained from my own particular point of view, or from some experience of the world … The whole universe of science is built upon the world as directly experienced' (1945: ii–iii; 1962: viii; 2002: ix). Similarly, he later objects to the Empiricist view of the world as existing independently from consciousness on the basis that, 'All knowledge takes its place within the horizons opened up by perception' (1945: 240; 1962: 207; 2002: 241). Passages like these have led theorists such as Baldwin to read Merleau-Ponty as claiming that, since all our knowledge of the world is based on experience, we can only know things-as-experienced, not things-in-themselves. Therefore, the nature of things is determined by our experience of them, that is, there are no things-in-themselves. It is clear that this is a bad argument. First, the bare fact that all knowledge of the world is based on experience does not preclude us from coming to know the world-in-itself. Experience might provide us with completely accurate information about the world-in-itself, allowing us to know facts about it. The second, more significant problem is that even if we can only know the world as we experience it, this does not show that the nature of worldly things is determined by our experience of them such that there are no things-in-themselves.

It seems to me, however, that Baldwin is wrong to attribute this argument to Merleau-Ponty. But contrary to Gardner's view, PhP *does* contain argument for the transcendental position. Moreover, Hyppolite is wrong to see the two parts of Merleau-Ponty's discussion as unconnected. The strategy pursued by Merleau-Ponty in PhP is instead as follows. It is usual to see his inquiry as wholly different from, and discontinuous with, scientific investigation. In various ways it is – I will say more about this shortly. Nevertheless, there is an important sense in which Merleau-Ponty's inquiry *is* continuous with scientific investigation. It thus satisfies Husserl's wish that phenomenology should be a kind of science. Moreover, an understanding of this continuity is important to fully appreciate how he reaches his transcendental position, and the role the scientific case studies play in his work.

Scientific inquiry begins with the observation of entities and events, which scientists then seek to analyse. They formulate hypotheses to explain what has been observed. The hypotheses yield predictions for future experience, stating what one will observe in such-and-such conditions. If the predictions conflict with what is actually observed, the hypothesis is modified, or rejected in favour of one that better fits the observed data. Of course, things are not quite so straightforward. It is generally acknowledged that theory is underdetermined by data: the same observed data is consistent with a number of different, conflicting hypotheses. Thus the observed data is only one of the factors that guide the formulation of a hypothesis. Considerations such as simplicity, coherence with other accepted hypotheses are also important. Doubt has also been cast on the idea that observation can be theory-neutral. Theories one accepts will, for example, dictate how one classifies what one observes. They may also affect what one looks for, and so what one finds.

Merleau-Ponty takes our ordinary way of thinking to be Objective Thought. Our conceptual framework is derived from Objective Thinking. Unsurprisingly, Merleau-Ponty sees the scientific investigation of his day as adopting this conceptual framework. Empiricism is the first species of Objective Thought. It endorses the following claims:

E1   The world is composed of determinate entities that stand in external relations to one another.

E2   This world is the world-in-itself.

E3   We can come to know about the world-in-itself.

E4   Consciousness is just another thing in the world, and so obeys its laws.

These claims are unquestioningly taken for granted by Empiricist scientists. However, Merleau-Ponty thinks that these are not truths that have been established beyond all doubt. These claims should instead be thought of as a hypothesis that informs Empiricist scientific inquiry in the following way.

Merleau-Ponty notes that 'All my knowledge, even my scientific knowledge is gained from my own particular point of view, or from some experience of the world' (1945: ii; 1962: viii; 2002: ix). Here, he points out that scientific knowledge stems from experience of the world. Scientists make *observations*. They formulate hypotheses to explain what they have *seen*. These hypotheses yield predictions for future *experience*. Hypotheses are modified or rejected if they conflict with what is *observed*. However, although Empiricist science deals with experience, it aims to study the world as it really is, independently of how anyone experiences it as being, that is, the world-in-itself. The supposition that this is a coherent enterprise is, of course, thesis E3. To fulfil this aim, Empiricist science separates what it considers to be personal and subjective in experience from what it takes to be information about the world-in-itself. This process of sifting is guided by its assumption that the world-in-itself is determinate – and thus measurable – causally determined, and nothing more than the sum of its most basic parts. In other words, the process is guided by claims E1 and E2. It follows that, where experience presents us with something indeterminate, Empiricist science holds that the thing itself is not indeterminate; it is just our experience of it that presents it as such. 'There are many unclear sights, as for example, a landscape on a misty day, but then we always say that no real landscape is in itself unclear. It is only so for us' (Merleau-Ponty 1945: 12; 1962: 6; 2002: 7). Finally, Empiricist scientists assume that consciousness is just another thing in the world – E4. Its doings can thus be explained by appealing to the laws of causation. This claim dictates the kind of theories they offer to explain the activities of consciousness.

A good scientific hypothesis is one that is supported by evidence; a bad hypothesis is one that is *not* supported by the relevant data (subject to the caveats mentioned above). Merleau-Ponty's strategy in PhP is to try and show that the Empiricist hypothesis is not adequately supported by the relevant data. He offers various examples where experience presents the world as indeterminate, ambiguous and populated by entities that stand in internal relations to one another, thus putting pressure on E1. He also presents data which conflict with the Empiricist conception of consciousness, and which cannot be explained within this framework. Since the Empiricist hypothesis conflicts with the relevant evidence, it should be rejected.

At this point, there are two options. One might reject the Empiricist hypothesis wholesale by rejecting all of the claims E1–E4. Or one might reject only part of the Empiricist hypothesis, and retain one or more of its theses. Merleau-Ponty's critique of Empiricist conceptions of consciousness shows – if it is successful – that the activities of consciousness do not admit of causal analysis. One might therefore deny that consciousness is just another thing in the world, so rejecting thesis E4 and replacing it with I4 – the claim that consciousness lies outside the world and is wholly different from it. As I stated above, Merleau-Ponty thinks that, once one has made this move, one is forced to hold that the world is constituted by consciousness. Thus rejecting E4 leads to Intellectualism, which is defined by the following theses:

I1   The world is composed of determinate entities that stand in external relations to one another.
I2   This world is constituted by consciousness.
I3   Thus we cannot come to know about the world-in-itself.
I4   Consciousness lies outside the world and is wholly different from it.

Again, Merleau-Ponty treats this as a hypothesis which informs Intellectualist inquiry. Once more, he seeks to show that this hypothesis is unsupported by the relevant evidence and must thus be rejected. In particular, he aims to establish that explanations of consciousness which take it to lie outside the world and to be wholly different from it are inadequate. Likewise, theories which take the world to be constituted by consciousness cannot properly account for it. It follows that modifying the Empiricist hypothesis by replacing E4 with I4 and, by implication, E2 with I2 is insufficient.

An alternative strategy is to modify the Empiricist hypothesis by rejecting E1: the view that the world is composed of determinate entities that stand in external relations to one another, and is causally determined. If one takes this route, one will present a different description of the world, but retain claims E2–E4 – the world so described is the world-in-itself, we can come to know the world-in-itself, and consciousness is just one of many things in it. A position which seems to adopt this view is Gestalt psychology. Merleau-Ponty makes extensive use of Gestalt ideas and discoveries. But he thinks that the Gestalt psychologists did not understand the full implications of what they discovered. In particular, they did not see that their results actually conflict with the claim that the world they describe is the world-in-itself, and that consciousness is just one of many things in the world. It follows that the Empiricist hypothesis cannot be modified to accommodate the recalcitrant data by simply rejecting E1. Merleau-Ponty's conclusion is that both Empiricism and Intellectualism should be rejected. Neither hypothesis is supported by the relevant data, and neither is capable of properly accounting for consciousness, the world and their relation. PhP is dedicated to developing a new hypothesis which *is* supported by the relevant evidence and can properly account for the world, consciousness and the manner in which they are related.

We can note some points about this strategy. First, as I suggested above, the inquiry Merleau-Ponty conducts in PhP is an empirical one. He proceeds on the basis of observation. He argues against certain hypotheses on the grounds that they cannot accommodate the observed data. He then formulates a set of alternative hypotheses based on observation. In this sense, Merleau-Ponty's investigation is continuous with scientific inquiry. It is, of course, discontinuous with it insofar as science presupposes the Empiricist and/or Intellectualist hypotheses that Merleau-Ponty rejects. Second, Merleau-Ponty does not carry out every part of this strategy systematically in PhP. Sometimes he takes for granted arguments that he has given elsewhere. This is particularly so with respect to his arguments against Gestalt psychology's acceptance of E2, E3 and E4. He gives these in the *Structure of Behaviour* (Merleau-Ponty 1963), and does not revisit them in PhP.

Third, I noted some complications with refuting/confirming hypotheses on the basis of evidence. Merleau-Ponty is well aware of these complications and, as we will see later, explicitly acknowledges that it is impossible to decisively refute or confirm a hypothesis on the basis of evidence. One can always explain away recalcitrant evidence by offering an auxiliary hypothesis to support the main theory one is trying to defend. It follows that Merleau-Ponty cannot offer any conclusive arguments against Empiricism and Intellectualism. Moreover, since Merleau-Ponty's target is not any specific theory, but our conceptual framework in general, the task of refuting our current ideas is made even harder. It is useful to see him as trying to bring about a paradigm-shift. A paradigm is a global way of thinking about some issue, which defines which questions can be raised and how they are to be answered. It is difficult, if not impossible, to argue conclusively for the replacement of one paradigm with another, since each will have different conceptual resources at its disposal. Merleau-Ponty's strategy is to put increasing pressure on the old paradigm of Objective Thought and so persuade us of the need for reform. But he is aware that it will always be possible for proponents of Objective Thought to resist his arguments.

Fourth, my account of Merleau-Ponty's strategy sheds light on the role that description plays in his phenomenology. The early Husserl held that the phenomenologist should simply *describe* experience as it is lived without going beyond what is immediately given. This is so that phenomenology can be 'rigorous'. He draws a sharp contrast between description and explanation, which, by its very nature, goes beyond what is given to the subject. However, the reader may have noticed that there is a problem lurking here. It is not immediately obvious that one *can* merely describe something so that one's description is free from assumptions, explanations, theories and so on. Describing something involves classifying it as being of a certain type and/or as having certain sorts of properties. In other words, it involves subsuming it under concepts. Many, if not all, of the concepts we have at our disposal imply or contain explanations and theories about the things that fall under them. To take just one example, the concept 'tree' includes or implies the information that trees really exist (unlike the concept 'phoenix', which arguably includes the information that those things which fall under it do *not* exist), and that they are living things that grow from seeds. But these facts are not given in a tree-experience. It follows that describing an object of experience as falling under the concept 'tree' imports certain assumptions and explanations into one's description.

Perhaps it is possible to develop concepts to capture the content of experience that do not contain any explanations or assumptions. However, although this may be a possibility for the early Husserl's phenomenology, it is ruled out by Merleau-Ponty's alternative conception of the phenomenological programme. For him, describing experience involves describing an experienced region of the world. It involves listing the worldly items that one experiences. Since these are worldly entities, they go beyond, or transcend, one's experience of them. A real chair, for example, is something over and above my experience of its front. In cataloguing worldly items, one cannot help but make claims about their nature – that they exist, that they have certain properties that distinguish them from one another in certain ways, and so on. In other words, it is impossible to describe them in a way that only captures what is given, and is free from assumptions and theories. There is no sharp line between describing something and offering an explanation of it. One might thus wonder if this is a difficulty for Merleau-Ponty. He certainly presents himself as engaged in the project of describing the phenomenal field, rather than providing explanations for the items it contains. He states, for example, that '[i]t is a matter of describing, not of explaining or analysing' (Merleau-Ponty 1945: ii; 1962: viii; 2002: ix).

However, what Merleau-Ponty does in PhP is not entirely consistent with what he claims to be doing in this quote. He offers us many explanations of the phenomenal field, and puts forward many theories about the world and consciousness. The claim that Merleau-Ponty is engaged in a loosely scientific inquiry sheds light on this issue. He begins his inquiry by collecting data to show that both the Empiricist and Intellectualist hypotheses are inadequate. It is important to report on the available evidence as accurately as possible. This involves describing one's observations as carefully as possible. One can do this whilst still acknowledging that there is no clear line between describing and explaining. What that means, of course, is that one's description of the data can always be defeated if it is shown that it presupposes an explanation that cannot be defended. But this is no big problem for Merleau-Ponty. Again, it just shows that Objective Thought cannot be decisively refuted – it is always possible for a proponent of Objective Thought to argue that a description of some recalcitrant evidence crucially depends upon a theory that Objective Thought rejects. But Merleau-Ponty acknowledges this.

Finally, we are now in a position to see how Merleau-Ponty uses the scientific case studies. These are part of the data that Merleau-Ponty uses to make his case against the Empiricist and Intellectualist hypotheses, and which he tries to explain with his alternative framework. Since the scientific case studies play a role both in his arguments against Objective Thought, and his case in favour of his own position, it will damage the account he offers if these case studies are no longer valid. But his theory can be defended if alternative evidence that does the same job can be found. Various theorists have offered contemporary evidence to support his theories. See, for example, Dreyfus (2000), Kelly (2001), and Carman (2008).

CONCLUSION

Merleau-Ponty is a phenomenologist, and he conceives of himself as bringing Husserl's philosophical project to completion. Like Husserl, he thinks that science and philosophy are in trouble. He holds that the conceptual framework that underpins them – that is, our conceptions of consciousness, the world and the relations between them – is a distorted reflection of the things it describes. He calls this way of thinking 'Objective Thought'. The aim of phenomenology is to reveal its shortcomings to us and provide an alternative conceptual framework. The object of phenomenological investigation is the phenomenal field: the worldly region perceived, as presented to the perceiver. The form of Merleau-Ponty's investigation is, broadly speaking, scientific. He treats Objective Thought as a set of hypotheses that inform nearly all scientific and philosophical investigation. Like all hypotheses, they are open to revision/rejection in the face of recalcitrant evidence. Merleau-Ponty proceeds by observing the world and consciousness. His data comprises descriptions of different forms of lived experience, including pathological cases. To carry out his investigation, he performs the Transcendental-Phenomenological Reduction. This involves suspending the assumptions of Objective Thought in order to describe lived experience in a way that does not presuppose them. The aim is to produce, as far as possible, a 'neutral' description of lived experience that can provide independent evidence for or against the hypotheses of Objective Thought. The evidence he collects cannot be adequately accommodated by Objective Thought. In this way, Merleau-Ponty shows us that Objective Thought must be rejected. He then develops a new conceptual framework, based on his observations of consciousness and the world. We now have an understanding of Merleau-Ponty's aims and the course his investigations will take. We are ready to look at his critique of Objective Thought, and the alternative conceptions of consciousness, the world, and their relation that he offers us. It is to these that I now turn.

2

TRADITIONAL PREJUDICES AND THE RETURN TO PHENOMENA

Merleau-Ponty begins his investigation with a critique of Empiricist and Intellectualist accounts of perception. This will be the focus of the present chapter. His aim is to show us that the traditional assumptions that are made about perception and the theories that rely on them – those of Objective Thought – cannot adequately account for perceptual experience. He thus clears the way to present his alternative account, and begins to put pressure on Objective Thought's conceptual framework.

SENSATION

We saw in Chapter 1 that Objective Thought takes the world to be composed of determinate entities that stand in external relations to one another. The world is thus reducible to its most basic components. This assumption informs Empiricist and Intellectualist accounts of perception in various ways. In particular, it motivates the claim that perceptual experiences – like everything else – are nothing more than the sum of their basic atoms. The most basic units of perceptual experience are *sensations*. The term is found in everyday language, but in Merleau-Ponty's discussion it has a restricted, technical meaning. Whilst perceptual experience is intentional, and presents the subject with something that appears to be an entity in, or a feature of, the world – e.g. cars, dogs, mud, sky – sensations are non-intentional. To have a sensation, in other words, is not to be presented with something that appears to be a part of the external world. Merleau-Ponty begins with a sustained attack on the idea of sensation. He claims that although the notion seems straightforward – we readily talk about sensations of blueness, redness, heat and cold – 'nothing could in fact be more confused' (Merleau-Ponty 1945: 9; 1962: 3; 2002: 3). He considers and rejects three ways that the notion might be understood.

Merleau-Ponty's first argument can be summarised as follows:

(1) Sensations must be homogeneous.
(2) Perception of a completely homogeneous area is impossible.
(3) Therefore, the smallest instant of perceptual experience cannot be sensation.

Premise (1) claims that a single sensation cannot be differentiated in any way; it must be completely uniform. Merleau-Ponty defends premise (1) by appealing to the thought that to experience something as having spatial properties such as shape, extension and location is to be presented with an external object. He then claims that, to experience something as differentiated, one has to experience it as spatial. To experience red and green, for example, one must be presented with a coloured patch – something that has extension. Since to have sensation is, by definition, not to be presented with any kind of external object, it follows that sensations must be homogeneous. Notice that this argument implies that there can be *no* sensations of colour because, to experience even a single, uniform colour, I must be presented with something that has extension.

Merleau-Ponty does not explicitly consider tactile and auditory sensations. But the points made above also apply in the tactile case. It seems that for tactile sensations, differentiation just *is* difference in spatial location. A painful itch is surely not a composite (i.e. differentiated) sensation composed of itching and pain, but rather a uniform sensation of painful itching. To distinguish between itching and pain, they must be located in different parts of my body. Moreover, tactile sensations are *always* experienced as located in the body – it is, for example, my hand that hurts, my foot that itches. An itching or pain that has no location seems inconceivable. Thus it seems that to experience even an undifferentiated tactile sensation requires the experience of spatiality. Again, this implies that there can be no tactile sensations. However, it appears that parallel arguments are *not* available for auditory sensations. I can hear a uniform whistling noise without experiencing that noise as located. Furthermore, I could experience a sound that changed in pitch, or two different sounds at the same time – for example, a whine and a whistle – without experiencing the sound(s) as located in space.

It follows that if premise (1) is supposed to apply to all types of sensation, Merleau-Ponty's defence of it on the grounds that experience of differentiation requires experience of spatiality is not wholly successful. One option is to read his argument as applying to only visual sensations. Since perceptual experience has a visual component, if Merleau-Ponty can show that there is a problem with the notion of a visual sensation, this is sufficient to create difficulties for the view that perceptual experience in general is composed of sensations. Alternatively, one might defend premise (1) differently. Sensations are supposed to be the most basic units of perceptual experience. One might argue they must therefore be indivisible. However, if a sensation is differentiated, it can be divided into more basic components. Thus sensations cannot be differentiated. They must be homogeneous as premise (1) claims.

Premise (2) states that perception of a completely homogeneous area is impossible. The conclusion that Merleau-Ponty wants to draw from this is that sensations cannot be perceived, and so cannot be the smallest instants of perceptual experience. His defence of premise (2) rests on the Gestalt psychologists' claim that every visual experience will have a figure-background structure, and, if an experience is structured in this way, then it is differentiated. The figure is the part of the visual field on which one's attention is focused, whilst the background is the rest of the visual field, to which one is not currently attending. The figure stands out from the background; it coheres and has a shape. The background appears relatively homogeneous, and is perceived as continuing behind the figure. The Gestalt psychologists discovered that both complex and very simple visual experiences have this structure. When I look at my dog, for example, I see him in detail. He stands out from the lawn and flowerbeds surrounding him, which appear fuzzy and indeterminate – I may see that there are flowers to his right, but they appear as an indistinct patch of yellow, I do not see each individual bloom. Although I do not explicitly see the grass beneath my dog's paws, I do not see his paws as located in paw-shaped holes in the lawn. Instead, I see the grass as continuing underneath him. Parallel points apply for very simple perceptions. Figure 2.1, for example, appears as a cross which stands out from a background that continues beneath it.

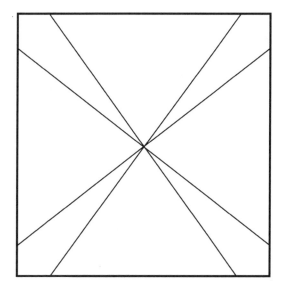

Figure 2.1

Merleau-Ponty argues that perception *necessarily* has a figure-background structure. It is not immediately obvious why he thinks this. Hamlyn (1957) argues, in his discussion of Gestalt psychology, that the figure-background structure of perception is logically necessary because perceiving an object involves identifying it, and to identify it is to distinguish it from other things. He takes this to follow from the definition of objects as individuals that are distinguishable from one another (Hamlyn 1957: 56). But there are problems with this argument. 'Seeing an object' is ambiguous between seeing something which is in fact an object, and seeing something *as* an object. In the latter case, Hamlyn's claim has some initial plausibility. Since objects are distinct individuals, it surely follows that to see something *as* an object is to see it as distinguished from other things. However, although this constraint will be satisfied by experience that has a figure-background structure, it does not show that experience of something as an object *must* be structured in this way. It merely requires that one see more than just that object – for example, to see my dog as an object, I must see the grass and the wall as well as my dog. But the claim that perception has a figure-background structure involves a further thesis about the different manner in which the parts of the visual field are presented – namely that the figure coheres, is unified and stands out from the background. Furthermore, it seems possible to have experiences where Hamlyn's constraint is not met, for example if I view my dog so that he takes up my whole visual field. In this case, I perceive what is in fact an object (my dog) but without perceiving him *as* an object, since he is the only thing that I perceive. It follows that Hamlyn's argument for the claim that perception necessarily has a figure-background structure is unsuccessful.

An alternative argument for premise (2) that seems to better capture what Merleau-Ponty has in mind is this. The Gestalt discovery that visual experience always has a figure-background structure points to the nature of vision. It shows that to see is to focus one's attention on some feature of one's visual field. To do this, there must be features upon which one can focus one's attention. In other words, one's visual field must be differentiated. Merleau-Ponty then appeals to the thought that what we mean by 'vision' is fixed by the actual nature of vision, which we discover empirically. Thus if visual experience in fact has a figure-background structure, then it necessarily has this structure. It follows that the visual field is necessarily differentiated, and perception of a completely homogeneous area is impossible.

However, it is *not* clear that visual experience always has a figure-background structure. Imagine that I walk to the top of a hill and lie down on my back, looking at the sky. The sky is uniformly blue, cloudless and takes up the whole of my visual field. In this case my visual field is undifferentiated, yet I see the sky. Thus it appears that one *can* see a completely homogeneous area after all. There are two related responses that may be offered to this objection. First, one might point to the fact that the visual experience of the sky – like any visual experience – does not occur in isolation from other forms of perception. At the time that one sees the sky, one is also proprioceptively aware of the position of one's limbs relative to one another. One has tactile experience of the ground beneath one's back. It is this experience that provides the background, against which one is able to see the sky as located above one. Without being embedded in this global perception – one might argue – my vision of the sky would not be possible. The second response points out that experiences are not isolated units; they are parts of a 'flow' of experience which is extended in time. The vision of the sky, for example, is preceded by experience of walking through the countryside to reach the hill, the experience of lying down on top of the hill, and so on. One might argue that the previous experience is the background which confers meaning on my current experience. Without the flow of previous experience, I would not be able to see the sky. The onus is thus on Objective Thought to show that it is possible to have an isolated visual experience of the sky. It is completely unclear how this could be established. It thus seems that Merleau-Ponty is right to claim that the perception of a completely homogeneous area is impossible.

Merleau-Ponty's argument shows that sensations cannot be experienced. To put the matter more precisely, sensations are not experiences. But, if sensations are not experiences, then they cannot be the smallest units of experience. This establishes his conclusion (3) that the smallest unit of perceptual experience cannot be sensation.

Merleau-Ponty then considers whether sensations can be understood as sensed qualities such as colours, lights and sounds. He makes two objections to this notion of sensation. First, he points out that sensed qualities such as red and green are presented as properties of the things experienced, not elements of consciousness – one does not have sensations of greenness, one sees green things. But, whereas sensations are supposed to be non-intentional or meaningless, to see a green thing is to have an intentional experience. Merleau-Ponty's second objection is that the qualities we experience are internally related to one another, so that they cannot be specified independently of one another. The colour of a carpet, for example, is affected by its texture so that it appears a specifically woolly red. Moreover, these qualities are again affected by the light falling across the carpet, so that the woolly red of the carpet is experienced as its appearance in sunlight. But sensations are supposed to be simple – the basic units of experience. Merleau-Ponty therefore concludes that sensations cannot be identified with sensed qualities.

Finally, Merleau-Ponty considers whether there is any theoretical support for the notion of sensation. In the last part of his discussion, he examines the Constancy Hypothesis. This theory takes perceptual experience to be an exact 'reproduction' of what is perceived. Perception is caused by objects stimulating our sense-organs, which passively receive information about the world. The effect produced depends on the nature of the stimulus, and the structure of the sense-organ it stimulates. The Constancy Hypothesis claims that there is a one-to-one correspondence between the stimuli and the effects they produce in us. Moreover, it asserts that the same stimulus will always produce the same effect. The Constancy Hypothesis accepts the view that the world is composed of objects with determinate properties that are externally related to one another. In perception, each property perceived stimulates the appropriate sense-organ to produce a sensory impression that corresponds to it. Since the properties of an object are reducible to basic, non-complex properties, so too the impressions that correspond to them are simple. The impressions caused by stimulation of the sense-organs are sensations.

An immediate problem for the Constancy Hypothesis is that there are counterexamples to it. Merleau-Ponty cites the following cases. The frequency of a sound wave is heard by humans as pitch. According to the Constancy Hypothesis, the sound wave stimulates our ears, producing a particular auditory sensation. The sensation produced by a sound wave of one frequency should always be the same. However, as Merleau-Ponty notes, this is not so. If the intensity of the sound wave increases (it gets louder), the sound is heard as changing in pitch.[1] Similarly, each atomic section of a figure on paper should stimulate a point on the retina to produce a visual sensation that corresponds with it, so that the same figure is seen in the same way each time it is viewed. However, two lines of equal length can be made to appear unequal by adding auxiliary lines to the diagram – as in the Müller-Lyer illusion. The differing chromatic thresholds on the retina should affect perception of a coloured area – such as the cover of a large red book – so that the colour is seen as red in some places, but orange or even colourless in others. But, in fact, the colour is perceived as a constant red. A red stimulus should always give rise to a red sensation, and a green one to a green sensation, but in certain circumstances red and green act together to produce an experience of grey. The size an object appears should correspond to the size of the image produced on the retina. But instead the apparent size of an object varies with its apparent distance. A toy cow held close to my face, for example, will produce an image on my retina that is the same size as the image produced by a real cow some distance away from me. Yet I will perceive the toy cow as smaller than the real cow, despite the fact that both produce retinal images of the same size.

Advocates of the Constancy Hypothesis deal with these cases in different ways. The last two examples – the variation of an object's apparent size with its apparent distance, and the grey produced in certain circumstances by combining red and green – are simply treated as rare exceptions to the Constancy Hypothesis. However, the other cases are brought into line with the Constancy Hypothesis by claiming that the expected sensations are produced, but are unnoticed by the subject. In some of the cases listed above, the expected sensations can be produced by practice, rest, being given more precise instructions by the experimenter, or simply paying closer attention to what is perceived. If one practises looking at the Müller-Lyer lines, for example, one can perceive them as being of equal length. Theorists who favour the Constancy Hypothesis cite this fact as evidence for the claim that the expected sensations are present but unnoticed.

Merleau-Ponty's first objection is that the decision to treat certain cases as exceptions to the Constancy Hypothesis, whilst bringing others into line with it by appealing to the auxiliary claim about unnoticed sensations, is ad hoc. There seems to be no principled difference between the two sorts of case, thus, if one is willing to accept two as exceptions to the Constancy Hypothesis, one should accept them *all* as exceptions to it – which, of course, makes the exceptions less rare and more damaging. Köhler (1971: 21) suggests that the decision to allow certain cases as exceptions is made when there seems to be a simple law relating stimuli and sensation.[2] There are, for example, very simple laws governing the mixture of colours, which may explain why advocates of the Constancy Hypothesis accept that red and green can be combined to produce a sensation of grey. However, the appeal to simple laws does not refute Merleau-Ponty's accusation that the decision to treat the cases differently is ad hoc. There is, for example, a simple law governing perception of the Müller-Lyer lines, namely, that the lines will first appear unequal, although one may train oneself to see them as equal through practice. One might try to argue that, although there are regularities in the appearance of the Müller-Lyer lines, there is too much variation – for example, in the amount of practice different people need to see them as equal – for there to be a simple law governing their appearance. But even if such an argument could be successfully developed, there are other problems.

Merleau-Ponty points out that the appearance which conflicts with the Constancy Hypothesis still needs to be explained. The fact that one can, with practice, perceive the Müller-Lyer lines as equal does not explain the first appearance of them as unequal. Advocates of the Constancy Hypothesis appeal to a further auxiliary claim at this point. They argue that the 'appearance' that conflicts with the Constancy Hypothesis is not a sensory experience at all, but a judgement. Thus the subject does not *perceive* the Müller-Lyer lines as unequal; they *judge* that this is so. Notice that since it seems to the subject that they *experience* the lines as unequal, the judgement that leads to error about the hypothesised sensations must also be unnoticed (Köhler 1971).

It should be clear at this point that the Constancy Hypothesis cannot be decisively refuted on the basis of experience. Recalcitrant data can always be explained by introducing auxiliary hypotheses. The same is true, Merleau-Ponty acknowledges, of all empirical theories.[3] Nevertheless, he holds that the Constancy Hypothesis can be *discredited* on the basis of experience. Merleau-Ponty does this by first identifying problems with the auxiliary claims that bring the recalcitrant data into line with the Constancy Hypothesis, then raising difficulties for the assumptions that underpin it. Merleau-Ponty objects to the auxiliary claims on the grounds that it is the Constancy Hypothesis alone which provides the rationale for accepting them; they have no independent support. It is only if one holds that the same stimulus always produces the same sensation that one has justification for claiming that there are unnoticed sensations in cases such as the Müller-Lyer lines. Similarly, it is the thesis that there is a one-to-one correspondence between stimuli and sensations that motivates the claim that certain 'appearances' are really false judgements – for example, the first 'appearance' of the Müller-Lyer lines as unequal. Advocates of the Constancy Hypothesis point to the fact that the expected sensations can be produced through practice, etc., as evidence for the claim that they are always present but sometimes unnoticed. However, as Merleau-Ponty points out, one could equally argue that the perceptions produced under these special conditions are non-standard. Rather than revealing sensations that were there all along, one could hold that these conditions produce non-standard appearances. Again, it is only prior acceptance of the Constancy Hypothesis that motivates the interpretation of these cases as revealing existing, but unnoticed, sensations. The phenomenon does not provide any independent evidence for this claim. It follows that the auxiliary claims required to save the

Constancy Hypothesis in the face of conflicting experience are ad hoc.

Merleau-Ponty identifies two central theses that underpin the Constancy Hypothesis. The first is a conception of the body and the way it functions. As we have seen, advocates of the Constancy Hypothesis take perceptual experience to be a faithful 'copy' of what is perceived. Worldly stimuli are detected by the sense-organs, which simply 'transmit' the information received to consciousness in the form of sensations. The nature of the stimuli, together with the structure of the sense-organs that detect them, completely determine which sensations are produced. Qualitatively identical stimuli, detected by the same sensory system, result in sensations of the same type. Conversely, a single stimulus will give rise to different sensations, if there is a change in the structure of the sensory system that detects it. Moreover, it is claimed that the sensory systems function independently from one another so that damage to one system results in the loss or modification of specific sensations – those produced by the damaged systems – whilst the rest of sensory experience remains unaffected.

However, injuries to the body show that this conception of it cannot be maintained. Rather than functioning independently, the sensory systems work together as a whole. When one system is damaged, the body compensates for the injury. Where, for example, injury/disease leads to a reduced number of skin receptors sensitive to temperature and pressure, the motor system compensates and the person unthinkingly moves their hands more vigorously across the surface of objects they touch. Similarly, damage to different parts of the visual system should affect experience differently, according to the Constancy Hypothesis. But, instead, visual experience is always affected in the same way, no matter which part of the visual system is damaged. The parts of the visual system do not function independently from one another, but work together to compensate for injury (Merleau-Ponty 1945: 15–16; 1962: 9; 2002: 10).

Likewise, the idea that perceptual experience is just a reproduction of the external world, where each component of the external world is represented by a sensation caused by it, must be rejected. Instead, perceptual experience is 'composed' (1945: 16; 1962: 9; 2002: 10). Information about the world is combined to produce sense-experience in a way that belies any simple one-to-one correspondence between elements of the world and perceptions of it. This is shown by the pattern of experience following damage to the visual system. First, the saturation of all colours is reduced. Next, the spectrum of colours experienced diminishes to four colours, then two. Finally, the subject experiences only a grey, monochrome colour, which is reportedly different from any colour normally experienced. In these cases, injury does not simply result in the loss of specific sensations. Instead, the richness of visual experience as a whole is affected. There is a 'change to a less differentiated and more primitive structure' (Stein 1928).[4] It follows that the body and its sense-organs cannot be thought of as transmitters that detect information and merely relay it to consciousness in the form of corresponding sensations, as the Constancy Hypothesis supposes.

The second thesis that underpins the Constancy Hypothesis is the idea that perceptual experience is atomistic, that is, nothing more than the sum total of its basic components. This is implied by the conception of perceptual experience as a reproduction of what is perceived, where each perceived property is represented by a perceptual atom (a sensation) caused by it. Merleau-Ponty's discussion of sensation has already raised considerable difficulties for this view. First, the qualities of perceived objects are internally related to one another so that the carpet, for example, appears a specifically woolly red. It follows that the redness and the woolliness cannot be specified independently. The same is true, Merleau-Ponty argues, of all perceived qualities. Second, the context in which something is seen affects the way it appears. The Müller-Lyer lines illustrate this point. Seen alone, the parallel lines appear equal, but, seen in a context that includes the auxiliary lines, they appear to be of different lengths. A third feature of perceptual experience that Merleau-Ponty draws to our attention is the fact that it contains 'gaps'. One can, for example, perceive a crystal as having a regular shape without having counted, even tacitly, its sides. Similarly, one can see someone's face on lots of different occasions without ever seeing the colour of the person's eyes. Moreover, these 'gaps' do not literally appear as holes in one's perceptual field – my friend's irises, for example, do not appear as blank spaces within his eyes.

Merleau-Ponty also observes that perception has both implicit and indeterminate aspects. Consider again, the fact that perception has a figure-background structure. The figure is perceived distinctly and in detail, whilst the background appears less determinate. One perceives the background as continuing behind the figure. It follows that one sometimes see things that are presented as vague something-or-others, for example the things one sees out of the corner of one's eye. The perceiver also sees things that are not presented explicitly, for example the parts of the background that are hidden by the figure. The latter claim requires more explanation. To see what is at issue, it will be helpful to reflect on two features of perceptual experience: one sees things from a point of view in space, and things one sees are presented as taking up space. If one accepts that we really *see* things with depth, rather than merely *inferring* that we see them, then it follows that parts of the things one sees will be both hidden – since it is impossible to see all of a three-dimensional object from one perspective – *and* somehow perceived. If I look down at a mug, for example, I can only see the rim of the mug, the top of the handle and the surface of the coffee it contains. But I do not experience it as a two-dimensional mug-slice. It presents me with an object that takes up a certain amount of space, seen from a particular point of view. It follows that my experience must present the mug as having hidden parts – a surface which rests on the table, a bottom half of a handle, and so on. Merleau-Ponty thus describes perceptual experience as having both explicit aspects (what is in view) and implicit aspects (what is hidden). Following Husserl, he calls the implicit aspects of perceptual experience its 'horizons'. All of these features of perceptual experience show that it cannot be reduced to a collection of perceptual atoms. Instead, the experience as a whole is something over and above the sum of its parts.

Having identified what he takes to be insurmountable problems with the notion of sensation, Merleau-Ponty then examines theories of perception that appeal to it. He divides these into two sorts: Empiricist theories and Intellectualist theories. Both theories assume that perceptual experience is atomistic, and then try to account for it in terms of its most basic constituents: sensations. The task facing both theories is thus to explain how sensations are combined to produce perceptual experience.

EMPIRICISM

Empiricism takes consciousness to be just another thing in the world, and thus answerable to the laws of causation. Perceiving is not something that consciousness *does*; it is simply something that happens. On this view, sensations are combined by causal processes. Merleau-Ponty's fundamental objection to Empiricism is that it faces a dilemma. On the one hand, the Empiricist can hold that it is the intrinsic properties of sensations which determine how they are combined. However, to take this line is to give up the idea that they are non-intentional, and so abandon the very notion of sensation. Suppose, for example, that I experience what appears to be a camel. According to the Empiricist, one component of my experience will be a sensation of beige. If one holds that it is an intrinsic property (or properties) of the sensation which determines that it is a part of my camel experience, one is effectively claiming that the beige sensation has the property of 'seeming to be part of a camel'. But, since to experience something that seems to be part of a camel is to be presented with what appears to be something in the world, this means that the beige sensation is intentional. One might object that sensations can determine how they are to be combined without seeming to be parts of things or other features of the world. Each sensation could instead have the property of 'belonging to a certain part of the perceptual field' (where 'the perceptual field' is simply the array of appearances given in perception). However, this suggestion does not overcome the problem that Merleau-Ponty has raised. The perceptual field has apparent spatial properties – things are experienced as located in space. The property of belonging to a certain part of the perceptual field will thus be the property of being located at a certain place in experienced space. But to experience something as located in space is to experience it as part of the world. Thus if sensations have the intrinsic property of 'belonging to a certain part of the perceptual field', they are intentional.

On the other hand, the other option is to hold that sensations are *not* combined in virtue of their intrinsic properties. Nothing about the sensations themselves determines that they are components of a camel experience, for example, rather than an experience of sand. The Empiricist who takes this line must say *what* determines how sensations are combined. The problem is that no matter what answer they give to this question, the claim that the organisation of sensations is determined by something external to them destroys the idea that there is any connection between perceptual experience and the things perceived. It follows that perception can no longer be thought of as a way of finding out about the world. Suppose, for example, that I have a train experience. According to the Empiricist, the sensations which constitute my experience are caused by things in the world interacting with my sense-organs. However, nothing about the sensations themselves determines their combination as a train experience. If it should turn out that the thing causing the sensations is in fact a train, this is no more than a happy accident. It is a complete coincidence that my perceptual experience reflects what the world is like.

One might suppose that the Empiricist can overcome this problem by claiming that the worldly things that cause the sensations also determine how they are combined. When I perceive a train, for example, the train both causes certain sensations and causes them to combine as a train experience. According to this proposal, the sensations are organised by something external to them – the train – but, since it is the thing perceived that causes them to combine, a connection is retained between the perceived thing and perceptual experience. However, there is a serious difficulty with this suggestion. To claim that a thing in the world acts upon sensations and causes them to combine is to effectively claim that the perceiver detects those worldly things. But it is wholly unclear how the things are detected. The method of detection certainly cannot involve the body's sensory systems, because the operation of the senses – on the Empiricist view – merely gives rise to sensations. Thus if it is perceived things which cause sensations to combine, perceivers must have some extrasensory means of detecting them. Moreover, since it is the organisation of sensations that results in perceptual experience, the claim that things in the world cause sensations to combine, effectively makes all perception extrasensory perception. This is not a credible position.

The dilemma facing the Empiricist is inescapable. But Merleau-Ponty also considers specific problems for various Empiricist accounts of how sensations combine to produce experiences. One Empiricist account holds that 'proximities or likenesses cause [the sensations] to associate' (Merleau-Ponty 1945: 23; 1962: 16; 2002: 18). Certain sensations appear similar and/or next to each other, and this causes them to be grouped together as things. A sensation of dark beige, for example, is both similar and near to a sensation of light beige, and this causes the two sensations to be associated as parts of a camel experience. Merleau-Ponty objects to this proposal on the grounds that the perception of things is prior to the perception of proximities and likenesses. There are various ways in which this is so. First, one in fact perceives things before one perceives proximities and likenesses. Merleau-Ponty writes,

> If I walk along a shore towards a ship which has run aground, and the funnel or masts merge into the forest bordering on the sand dune, there will be a moment when these details suddenly become part of the ship, and indissolubly fused with it. As I approached, I did not perceive resemblances or proximities which finally came together to form a continuous picture of the upper part of the ship. I merely felt that the look of the object was on the point of altering ... Suddenly the sight before me was recast in a manner satisfying to my vague expectation.
>
> (Merleau-Ponty 1945: 24; 1962: 17; 2002: 20)

He notes that once the perceptual 'switch' has occurred, one notices the resemblances between the ship and its funnels and masts, and sees that the funnel and masts are next to the ship.

However, these are observations one makes *after* one sees the funnels and masts as parts of the ship.

Merleau-Ponty also argues that there is a conceptual problem with supposing that the perception of proximities and likenesses is prior to the perception of things. In the case of proximity, to see something as next to something else, one has to see both of them as located in space. Thus it is only if the subject is already presented with a spatial world, that they can experience proximity. There is also a problem in the case of resemblance. Items resemble one another if they share their properties; they do not resemble one another if their properties diverge. For resemblance to cause certain of the perceiver's sensations to associate as a thing, those sensations must possess properties that they share with each other and not with the other sensations the perceiver has at that time. However, the sensations that associate with one another as a particular thing cannot share *all* their properties. It is generally accepted that if an individual *a* has exactly the same properties as an individual *b*, then *a* and *b* are one and the same individual – that is, they are numerically identical.[5] Moreover, all sensations share at least one property – the property of being a sensation – and many sensations will share further properties, for example the property of being a visual sensation, the property of being a tactile sensation, and so on. Thus the sensations which associate with one another as a thing will share some of their properties with other sensations. Moreover, it seems that the only property shared by all, and only those sensations which associate as a thing, is the property of being associated as that thing. But this is a property those sensations have only *after* they are associated. It is not a property that can explain how they are caused to associate. It follows that the association of sensations cannot be caused by proximities and likenesses.

A second Empiricist proposal is that the experience of motion allows certain sensations to become associated with one another to yield the experience of a thing. In other words, the perceiver experiences a cluster of sensations moving across their perceptual field, and this leads to those sensations being associated so that they experience them as a single thing – a red car, for instance. However, it is clear that this suggestion is hopeless. For one thing, the perceiver sees as things many entities that they never see in motion, for example houses, the sun, and mountains (Merleau-Ponty 1945: 23; 1962: 15; 2002: 18). The Empiricist might respond by claiming that the perceiver first gains the ability to associate groupings of sensations as things through seeing entities in motion. They then transfer this ability to static things, associating certain groupings of sensations as mountains, houses and so forth. But Merleau-Ponty points out that, for the transference to occur, it must be brought about by some property (or properties) of the sensations that the perceiver associates as motionless things. If so, then this property is sufficient to bring about the association of those sensations as a thing without the need for the transference. It follows that the appeal to motion is redundant.

A further problem is that the experience of motion is the experience of some*thing* moving, which means that the perception of things is prior to the experience of motion. The subject has to already see the red sensations, for example, as a red thing in order to see them as *moving* across her perceptual field. If they do not already see them as a red thing, then they merely experience a changing flux of colours, rather than motion. Thus it cannot be the experience of motion that brings about the association of sensations as things.

Finally, Merleau-Ponty considers the Empiricist claim that 'the sense-data [i.e. sensations] must be filled out by a projection of memories' (1945: 27; 1962: 19; 2002: 22). Certain sensations are experienced as a thing of a particular sort because I have experienced a similar thing in the past – for example, I experience certain sensations as a camel because I have previously experienced camels. However, as Merleau-Ponty notes, this proposal gets us nowhere. There must be something about the current sensations which explains why certain memories are evoked and not others. But for my current sensations to remind me of camels they must already be organised as a camel or something that looks like one. If there is nothing about the sensations that places constraints on which memories are evoked, any memories could surface and perception will not have any determinate content. It follows that the Empiricist's appeal to memory is unsuccessful.

INTELLECTUALISM

Merleau-Ponty then considers Intellectualist theories of perception. Like Empiricism, Intellectualism conceives of the world as
constituted by entities that stand in external relations to one
another and interact causally. But Intellectualists disagree with
the Empiricist view that consciousness is causally determined. In
the first instance, Intellectualism accords consciousness an active
role – it can *do* things; conscious events are not merely caused to
come about. An implication of this view is that consciousness
cannot be just another thing in the world, since everything in the
world is causally determined. If one follows this view to its logical conclusion, Merleau-Ponty thinks that one is forced to
embrace transcendental idealism: the thesis that consciousness lies
wholly outside the world and constitutes it.

Merleau-Ponty considers two forms of Intellectualist thinking
about perception. The first is a strict counterpart to Empiricism.
Both theories claim that perceptual experience is composed of
sensations. They differ in their explanation of how these sensations are combined to form perceptual experiences. Whilst the
Empiricist claims that sensations are combined by automatic,
causal processes, the Intellectualist argues that the perceiver
interprets the sensations and makes judgements about what they
see. Merleau-Ponty calls this position 'the Intellectualism of the
psychologists' (1945: 46; 1962: 36; 2002: 42), since many psychologists of his time endorsed it. Intellectualism of this sort has
not yet moved away from scientific realism. It accepts the objective existence of the external world, and takes the subject to be an
entity within it. The second Intellectualist view of perception is
that found in the work of transcendental idealists such as Kant
and the early Husserl. This version of Intellectualism holds that
the world we perceive is constituted by consciousness. The sen-
suous matter of experience – sensations – is combined in accordance with intelligible rules to form whole perceptual experiences
in acts of *synthesis*. These are still acts of consciousness – synthesis
is not a causal process – but they occur below the level of ordinary awareness. The combination of sensations is no longer held to
be the result of judgement. Intellectualist accounts of this sort

aim to identify the rules that order sensations. Their goal is to provide an account of the essential, intelligible structure of experience. Merleau-Ponty holds that both forms of Intellectualist thinking about perception are untenable.

The first sort of Intellectualism takes all perception to involve judgement, which is introduced by theorists as 'what sensations lack to make perception possible' (Merleau-Ponty 1945: 40; 1962: 32; 2002: 37). Merleau-Ponty offers two examples of this kind of Intellectualist thinking about perception. Both are from Descartes's *Second Meditation*. The first one is Descartes's analysis of perceiving a lump of beeswax. Merleau-Ponty reads Descartes as identifying sense-experience with atomic sensations of what he takes to be the wax's perceptible properties – a visual sensation of yellow, a smell of flowers, a taste of honey, a sensation of hardness, a sensation of coolness. Descartes then reasons that the wax, that is, the worldly item perceived, is not identical with this cluster of properties because it can lose all of them. If it is heated, it will become warm and soft; if it is burnt, it will change its colour to a deeper brown; over time it will lose the taste of honey and the scent of flowers. He concludes from this that sensations do not present the perceiver with the wax itself. Thus perceiving the wax involves judging that I see it. The second example is Descartes's analysis of perceiving people in the street. We take ourselves to perceive *people*. But Descartes argues that, since the people are completely hidden inside their clothes, it is only their garments and not the people themselves that can cast an image on the retina. Thus we only have sensations of their hats and coats. It follows that we must judge that we perceive people (Descartes 1996: 20–21).

Merleau-Ponty notes that Descartes's reasoning betrays an acceptance of Objective Thought. In the case of the beeswax, Merleau-Ponty argues that Descartes misses the actual perceptual experience of the beeswax from two directions. First, he identifies sense-experience with atomic sensations of discrete properties, when in fact the properties presented to us in perception are internally related and cannot be specified independently from one another. The colour of the wax, for example, is that of something which is soft to the touch, and one literally *sees* that it will make a

dull sound if one pats it with one's finger. One also sees that the
wax can change its shape; it appears to the perceiver as something
that can be manipulated and moulded. Second, Descartes assumes
that the thing perceived is the thing as described by science.
Once he has made this assumption, he does not examine the
object of perception as it is perceived. He simply concludes that,
since the beeswax as described by science is a certain physical
structure whose essential properties can only be detected with
scientific instruments, one must judge that one is confronted with
it. In this way also, Descartes misses what it is actually like to
perceive the beeswax. There are similar problems with Descartes's
analysis of perceiving people. He again makes the mistake of
identifying sense-experience with sensations. He also argues from
considerations about which things in the world can throw light
on the retina to conclusions about what must be sensed. In so
doing, Descartes reveals that he is prejudiced in favour of the
world: he starts with objects in the world – hats, coats, the retina,
etc. – and tries to construct perceptual experience from them.
Merleau-Ponty has already shown that this strategy distorts the
actual nature of perceptual experience. Reasoning from objects in
the world will not allow one to draw accurate conclusions about
perception.

Descartes's reasoning about perception illustrates the problems
that face Intellectualism. Notice first that the Intellectualist faces
the same fundamental dilemma as the Empiricist. In Descartes's
analyses, the perceiver's sensations ground their judgements about
what they perceive. However, for the perceiver to judge that they
perceive p on the basis of their sensations, p must have the property of appearing to be p. For my beige sensations, for example, to
motivate my judgement that I am looking at a camel, those beige
sensations must look like a camel. If this is so, then the subject
already has perceptual experience of p; the judgement that they
perceive p is redundant. Furthermore, to claim that the sensations
have the property of appearing to be p is to give up the idea that
they are non-intentional, and so to give up the very notion of
sensation. The alternative is to hold that the perceiver's judgement about what they perceive is *not* motivated by her sensations.
But if the Intellectualist takes *this* line, perception loses any

contact with the world perceived. The Intellectualist must either hold that the subject's judgements about what they perceive are groundless, in which case they are not judgements at all, but just wild guesses. If the subject guesses correctly, this is purely coincidental. Or the Intellectualist must take the subject's judgements to be grounded in something other than their sensations. However, whatever it is that grounds their judgements cannot have any connection with the world, or else the subject has been attributed with an extrasensory means of sensing the world, which is utterly implausible. Thus, in both cases, the connection between perception and the world is lost.

The Intellectualist claim that perceiving involves judgement also faces difficulties. As Descartes's reasoning illustrates, the perceiver interprets 'the evidence' provided by their senses in the form of sensations, and draws a conclusion about what they perceive (Merleau-Ponty 1945: 42; 1962: 33; 2002: 39). Consequently, the Intellectualist must reject a claim we ordinarily make about the difference between perceiving and judging. Ordinarily, we think that 'judgement [is] the taking of a stand' (1945: 43; 1962: 34; 2002: 39). To judge that p, in other words, is to endorse p as true; it is to accept the truth of p. But 'sense experience, on the contrary, is taking appearance at its face value' so that one can perceive p without endorsing p as true (1945: 43; 1962: 34; 2002: 39). Clearly, one can no longer maintain that perception and judgement differ in this way, once perceiving p is understood as judging that one perceives p.

The rejection of this distinction makes it difficult to account for cases where the perceiver's judgement about how things are is different from how they see things as being. This sometimes happens in the case of figures that can be seen in more than one way, for example the duck-rabbit, where the perceiver may judge that the figure can be seen in two ways, whilst only being able to see it in one. It also occurs in cases of optical illusions, for example Zöllner's illusion, where the perceiver may judge that the long lines are parallel, whilst seeing them as converging. Since seeing that p also involves judging that p on the Intellectualist view, the perceiver must make a pair of inconsistent judgements. In the case of Zöllner's illusion, for example, they judge,

(1)   The long lines are parallel.
(2)   The long lines converge.

But the Intellectualist can offer no explanation for this incon-sistency. Moreover, inconsistency in one's judgements usually constitutes some form of irrationality. However, there seems to be nothing irrational about the mismatch between one's judgements and one's perceptions in cases like Zöllner's illusion.

Figures like the duck-rabbit that can be seen in more than one way present an additional problem for the Intellectualist. The 'look' of these diagrams is apt to change so that, for example, one sees a rabbit, and then suddenly it looks like a duck. No satis-factory explanation of this phenomenon can be given once per-ception is understood as judgement. The Intellectualist has to claim that the perceiver first judges that the figure is a drawing of a rabbit, then revises their judgement to hold that it is a drawing of a duck. But the Intellectualist cannot explain *why* the subject revises their judgement. The claim that sensations are combined by judgement must be rejected.

Merleau-Ponty then considers the second sort of Intellectual-ism, which holds that perceptual experience is the result of synthesis. Sensations are combined in accordance with intelligible rules to form whole perceptual experiences. This is done below the level of ordinary awareness. The combination of sensations is no longer held to be the work of judgement. Intellectualist accounts of this sort aim to identify the rules that order sensa-tions. Their goal is to provide an account of the essential, intelli-gible structure of experience. Since this kind of Intellectualism denies that experience is of an independently existing world, this view does not face the fundamental dilemma that confronts Empiricism and the first kind of Intellectualist analysis. However, there are other problems.

Merleau-Ponty observes that perceptual experience *does* have a structure or follows certain rules – certain arrangements and con-junctions of phenomena regularly give rise to certain perceptual meanings. In Zöllner's illusion, for example, a certain arrange-ment of lines gives rise to the appearance that the longer lines are converging. Similarly, paralysis of the oculo-motor muscles makes the landscape appear to be moving to the left, whenever the perceiver believes they have turned their eyes to the left. Again, a distant church looks nearer if the objects between it and the perceiver are hidden with a screen; the church suddenly looks further away if the screen is removed so that the objects in between are visible. Merleau-Ponty calls the regularities that hold between arrangements of phenomena, and the perceptual meanings that emerge from them, a 'perceptual syntax' (1945: 45; 1962: 36; 2002: 42).

But, although perceptual experience is organised according to this 'syntax', its structure cannot be accounted for by Intellectualism. The problem is that, for Intellectualism, the principles by which perceptual experience is structured must be amenable to reason. Intellectualism in its first phase appeals to judgement to explain how perceptual experience is constructed from sensations. Judging is a rational activity. A central aim of judgement is truth. Thus one judges that p when one has reason to believe that p is true. In its second phase, Intellectualism no longer aims to explain perceptual experience. Instead, the aim is to uncover its essential structure. However, the principles by which perceptual experience is organised are still assumed to be rational principles that can be grasped by conceptual thought. We can see this assumption at work in Kant's approach, where he reaches claims about how experience must be structured on the basis of *a priori* argument. The problem with perceptual syntax is that it is *not* comprised of a set of rational principles. Another way of putting the matter is this – the arrangements of phenomena are not reasons for the perceptual meaning that emerges. As Merleau-Ponty remarks, 'there is *no reason* why a steeple should appear to me to be smaller and farther away when I am better able to see in detail the slopes and fields between me and it' [italics in original] (1945: 60; 1962: 48; 2002: 56).

One might object at this point that, although there is no reason why a steeple appears smaller when it is farther away, the steeple's being smaller is a *cause* of my seeing it as farther away. But, if one takes this line, then one has given up the Intellectualist position, which holds that acts of consciousness are not caused. More importantly, Merleau-Ponty observes that perceptual syntax cannot be understood as a set of causal laws relating arrangements of phenomena (the causes) to perceptual meanings (their effects) either. Consider, for example, the Müller-Lyer lines. Perceivers tend to see one as shorter than the other. The arrangement of the parallel and auxiliary lines gives rise to the impression that the longer lines are unequal in length. However, the lines' arrangement cannot be understood to *cause* this appearance. For this to be so, the arrangement of lines would always have to produce the same effect. But we have already seen that this is not so; with practice, the parallel lines can be seen as the same length. Moreover, practice cannot be thought of as a causal factor that combines with other such factors to produce some effect. Practice cannot be determinately measured, and there is no fact of the matter about how much practice is required to see the lines as equal in length.

The arrangement and conjunction of phenomena does not provide a *reason* for the perceptual meaning that emerges from it; neither does it *cause* the meaning to appear. Merleau-Ponty uses a notion developed by Edith Stein (1922) in her doctoral thesis to capture the relation: 'motivation' (Merleau-Ponty 1945: 40; 1962: 31; 2002: 36). Motives bring about, that is, motivate, acts of consciousness. They have two defining characteristics. First, a motive is 'an antecedent which acts only through its significance' (1945: 299; 1962: 259; 2002: 301). In other words, its motivating force is not the result of its brute physical characteristics. If this were the case, a motive with certain physical characteristics would always bring about the motivated phenomena, but, as we have just seen, this is not the case. Instead, it is the motive's meaning that brings about the motivated phenomena. This will become clearer later on, when we have more examples of motivation in front of us. Second, the motive and what it motivates are internally related.

As we will see later, there are different kinds of motive, and the way in which they are internally related to what they motivate varies. One sort of internal relation obtains between a thing and its parts if the thing is more than the sum of its parts and so cannot be reduced to them. In the case of the Müller-Lyer lines, the motivated phenomenon is the perception of the lines as either unequal, or – if one is practised at viewing them – equal. The overall perception of the lines is motivated by its components: the experience of the long lines combined with the auxiliary lines. But the perception taken as a whole is not reducible to the simple sum of its parts; it is something over and above the sum of its basic components. Another sort of internal relation obtains between two things if one or both of them could not retain their identity without standing in this relation. In the case of the steeple, Merleau-Ponty holds that the experience of its apparent size is just an experience of its distance. One sees distance because one sees apparent size – in this sense, apparent size motivates the experience of distance. But the experience of apparent size cannot retain its identity as this experience without being a perception of distance. We will examine Merleau-Ponty's account of depth perception in more detail in Chapter 4.

CONCLUSION

Merleau-Ponty's conclusion is that Objective Thought cannot account for perception. The claim that perceptual experiences are nothing more than the sum of their basic, non-intentional parts (sensations) cannot be upheld. The notion of sensation is deeply problematic. Theories which try to account for perceptual experience in terms of sensation face insurmountable difficulties. Finally, the analysis of perceptual syntax reveals that Objective Thought does not have the conceptual resources at its disposal to capture the way in which perceptual experience is organised. Intellectualism tries to account for it in terms of rational principles that can be grasped by conceptual thought. But, as we have seen, the structure of perceptual experience is not amenable to reason. The only other option available to Objective Thought is to try and account for perceptual syntax by appealing to causation – this is an Empiricist strategy. But the arrangement and conjunction of phenomena are not the cause of the perceptual meanings that emerge from them. It follows that we must reject Objective Thought if we are to provide an adequate account of perception.

3

THE BODY

One of Merleau-Ponty's most important ideas is his thesis that
the body is a form of consciousness. As we have seen, both var-
iants of Objective Thought – Empiricism and Intellectualism –
conceive of the body as a physical object, which is answerable to
causal laws, and does not differ in any significant respect from
other physical objects like tables and rocks. Empiricism takes
consciousness to be the result of causal goings-on in the body.
Intellectualism argues that consciousness cannot be understood as
the outcome of causal processes. However, since it accepts the
notion of the body as a mere physical object, Intellectualism has
to conceive of consciousness as non-physical. Merleau-Ponty
argues in contrast that the body cannot be thought of as a mere
object. Instead, it is a subject: a form of consciousness. Moreover,
bodily consciousness underpins those states and activities that we
tend to think of as mental, for example beliefs, desires, thinking.
Bodily consciousness is manifest in perceiving and acting, and it
is through his analyses of perception and action that Merleau-
Ponty develops his notion of bodily subjectivity. An important
part of his discussion of these topics focuses on a pathological case
studied by Goldstein and Gelb (1920): a First World War

veteran named Schneider whose brain was injured by shrapnel. Much of this chapter will focus on Merleau-Ponty's treatment of Schneider, although I will also refer to ideas developed elsewhere in Merleau-Ponty's work. Typically, Merleau-Ponty does not present an explicit, fully worked out theory or set of principles at the outset. Instead, he begins with some initial ideas, then slowly develops and refines them through the course of the discussion. His conceptions of perception and action thus emerge gradually as he considers Schneider's case.[1]

THE CASE OF SCHNEIDER

Schneider's brain injury impaired his capacity for action in rather odd ways. Experiments reveal that he cannot point to a part of his body unless he is allowed to grasp it (Merleau-Ponty 1945: 120; 1962: 103; 2002: 118). If he is stung by a mosquito, he can immediately scratch the place where he was stung (1945: 122; 1962: 105; 2002: 121). However, if a doctor presses a ruler on a part of his body, Schneider cannot point to the part that has been touched unless he goes through preparatory movements, which involve moving his whole body, then gradually confining the movements to the part pressed by a doctor (1945: 124; 1962: 107; 2002: 122). Likewise, Schneider has great difficulty moving the parts of his body when asked to do so by an experimenter. He needs to either watch the relevant limb or perform preparatory movements, which again consist in moving his whole body, then confining movement to the part he has been asked to move (1945: 120; 1962: 103; 2002: 118). Surprisingly, however, Schneider can perform those habitual actions needed in his day-to-day living – for example, taking a match from a box and lighting a lamp, taking a handkerchief from his pocket and blowing his nose – without any problem. He even has a job manufacturing wallets, where his production rate is three-quarters that of a normal workman (1945: 120; 1962: 103; 2002: 118). Goldstein and Gelb (1920) label those actions that Schneider cannot easily perform 'abstract' and those with which he has no difficulty, 'concrete'.

Two preliminary points can be made about Schneider's disability. First, Schneider does not experience difficulties acting at random. He is *consistently* able to grasp, but not point; immediately identify the site of a mosquito bite, but not the touch of a ruler; perform actions in his day-to-day life, but not move his body to order. It is thus implausible to think that the only difference between abstract and concrete actions is the mere fact that Schneider can perform the latter with ease, but not the former. Instead, there must be some independent means of distinguishing between the things that Schneider can and cannot do, which helps explain his impaired abilities. It follows that a proper understanding of Schneider's case requires a grasp of what distinguishes concrete from abstract actions. Second, it is obvious that acting requires a grasp of how one's own body is orientated in space and with respect to one's surroundings. To kick a ball, for example, I must know (in some sense) where my leg is in relation to the ball; to raise my arm, I must have a grasp of where my arm is and which direction is up. This thesis provides a way to understand why Schneider, when ordered to move part of his body by an experimenter, must watch the relevant limb or perform preparatory movements. These movements enable him to '"find" the operative limb, the direction or pace of the movement, and finally the plane in which it is to be executed' (Merleau-Ponty 1945: 127; 1962: 109; 2002: 126). He finds out the same information by looking. Since normal people do not need to look, nor engage in preparatory movements, before moving parts of their bodies to order, Schneider must lack the ordinary 'knowledge' individuals normally have of their body's orientation in space – at least when it comes to abstract actions.

SCHNEIDER AND OBJECTIVE THOUGHT

Merleau-Ponty argues that no satisfactory account of Schneider's case can be given by Objective Thought. He reaches this conclusion by criticising what were, at the time he was writing, contemporary analyses of Schneider, which he takes to be representative of Objective Thought in its two forms – Empiricism and Intellectualism.

Empiricism takes the world to be causally determined and atomistic – that is, constituted by, and nothing more than the sum of, its basic parts. Empiricism holds that human subjects are things in the world like any other. Their doings are entirely determined by causal laws, and they are composed of externally related basic constituents. Empiricist accounts of Schneider's case therefore attempt to give a causal explanation of his disabilities. They assume that his various capacities can be identified separately, and function in relative isolation from each other. Merleau-Ponty considers two Empiricist analyses. Both claim that the difference between abstract and concrete actions is that their performance requires different sensory information. The first holds that the performance of abstract actions relies primarily on visual information. The agent must be able to *see* how their body is orientated in space to perform an action of this sort. The grasp of bodily orientation required to perform concrete actions, on the other hand, is held to be primarily tactile (Merleau-Ponty 1945: 131–2; 1962: 113; 2002: 130). On this account, Schneider's disability is caused by visual deficits: he cannot see properly, and this results in difficulties when he tries to perform abstract actions. But his sense of touch is intact, thus he can perform concrete actions with no problem. The second Empiricist analysis that Merleau-Ponty considers claims, in contrast, that the performance of abstract actions requires a tactile grasp of bodily orientation. On this account, Schneider's impairment is caused by tactile deficiencies.

Merleau-Ponty points out that these two hypotheses are clearly incompatible. Moreover, there is evidence which supports and conflicts with both hypotheses. Schneider's brain injury, for example, resulted in a condition that Merleau-Ponty calls 'psychological blindness' (1945: 134; 1962: 116; 2002: 133). His description indicates that it is what is more commonly known as 'visual agnosia'. It typically results from damage to the occipital lobe, which is an area of the brain responsible for processing visual information. It is this area that is damaged in Schneider. People who suffer from this condition typically see the shape, colour and texture of objects, but are unable to see them as things of particular sorts (1945: 152; 1962: 131; 2002: 151). This supports the first hypothesis and tells against the second. However, other patients share Schneider's disabilities, but, unlike Schneider, their impairments result from damage to the cerebellum, which is an area of the brain responsible for coordinating movement. Damage to this area typically leads to tactile and motor deficits. This fact tells against the first hypothesis and supports the second.

We therefore have two competing causal explanations of Schneider's case. They are incompatible with one another, and each is supported by some – but not all – of the evidence. One might suppose that this is not a particular problem. Any theory can be made consistent with observation by adding auxiliary hypotheses to explain away any conflict. We have seen, for example, how defenders of the Constancy Hypothesis deal with apparent counter-examples to the theory by appealing to the claim that there are unnoticed sensations. Thus one can appeal to auxiliary hypotheses to explain the data that conflicts with each account of Schneider's disability. Since any theory can be made consistent with the data, other factors aside from consistency are also relevant when choosing between competing hypotheses. One must also consider such things as how simple the theory is, how many auxiliary hypotheses it requires to bring it into line with the data, whether there is any independent support for these hypotheses, and so on. Thus one may suppose that we can choose between the competing causal explanations of Schneider's case on this basis (Merleau-Ponty 1945: 137; 1962: 117; 2002: 135). However, Merleau-Ponty argues that one cannot choose between them in this way. Neither is simpler than the other. Neither appeals to problematic auxiliary hypotheses to explain recalcitrant data. The explanations are exactly parallel.

Merleau-Ponty provides the following diagnosis of the situation. The claim that it is damage to Schneider's sight – and not to his sense of touch – that causes his impaired capacity for action, presupposes that vision and touch are independent so that damage to one does not affect the other. The independence of sight and touch is also presupposed by the alternative claim that Schneider's impaired capacity for action is caused by damage to his tactile sense, rather than any visual deficiencies. Merleau-Ponty suggests that the fact that there is no principled way of choosing between these explanations shows that sight and touch are *not* independent, but internally related so that 'there is not in the normal subject a tactile experience and also a visual one, but an integrated experience to which it is impossible to gauge the contribution of each sense' (1945: 138; 1962: 119; 2002: 137). The same is true of the other senses.

Merleau-Ponty's diagnosis is confirmed by the nature of ordinary sense experience. Notice first that, when I experience something in more than one sensory modality, I do not have two different experiences which I then judge to be of the same thing. Instead, I am simply presented with an entity that has various sensible properties – that is, a colour, a smell, a texture and so on. Suppose, for example, that my dog is standing in front of me barking. I both see and hear him. But I do not have a visual perception of a dog opening and shutting his mouth, and an auditory perception of barking, which I judge to be experiences of the same entity. I simply see and hear my dog barking. Moreover, each of my senses presents me with more than just those properties which strictly correspond to it. Merleau-Ponty has already observed that I *see* the carpet as being a woolly red. Notice that this means that vision presents me with how the carpet feels to the touch. Similarly,

> One sees the hardness and brittleness of glass, and when, with a tinkling sound, it breaks, this sound is conveyed by the visible glass. One sees the springiness of steel, the ductility of red-hot steel, the hardness of a plane blade, the softness of shavings ... The form of a fold in linen or cotton shows us the resilience or dryness of the fibre, the coldness or warmth of the material ... In the jerk of the twig from which a bird has just flown, we read its flexibility or elasticity, and it is thus that a branch of an apple-tree or a birch are immediately distinguishable. One sees the weight of a block of cast iron which sinks in the sand, the fluidity of water and the viscosity of syrup. In the same way, I hear the hardness and unevenness of cobbles in the sound of a car, and we speak appropriately of a 'soft', 'dull' or 'sharp' sound.
>
> (Merleau-Ponty 1945: 265; 1962: 229–30; 2002: 266–7)

Each sensory modality is able to present me with properties that do not strictly correspond to it because the senses are not discrete modes of experiencing the world. Instead, they are integrated with, and transform one another, so that we should think of them as internally related components of a unified perceptual system.

The discussion so far has focused on the five senses: sight, touch, taste, hearing and smell. However, the normal subject also has proprioceptive awareness of their own body. The proprioceptive systems include those which provide information about nutrition and fatigue – resulting in feelings of hunger and tiredness – the sense of balance, the kinaesthetic sense we have of our own movements, the 'internal' sense we have of the position of our limbs relative to one another, and so on. Proprioception is also integrated with the five senses in various ways. I am, for example, proprioceptively aware of my right hand. If I also look at it, I simply see the hand of which I am proprioceptively aware. I do not have two different experiences – one visual, one proprioceptive – which I judge to be of the same thing.

Perhaps more significantly, proprioception is an integral component of other modes of sense experience, such that some authors are led to deny that it is a separate sensory modality at all – indeed, Carman (2008) attributes this thesis to Merleau-Ponty. Consider the sense of touch. Tactile awareness of things in the world is given via proprioceptive awareness of one's own body. Running my hands along my cat's body, for example, gives me an awareness of her shape, texture and temperature. It is the proprioceptive awareness of the shape of my hands as I hold my cat that gives me an awareness of *her* shape. My awareness of her texture and temperature is constituted by sensations of warmth and furriness, which I feel in my hands. We can see from this example that proprioception is an integral part of the sense of touch. Merleau-Ponty also emphasises the role of proprioception in vision. He writes,

> When I walk round my flat, the various aspects in which it presents itself to me could not possibly appear as views of one and the same thing if I did not know that each of them represents the flat seen from one spot or another, and if I were unaware of my movements, and of my body as retaining its identity through the stages of those movements.

> (Merleau-Ponty 1945: 235; 1962: 203; 2002: 235)

He points out here that one sees changing aspects of the entities around oneself. I see the front of the chair, followed by the side of the chair, then the back of the chair as I walk around it. For these to be experienced as stable objects rather than fleeting appearances requires an awareness of how one is moving relative to those objects. This is provided in part by one's proprioceptive awareness of one's own body.

The integration of the senses means that one cannot take Schneider's impaired capacity for action to be caused by damage to just one of his senses. However, Merleau-Ponty makes a much stronger claim in his discussion of the competing explanations. He claims that *no* causal account of Schneider's case can be given: 'behaviour ... [is] inaccessible to causal thought' (1945: 139; 1962: 120; 2002: 138). It is not immediately obvious how Merleau-Ponty reaches this conclusion. It is certainly stronger than is warranted by his examination of the two Empiricist accounts outlined above. One way of understanding his argument here is this. The fact that the senses are integrated and do not function in isolation from one another conflicts with Empiricism's atomistic conception of human subjects. This puts a certain amount of pressure on the Empiricist position, and loosens the hold that this perspective may have on us. The way is thus open for Merleau-Ponty to offer his alternative analysis of Schneider's case. As we will see below, Merleau-Ponty's account of Schneider is incompatible with a causal explanation of his disability. We can then see Merleau-Ponty as relying on inference as the best explanation to make his case. He holds that his account is the best analysis of the evidence and should thus be accepted. Since it is incompatible with causal explanations, we should reject any causal (i.e. Empiricist) analysis of Schneider's impairments.

Objective Thought's alternative to Empiricism is Intellectualism. One sort of Intellectualism accepts the Empiricist's view of the world, but identifies consciousness with mental states and activities. Merleau-Ponty takes this view of consciousness to be incompatible with thinking of it as causally determined. Since all physical things are causally determined, this view implies a non-corporeal conception of consciousness, although theorists may have Intellectualist tendencies, without explicitly endorsing the view that consciousness is non-physical. Intellectualist analyses of Schneider take his disability to result from a failure of what they variously call his 'symbolic function', 'abstract attitude', 'categorial attitude' and 'power of objectification' (Merleau-Ponty 1945: 140–41; 1962: 121; 2002: 139). Merleau-Ponty takes all of these terms to refer to basically the same capacity, despite some slight differences between the notions. These terms refer to the ability to abstract from the particulars of a situation and subsume entities under general categories. In short, these terms refer to the capacity for conceptual representation. Intellectualism, in other words, understands Schneider's impairment to be a failure of thought. Merleau-Ponty makes a case against the Intellectualist treatment of Schneider and argues for his own analysis in tandem. Step by step, he offers an interpretation of the evidence – which he takes to be the best analysis of it – showing how it is incompatible with an Intellectualist account. Thus his case against Intellectualism can again be viewed as resting on inference to the best explanation.

The view of action that is held by the majority of contemporary theorists is one that Merleau-Ponty would class as Intellectualist. It holds that actions are essentially brought about by thoughts that represent their performance. Actions are distinguished from things that merely happen to the agent on this basis. Generally speaking, theorists claim that intentions are responsible for bringing about action. But it does not matter for Merleau-Ponty which kind of thought is taken to have this role. In what follows, I will talk about intention for ease of reference, but what I say should be understood as applying *mutatis mutandis* to whichever kind of thought is held to bring about action.

The nature of thought is itself controversial. But it is sufficient for our purposes to conceive of thoughts as conceptual representations, where these are such that the capacity to form them is independent of context. Someone who, for example, possesses concepts of the Queen, ownership and pet kangaroos can represent the Queen as having a pet kangaroo irrespective of the context in which they finds themselves. Some care is needed here. There are rational constraints on thinking which dictate when a subject should *not* have certain thoughts and when they *should* have others. It is widely claimed, for example, that beliefs aim at the truth, and so a subject should not believe that their dog is ill unless they have good reason for supposing that this is the case. A subject should intend to stop visiting the casino if they believe that this is possible, and that it would be beneficial to do so. However, the rational constraints on thought can be accommodated without giving up the idea that thinking is independent of context. It is common to hold that different types of thought involve taking up different attitudes to represented states of affairs. It can thus be maintained that a subject can, at any time, form a conceptual representation of something for which they possess the relevant concepts. But rationality dictates when they should, or should not, take up a certain attitude – believing, desiring, intending and so forth – to the states of affairs they represent.

Given this conception of action, one may account for Schneider in two ways. One option is to claim that, whilst Schneider can form conceptual representations of actions in contexts where those actions are concrete, he cannot do so in contexts where the actions are abstract. But the ability to form a conceptual representation is supposed to be independent of context. Thus an account of Schneider along these lines must be rejected. A second option is to argue that Schneider's difficulty lies not with his ability to form conceptual representations, but with his capacity to take up the right attitude – that is, the one that initiates action – towards them. Thus, whilst Schneider can form a conceptual representation of, for example, an arm-raising whenever he likes, he can only intend to raise his arm in contexts where this action is concrete. However, this suggestion fares no better than the previous one. There are two ways to account for Schneider's impaired capacity in terms of an inability to form the relevant intentions. In both cases, Schneider's disorder becomes primarily a failure of rationality.

Rational constraints prohibit intending to φ in cases where one does not believe that one can φ and/or one's various reasons for action, for example, moral considerations, practical concerns and so on, combine so that one's overall preference is for not φ-ing. On the one hand, one might argue that Schneider is rational in what he intends, so that he is unable to form intentions when this contravenes the rational constraints on intending. His inability to raise his arm when the psychologist asks him will therefore result from the belief that he cannot do so, or because he has reasons that weigh heavily against this course of action. But, if the former is the case, then Schneider has an irrational belief, because he has no good reason for thinking that he cannot raise his arm in response to the psychologist's order. In particular, this belief cannot be justified on the grounds that he experiences difficulties doing so. According to the present suggestion, the belief is what brings about the difficulties, thus the difficulties cannot justify the belief. If Schneider cannot intend to raise his arm because he has reasons that weigh heavily against doing so in a context where this action is abstract, then this preference is irrational, because there are no reasons that should weigh so heavily with Schneider.

On the other hand, one might hold that it is not the rational constraints on intention that prevent Schneider from intending to raise his arm. There are other factors that may prohibit a subject from having certain thoughts. They may, for example, be unable to understand them, or be ignorant of the state of affairs they represent. My limited mathematical powers mean that I cannot believe Fermat's Last Theorem. Moreover, a subject who is prevented from thinking about particular things by such factors is not irrational – I am not irrational because I cannot believe Fermat's Last Theorem. However, these prohibitions on thought all involve an inability to form a conceptual representation of the state of affairs concerned. An inability to form conceptual representations of certain actions has already been ruled out as an explanation of Schneider's disability. Thus it cannot be factors such as ignorance or lack of understanding that result in Schneider's impairment. Thus one must accept that Schneider is able to form conceptual representations of abstract actions, is not rationally prevented from intending to perform these actions, but is nevertheless unable to intend to perform them. A subject in this position is irrational. Consider, for example, the following case. Nicky is able to conceptually represent Jo's owning a black dog. She has good reason to think that Jo owns a black dog (i.e. she is not rationally prevented from believing that Jo owns a black dog). But she is unable to believe that this is the case. It is clear that Nicky's inability to believe that Jo owns a black dog is irrational.

The same is true of Schneider's hypothesised inability to intend to raise his arm when a psychologist asks him.

There are (at least) three serious problems with the claim that Schneider's impairment results from an inability to intend to perform abstract actions. First, these explanations do not explain why it is only abstract actions that create difficulties for Schneider. They offer suggestions as to what goes wrong when Schneider has difficulty acting, but they shed no light on *why* this happens on certain occasions, but not others. Second, the claim that Schneider's impairment is a failure of rationality does not fit the facts of his case. Merleau-Ponty tells us that 'Schneider's general intelligence is intact; his replies are slow, never meaningless, but those of a mature, thinking man who takes an interest in the doctor's experiments' (1945: 156; 1962: 134; 2002: 155). Third, it is implausible to hold that it is thought which Schneider lacks. When Schneider is asked by a psychologist to raise his arm, he clearly understands the order and tries to obey it – this is evidenced by the fact that he engages in a process which eventually leads to his raising his arm. These considerations may not be absolutely fatal, but they do strongly suggest that no satisfactory account of Schneider's impairment can be given if one holds that actions are essentially brought about by the agent's thoughts. It follows that some alternative account of action is needed.

ABSORBED COPING

Merleau-Ponty develops an alternative account of action through further consideration of Schneider. A proper understanding of his disability requires an account of the difference between concrete and abstract actions. Merleau-Ponty distinguishes them on the grounds that concrete actions are – and abstract actions are not – 'relevant to an actual situation' (1945: 119; 1962: 103; 2002: 118). One might initially suppose that 'an actual situation' is the agent's actual environment. One might then understand actions that are relevant to one's actual situation as those that have some connection with one's actual surroundings – for example, by being responsive to, or involving interaction with, things in one's immediate vicinity. But psychologists are as much a feature of Schneider's environment as anything else. It is thus hard to see how one could exclude arm-raising in response to a psychologist's order – an abstract action – from the class of actions that are relevant to one's actual surroundings, no matter how one construes 'relevant'.

In fact, Merleau-Ponty does not mean the agent's actual surroundings, by 'actual situation'. Instead, the notion is linked to his ideas about perception, which he takes to have been established by the Gestalt psychologists. Merleau-Ponty holds that perceptual experience presents the perceiver with things that have a meaning or value for them, in terms of their capacities to interact with these things. The perceiver perceives their environment as 'inviting' them to interact with it in certain ways, as 'offering' certain possibilities for action and 'disallowing' others. In other words, the perceiver is not confronted with things that have merely 'objective' properties such as size, shape and so on. Instead, things look edible, reachable, kickable, etc. This fact about perceptual experience is reflected in ordinary claims we make about the way things look. We talk, for example, about certain kinds of food as looking delicious and appetising, which is to say that we perceive it as inviting us to eat it. Similarly, a dog can be described as looking dangerous, that is, we perceive it as not-to-be-stroked, as 'forbidding' us to go near. Merleau-Ponty cites Koffka's (1928) example of a candle flame that literally looks repulsive to a child who has been burnt by it – the child perceives the flame as to-be-avoided (Merleau-Ponty 1945: 64; 1962: 52; 2002: 60). We can also see from these examples that perception has an affective or emotive dimension. The affective values of perceived things contribute to the perceiver's sense of what behaviour is appropriate or required. A city, for example, can feel foreboding, and this diffuse sense of danger 'invites' the perceiver to pay close attention to their surroundings, to walk quickly, not to linger. One's home, in contrast, feels familiar and safe. It invites one to relax, to let down one's guard.

The behaviour one perceives one's surroundings as requiring is partly determined by one's current task or project. Consider this example from the *Structure of Behaviour*,

> For the player in action the football field is not an 'object' ... It is
> pervaded by lines of force (the 'yard' lines; those which demarcate the
> 'penalty area') and articulated into sectors (for example the 'open-
> ings' between the adversaries) which call for a certain mode of action.
>
> (Merleau-Ponty 1963: 168)

In this passage, Merleau-Ponty observes that, to the player
engaged in a game of football, the pitch is presented as a dynamic
space that offers the player opportunities to perform various
actions. The player does not simply perceive the yard lines and
those that mark out the penalty area as white lines with a particular location in space. Instead, they perceive them as real
boundaries that mark out areas of the pitch that have significance
for their behaviour. They do not merely see the spaces between
the players on the opposing team as places where no one is standing, but as 'openings', that is, opportunities to pass the ball to a
team mate or to progress towards the goal. However, the player only
perceives the pitch like this when they are playing football. If
they accidentally wander on to the pitch during a game whilst
walking their dog, they will see the ball as to-be-avoided, rather
than as to-be-intercepted.

It follows that, at any one time, the agent does not perceive
their surroundings as offering a disparate collection of actions.
Instead they perceive it as demanding a certain form of behaviour.
The agent's environment, perceived as requiring a particular kind
of behaviour, is their actual situation. Merleau-Ponty writes of
Schneider's experience at work,

> [T]he space is given to him in the form of the world at this moment; it
> is the piece of leather 'to be cut up'; it is the lining 'to be sewn'. The
> bench, scissors, pieces of leather offer themselves to the subject as
> poles of action; *through their combined values they delimit a certain
> situation* [my italics] ... which calls for a certain mode of resolution, a
> certain kind of work.
>
> (Merleau-Ponty 1945: 123; 1962: 106; 2002: 122)

Schneider perceives things that present him with particular
opportunities for action. His current task is making wallets, and

so he perceives opportunities to engage in this task. Thus Schneider's actual situation is a wallet-making situation.

Concrete actions – those that are 'relevant to an actual situation' – are actions that correspond to the agent's perception of their surroundings at the time they act. Abstract actions are those that do not. Thus the actions Schneider performs in his day-to-day living are concrete because they correspond to the opportunities for action he perceives his environment as offering, whilst actions such as raising his arm in response to a psychologist's order do not correspond to any of the opportunities for action that Schneider perceives. Having described the difference between concrete and abstract actions, we need to know why this difference affects Schneider's capacity for action. Merleau-Ponty offers the following account of Schneider's case. He claims that certain actions are not brought about by thought, but by perceived opportunities for action. The agent perceives their environment as requiring a certain action, and this perception immediately brings about their performance of it. The capacity to respond to one's perceived surroundings by engaging in the behaviour they require is intact in Schneider, which is why he can perform concrete actions with ease. They are brought about by his perceived environment.[2]

It is not unusual to experience one's behaviour as occurring in response to the perceived situation, without the guidance of thought. Consider what it is like to behave in accordance with social norms. Merleau-Ponty observes, 'the conventions of our social group, or our set of listeners, immediately elicits from us the words, attitudes and tone which are fitting ... by a sort of remote attraction' (1945: 124; 1962: 106; 2002: 122). I do not have to constantly *think* about how to behave when I am, for example, at a dinner party. Instead, I have a sense that it is a formal occasion and unthinkingly modify my behaviour to suit. Similarly, I do not think about behaving in a more relaxed manner with my close friends. I just feel at ease and spontaneously relax. There are many other examples. A driver may unthinkingly swerve to avoid hitting a dog they see in the middle of the road. A goalkeeper may automatically dive to catch the ball they see coming towards them. A person may absentmindedly wander into the kitchen to make a cup of tea whilst wondering where to go for dinner. Merleau-Ponty claims that in these cases where the agent experiences their actions as occurring without the guidance of thought, it is their perceived environment that initiates and controls their behaviour. Thus it is the sense of formality or ease that regulates my social behaviour; the driver's perception of the dog as to-be-avoided that brings about their swerving action; the goalkeeper's perception of the ball as to-be-intercepted that initiates their dive; and the person's perception of the kettle as for-boiling-water, the mug as for-holding-tea and so on that brings about their action of tea-making.

The ability to see opportunities for action, and respond to them by acting, is conferred upon the agent by their motor skills. These are physical abilities. To possess a motor skill is to be able to *do* something. They encompass very simple capacities, such as the ability to scratch oneself, through to more complex skills, such as the ability to play guitar. Motor skills contribute to the content of perception as follows. To exercise any motor skill, one must be in the right kind of environment – for example, to exercise my skill at horse-riding, my surroundings must contain a horse. Since exercising a motor skill requires a certain sort of environment, possession of that skill essentially involves the ability to identify environments that are appropriate for exercising it. Merleau-Ponty holds that recognising an opportunity to engage in some activity is not a matter of judging that one may do so. Instead, the sub- ject immediately perceives suitable surroundings as offering an opportunity to exercise their skill. Acquiring a motor skill is thus partly a matter of learning to perceive opportunities to exercise it. Consider, for example, what is involved in learning to climb. One of the things one must learn is to see fissures and ledges in the rock as hand and foot holds. When one is a beginner, only the wider ledges and larger fissures will look suitable. But, as one gets better at climbing, one will perceive smaller fissures as offering passage up the rock face. In this way, one progresses from seeing the rock as an impassable mass to seeing it as climbable. The better one becomes at climbing, the better one becomes at perceiving opportunities to do so and discriminating between rock faces that are more or less difficult to climb. Thus motor skills furnish the subject with ways of perceiving the world.

Motor skills are gained through practice. One learns to do x by attempting to do x, and practising until one becomes proficient. Practice involves familiarising oneself with an activity so that, eventually, engaging in it feels like 'second nature'. Consider, for example, learning to roller-skate. I cannot become skilled at roller-skating by simply thinking about doing so; I must actually try to skate. To begin with, I feel awkward with the skates strapped to my feet. I feel unusually tall, ungainly and encumbered. I find the sensation of being on wheels strange, and the bodily movements required to propel myself along feel unnatural. I move tentatively and without confidence. I often stumble over. But, as I practise, wearing roller skates starts to feel more comfortable. I cease to be aware of my added height. I manage to stay upright, and no longer feel that I might fall at any moment. I start to move confidently as the bodily movements needed for skating feel less awkward. The more I practise, the better I become at making minute adjustments to my posture to keep my balance. I start to lean forward and crouch down slightly when I am skating along. As I move my legs to propel myself forward, I learn to shift my weight just enough to aid propulsion without overbalancing. Through practice, I become familiar with roller-skating so that it feels natural to me. The same applies to other motor skills.

Merleau-Ponty includes one's habits amongst one's motor skills. His account of how we acquire motor skills explains this categorisation. Like motor skills, habits are acquired through 'practice': one develops a habit by doing something in the same way several times. As with motor skills, one's habitual ways of behaving feel like second nature. They also contribute to the content of perceptual experience. Consider, for example, a woman who habitually wears a hat with a large feather. She is so used to wearing it that she no longer notices the extra weight of the hat on her head, and immediately sees whether her hat will fit through the doorway (Merleau-Ponty 1945: 167; 1962: 143; 2002: 165).

Merleau-Ponty describes perceptual experience as having an affective dimension which contributes to the subject's perception of their surroundings as requiring certain forms of behaviour. Since the subject's skills and habits enable them to perceive their environment as offering certain opportunities for action, we should expect them to also contribute to the affective values of perceived things. This is the case. Objects one is skilled at manipulating *feel* familiar; interacting with and using them feels entirely natural. But one's habitual interactions with things also results in their having more specific affective values. My repeated interactions with my dog, for example, result in my perception of him as lovable and friendly – a being for which certain kinds of caring behaviour are appropriate.

Once an agent has become skilled at some activity, they can perceive opportunities to engage in it, and immediately respond to those perceptions by acting, without the need to think about what they are doing. It is because I have acquired the necessary social skills that I can behave politely at the dinner party, and relax with my friends. It is the agent's skill at driving that allows them to immediately react to the perceived demands of the road. The goalkeeper's football skills enable them to unthinkingly dive as they see the ball sailing towards the goal. Someone who repeatedly brews tea in their kitchen can do so 'on automatic pilot' without needing to think about where the teabags are kept, how much water to put in the kettle and so forth. Dreyfus (2000) calls this sort of activity 'absorbed coping'.

INTELLECTUALISM AGAIN

At this point, the Intellectualist may offer an analysis of Schneider's case. Merleau-Ponty has argued that Schneider's concrete actions are performed in immediate response to his perceived environment; they are not initiated or guided by thought. The Intellectualist may thus argue that Schneider's concrete actions are *caused* by his environment – they are mechanical responses to a stimulus. Abstract actions, on the other hand, *are* initiated and guided by thought. Schneider's brain injury has interfered with his ability to form conceptual representations, and this is why he has difficulties performing abstract actions. Furthermore, one might think that Merleau-Ponty's account of how it is possible to act in response to one's perceived environment provides some support for this hypothesis. Responding to one's perceived surroundings by acting is made possible by the acquisition of motor skills, which one acquires through practice. One might argue that practice is in fact conditioning and the resulting motor skill is a conditioned reflex. The behaviour is produced causally by an appropriate environmental stimulus. Motor skills are thus comparable to the reflex Pavlov produced in his dogs. He conditioned them to associate a bell with receiving food, so that, eventually, hearing the bell caused them to salivate.

Merleau-Ponty objects to such an analysis in the following passage,

> Any mechanistic theory runs up against the fact that the learning process is systematic; the subject does not weld together individual movements and individual stimuli but acquires the power to respond with a certain type of solution to situations of a general sort of form. The situations may differ widely from case to case, and the response movements may be entrusted sometimes to one operative organ, sometimes to another, both situations and responses in the various cases having in common not so much a partial identity of elements as a shared meaning.
>
> (Merleau-Ponty 1945: 166; 1962: 142; 2002: 164–5)

Objective Thought takes causes to completely determine their effects; identical causes will always bring about identical effects. It claims that it is the purely physical characteristics of entities that enter into causal processes. (The only thing held to have non-physical characteristics is, of course, consciousness as conceived by Intellectualism.) Consider, for example, a billiard ball that is hit by a cue and so caused to move across the table. The way in which it moves – speed, direction and so forth – is entirely determined by the manner in which it is hit. Hit the ball the same way a second time and its movement will be identical. The ball is caused to move because of such things as the ball's weight and shape, the texture and gradient of the table, etc. If one holds that motor skills are conditioned reflexes, one is committed to the following two claims. Given any two instances of exercising a particular motor skill, those two sequences of behaviour will be identical in all the relevant physical respects – that is, they will share all of those physical properties that are claimed to enter into the causal process. The stimuli that are claimed to bring about those two sequences of behaviour will also share all of their relevant physical properties.

The problem with this, as Merleau-Ponty points out, is that it is simply false. Consider, for example, the ability to play the organ. There is great variation in the skilled organist's responses – they can play a number of different tunes. There is also variation in the organs that they are able to play. With just an hour's rehearsal, they are capable of giving a performance on an organ whose pedals and stops are arranged differently to those of the organ on which they practise (Merleau-Ponty 1945: 169; 1962: 145; 2002: 168). But an hour is nowhere near long enough to develop another set of conditioned reflexes. Even very simple motor skills exhibit this variation. Doors, for example, vary in their size, heaviness, handle shape and position, whether they open inwards or outwards, and so on. An agent who has learnt to open doors can contend with doors in all their variety. Once they have acquired the ability to open doors, they can open those whose physical elements are different from any they have previously encountered. Moreover, the agent is able to open doors in different ways – with their left hand, with their right hand, with their foot if they have their hands full, and so on.

There is yet a further problem with the claim that motor skills are conditioned reflexes. As noted above, causes are physical and they completely determine their effects. It follows that, if certain physical conditions obtain, the behaviour they supposedly cause must occur. However, motor skills are not exercised in response to the agent's environment where this is understood in merely physical terms. They are exercised in response to the agent's *perceived* surroundings. The football player, for example, does not kick the ball in response to the ball, conceived as an object with a certain size, shape, made from a certain material, etc. They kick it in response to their perception of it as requiring them to boot it towards the goal. It follows that the supposition that motor skills are conditioned reflexes is completely implausible. The

Intellectualist cannot maintain that Schneider's concrete behaviour is merely caused by his environment, whilst the problems
he experiences when trying to perform abstract actions consists in
some disorder of thought.

MOTOR SKILLS AS PRACTICAL KNOWLEDGE

Merleau-Ponty holds that motor skills are practical knowledge.
He talks of a skilled typist, for example, as having 'knowledge in
the hands' (1945: 168; 1962: 144; 2002: 166). Theorists sometimes distinguish between two types of knowledge: knowing *that*
such-and-such is the case, and knowing *how* to do something
(Ryle 1949). Knowledge that *p* is propositional knowledge. It is
constituted by beliefs, where these are thoughts as traditionally
conceived. The subject forms a conceptual representation of *p* and
endorses it as true (that is, they take up the attitude of believing
towards the proposition that *p*). The subject's beliefs must be true
and they must have adequate justification for them, or have
formed them using an appropriate method for them to be classed
as knowledge. Knowing how to φ, on the other hand, consists in
being able to φ when one is in the right kind of environment for
φ-ing. Know-how is supposed to be a distinctive form of knowledge that cannot be reduced to φ. The concept of know-how is
useful for understanding Merleau-Ponty's claim that motor skills
are a kind of practical knowledge. To be skilled at φ-ing involves
being able to φ when circumstances permit, that is, it involves
knowing how to φ. Moreover, Merleau-Ponty argues that the
kind of knowledge comprised by motor skills does not consist in
conceptual beliefs. He offers various considerations in support of
this view.

First, the subject may not be able to state the knowledge which
is manifest by their ability to φ. 'It is possible to know how to
type without being able to say where the letters which make the
words are to be found on the banks of keys' (Merleau-Ponty 1945:
168; 1962: 143–4; 2002: 166). The thought here is that the
subject's inability to state where the keys are indicates that they
have no beliefs about their position. Since this makes no difference to their ability to type, it follows that knowing how to type

is not constituted by beliefs about how to do so. It is generally accepted that being able to say what one believes is a good test for whether or not one believes it – one can find out what someone believes by asking them. Nevertheless, one might object that Merleau-Ponty moves too quickly from the fact that the subject is unable to state that *p* to the conclusion that they lack the belief that *p*. There are cases where we ascribe beliefs to a subject who cannot express them. Suppose, for example, that Giles sees Joan murder the butler. He blocks this distressing event from his mind, and, if asked, cannot say who murdered the butler. But he starts to behave fearfully towards Joan. A common way to analyse cases like this is as involving suppressed beliefs. On this account, Giles is ascribed the belief that Joan killed the butler, even though he cannot say who the murderer is.

However, the existence of suppressed beliefs does not show that Merleau-Ponty's treatment of the typing case is flawed. For one thing, cases of suppressed belief typically involve facts that are too distressing for the subject to acknowledge, but there is no reason why the position of the letters on the keyboard should result in anguish for the typist. Perhaps, more importantly, one may question whether having a suppressed belief that *p* should be analysed as conceptually representing *p*, and endorsing this proposition as true. I will say more about this below. But for now we can note that if there is a question over whether or not Giles has a conceptual belief that he cannot express linguistically, then his case cannot be used to show that Merleau-Ponty's treatment of the typist example is problematic. The same is true of other cases where we might be inclined to say that the subject believes *p* although they cannot say so – for example, where the subject has no linguistic capacities. It is not clear that the subject should be ascribed a conceptual belief in these cases. Thus they do not tell against Merleau-Ponty's treatment of the typist.

The fact that subjects may not be able to state the knowledge that is manifest by the exercise of their motor skills does not show conclusively that it is not constituted by beliefs. However, Merleau-Ponty offers another, more compelling reason for this conclusion. Consider how motor skills are acquired. One engages in repeated bodily activity until one becomes proficient. An important aspect of this process is coming to experience the movements as familiar and 'right'. Moreover, one acquires such skills gradually – there is not a definite point at which one moves from being unskilled to skilled. None of this applies to the acquisition of conceptual belief. Suppose, for example, that I come to believe that Elvis is alive. I do not need to repeatedly move my body to acquire this belief; nor does my belief confer a sense of rightness and familiarity on any set of my bodily movements. I can also come to believe that Elvis is alive at a definite time, such as the time I see him in the supermarket. Thus it is hard to see how one could account for these facts about the acquisition of motor skills if one takes them to be constituted by conceptual beliefs.[3]

Merleau-Ponty claims that motor skills constitute a practical form of knowledge. As I have indicated, there are obvious parallels with the notion of know-how. Knowing how to φ involves being able to do so when one is in a suitable environment for φ-ing, and it cannot be reduced to conceptual beliefs about how one φ's. The same is also true of motor skills. However, Merleau-Ponty's notion does not map exactly on to the idea of know-how. Knowing how to do something is typically contrasted with knowing *that* things are thus and so, where this involves conceptual belief about the world. Although Merleau-Ponty holds that practical knowledge is distinct from that comprised by conceptual beliefs, it nevertheless constitutes understanding of the world – knowledge *that* things are a certain way. The subject understands their environment, in this practical sense, solely in terms of its potential for their actions. As we have seen, motor skills are exercised in perception and action. The skilled climber, for example, can both climb a rock face and see little cracks and fissures in the rock as hand and foot holds – as offering an opportunity to climb it. Merleau-Ponty claims that when the subject exercises a motor skill, this constitutes an understanding of the environment in which they exercise it. The climber's perception of the rock face as climbable, and their engagement in the activity of climbing it, constitute an understanding of the rock face as appropriate for the activity of climbing it, or practical knowledge *that* it can be climbed.

Merleau-Ponty also claims that the subject's apprehension of space is bound up with their perception of the world as requiring certain actions from them. The subject is aware of the position of objects in space around them by perceiving them as reachable in certain ways. To be aware of an object as located to one's left, for example, is to perceive it as requiring a certain kind of reaching movement to pick it up with one's left hand, a certain kind of kicking movement to move it with one's right foot, and so on. Again, Merleau-Ponty describes this apprehension of space as a practical understanding or knowledge of how the objects around one are located.

One may raise the following objection at this point. It is certainly the case that the agent who is skilled at φ-ing is *aware* of their environment as suitable for φ-ing – they perceive it as offering an opportunity to φ – and *aware* of how objects are located in space, but it is not so clear that this awareness should be classed as knowledge or understanding. However, two related points can be made in response to this objection. First, as we have already seen, perception is not, for Merleau-Ponty, the mere registering of objective features of the world. The subject perceives the world in relation to their capacities to interact with it. They exercise their motor skills to see the world as requiring certain sorts of behaviour and disallowing others, which, in turn, provides the subject with awareness of where objects are located in space. It follows that when the subject perceives a rock face as suitable for climbing, they are not just registering the presence of the rock face. They are also categorising it as suitable for climbing. Second, Merleau-Ponty has shown that the environments which are appropriate for φ-ing will not share their exact physical characteristics. No two rock faces, for example, will be exactly alike. In fact, rock faces may have quite different configurations, and be composed of different sorts of rocks, yet still be climbable. Instead, Merleau-Ponty holds that the environments in which one can φ share 'a general form' (1945: 166; 1962: 142; 2002: 164). It follows that when the subject – through their perceptions and actions – categorises a rock face as suitable for climbing, they are not doing so because it possesses an exact list of physical characteristics, shared by all climbable rock faces. They categorise it instead as suitable for climbing in virtue of its general form. For these reasons, the exercise of one's motor skills in one's awareness of, and interactions with, one's surroundings can properly be called understanding of them.

The claim that the subject's apprehension of, and interactions with, their surroundings constitutes a practical understanding of them allows for an alternative interpretation of cases such as that of Joan and Giles. Giles sees Joan murder the butler, but blocks the event from his mind. If asked, Giles is unable to say who killed the butler, but he starts to behave fearfully towards Joan. It is usual to interpret such a case as involving a conceptual belief – that Joan murdered the butler – which is unavailable to the subject's conscious reflections. The alternative that Merleau-Ponty's account makes available is that Giles has no conceptual belief about who murdered the butler, but has a practical understanding of the fact that it was Joan. This is manifest in his perceptions of her as a murderer – as dangerous, as someone who should be treated fearfully – and in Giles's fearful behaviour towards her. Other examples where the subject intuitively believes p but cannot state this belief can be treated in the same way, although it is a matter for further discussion whether or not this analysis is correct for every case of this sort.

Merleau-Ponty claims that this practical understanding of one's environment is also, at the same time, a practical form of *self*-knowledge. It is knowledge of one's own body. The subject understands their body, like they understand their environment, in terms of their behaviour. I perceive my environment as demanding certain actions; I perceive it as requiring *me* to act in certain ways – for example, I see the incoming football as demanding that *I* move *my* left leg to kick it away from goal. My experience of things around me as requiring particular actions is thus at the same time an awareness of my body as possessing the power to perform them. This thesis is nicely illustrated by Merleau-Ponty's account of phantom limbs. A phantom limb is the experience of a limb that does not exist. Perhaps the most well-known cases are amputees who continue to experience the limb that is amputated, but there are also reports of people who are born with phantom limbs (Ramachandran and Blakeslee

1998). Merleau-Ponty claims that people with phantom limbs perceive the world as offering opportunities to act with the non-existent arm or leg. A person with a phantom right arm, for example, perceives a mug of tea as reachable with their right hand. Merleau-Ponty holds that the perception of the world as offering one opportunities to act with what is in fact a non-existent limb is simultaneously an awareness of oneself as capable of performing the actions, and so as having the limb with which to perform them. Thus one's perception of opportunities to act with one's non-existent right arm gives one a sense that one has a right arm (Merleau-Ponty 1945: 96–7; 1962: 81–2; 2002: 94–5).

One perceives objects, not just as located in space, but as located in space around one. In other words, perception is egocentric. The subject sees, touches and tastes things that are presented around them in space. They hear sounds as coming from certain directions. They smell scents that emanate from particular places. By presenting them with things located around them in space, perception also thereby presents the subject as located in space with respect to the things they perceive. For Merleau-Ponty, the subject perceives objects as located in space around them by perceiving them as reachable in various ways. The subject's awareness of how they must move to reach the objects around them is simultaneously an awareness of how they are situated with respect to those objects. To perceive a ball, for example, as requiring a small jerk of one's right leg to kick it is to perceive the ball as located a small jerk away from one's right leg, and to have a sense of one's right leg as located a small jerk away from the ball. Just as one is aware of objects in space in terms of the opportunities for action they offer, so too one is aware of one's own body and its orientation in terms of its power to perform the actions one sees the objects around one as requiring. The perception of the ball as requiring a small jerk of one's right leg to kick it is – as we have seen – simultaneously an awareness of one's leg as capable of performing this action. It is the apprehension of one's leg as so capable that constitutes one's awareness of it as located at a particular point in space.

It is usual for a subject's perceptions of and interactions with the world to include proprioceptive awareness of their own body as an essential element (*un*usual cases are people with damaged nervous systems). As we have seen, proprioception is integrated with the rest of the perceptual system and is essential to the sense of touch. It also plays a key role in the normal capacity for action. To act requires awareness of both one's environment and one's body – I cannot pick up a glass, for example, unless I am aware of both the glass and my hand. In the normal case, an important dimension of this awareness is tactile experience of one's surroundings, and proprioceptive awareness of one's own body. Agents who lack proprioception and the sense of touch highlight its significance for normal actions. Cole and Paillard (1995) describe one such agent, IW. He uses vision to locate his limbs, coordinate his movements, and guide his actions. This requires a great deal of concentration, and even very simple actions are difficult for him. If he holds an egg, for example, he has to continually concentrate on exerting just enough pressure to grip it without breaking it. If his concentration is broken, the egg is crushed.

Merleau-Ponty points out that my proprioceptive awareness of my body is always an awareness of it doing something. I experience my body as a whole, as it is engaged in some task. I am only aware of my body parts in relation to this experience of bodily purpose. Thus I experience the parts of my body as having a different 'value' depending on the role they perform in my behaviour. Suppose that I am an experienced tennis player engaged in a tennis match. My opponent hits the ball over the net towards me. I run towards it and leap to meet the ball with my racket. In this case, I am aware of my body as it is engaged in the task of leaping and stretching to hit the ball. I experience the racket as an extension of my body. I am not aware of my right arm being a certain distance from my head at a certain angle relative to my trunk. I am simply aware of reaching for the ball with the racket. I do not experience my left leg as bent at a particular angle relative to the ground, and located in space a certain distance from the right. Instead, I experience my left leg simply as it is involved in propelling me off the ground towards the ball. My racket and the arm holding it are emphasised as they 'lead' the movement. I am aware of the rest of my body simply as 'it follows' my racket and arm. Thus my bodily experience is not constituted by awareness of each individual limb and its position relative to the others. Instead, it can be described as awareness of a movement of propulsion and reaching that involves my whole body.

In summary, the subject's perceptions of their environment and their interactions with it go hand-in-hand with awareness of their own body. The experience of their body is the inverse of their actions and awareness of the world. Since the subject perceives and acts by exercising their motor skills, it follows that the exercise of their skills is also what provides them with awareness of their own body. The skilled climber, for example, sees a ledge above their head as offering an opportunity to reach up with their right hand and pull themself up. Their perception of the ledge as offering this action gives them a sense that the ledge is above their head. Their experience of the ledge is simultaneously an awareness of their right hand as capable of reaching the ledge to pull themself up. This in turn gives them a sense of how their right hand is located with respect to the ledge – they are aware of it as located a 'reaching distance' away. They perceive the ledge as offering passage up the rock face by exercising their skill at climbing. Since this is, at the same time, an awareness of their body as capable of performing the actions they perceive their environment as requiring, it follows that they are aware of their body's powers and thereby its orientation, through exercising their climbing skills. Similarly, the tennis player's actions essentially involve proprioceptive awareness of their body, which is an awareness of it in action. The player exercises their tennis skills to jump and reach for the ball with their racket, and it follows that their awareness of their body in the performance of this action also results from the exercise of their tennis skills. We saw above that the exercise of motor skills can be properly classed as a practical form of understanding. It follows that the subject's awareness of their own body in perception and action is likewise a practical understanding of it: its configuration, capacities and orientation.

TWO ISSUES: ACTION GENERATED BY THOUGHT, AND SCHNEIDER AGAIN

Merleau-Ponty has described a level of engagement with the world that does not involve conceptual representations, that is, that does not involve thought (at least not in the traditional sense). The agent perceives the world by exercising their motor skills. The world appears to them as requiring certain actions. These perceived demands for action immediately draw forth the agent's behaviour without the need for any intervening thought. Motor skills are not mechanical responses to stimuli that always have the same physical properties. Instead, they are flexible ways of dealing with the world. The skilled agent can exercise their skill in novel ways – both varying the movements involved in exercising it and using it to cope with various environments. It follows that the exercise of motor skills cannot be explained in terms of causation. The flexibility exhibited by the exercise of motor skills allows us to think of them as a form of knowledge. The agent who is skilled at φ-ing knows how to φ. Moreover, this knowledge is different in kind from that constituted by conceptual beliefs. The exercise of their skill at φ-ing also manifests an understanding of both their surroundings and themself. But this understanding is practical, rather than conceptual; it is simply constituted by the exercise of their skill in perception and action.

The reader may be puzzled by two issues at this point. First, Merleau-Ponty has argued that some actions are driven entirely by the subject's perceptions. The subject perceives an opportunity to φ and this perception initiates and guides their φ-ing without any intervening thought. His analysis nicely captures certain kinds of cases, for example swerving to avoid hitting a dog lying in the road, or shuffling in a lift until one is standing the socially appropriate distance from the other people in it (Dreyfus 2000). But not all actions fit this model. There are cases where we want to say that the agent's actions are brought about by their thoughts. Suppose, for example, that Joni deliberates about whether or not she has enough time to visit Jason before going to the dentist. She works out how long it will take to get to Jason's house, realises there is enough time, forms an intention to now visit Jason, and so leaves the house. Here, we want to say that Joni's leaving the house is initiated by her intention to do so. Yet it is unclear how this case can be accommodated on Merleau-Ponty's model as it has been expounded so far. Indeed, cases like this seem to present him with a problem. During the time that Joni forms her intention and carries it out, she also perceives the world. Her perception of her surroundings plays *some* role in the execution of her intention – her action of visiting Jason must be guided at least in part by her perceptions of her front door, the road, Jason's house and so on. The difficulty is that, according to Merleau-Ponty's analysis, perception has the power to immediately initiate action, without the need for any thought. But, if this is so, then it is unclear what role Joni's intention can have in bringing about her behaviour. The relation between perception and action looks too tight; there seems to be no room for thought to intervene.

Merleau-Ponty's account of absorbed coping provides a partial response to this problem. In absorbed coping, the agent's behaviour is brought about by their perceptions. The content of perceptual experience is shaped by the agent's current task in combination with their surroundings and their motor skills – they perceive their environment in the light of what they are doing, and so perceive opportunities to exercise those of their skills that are relevant to their current project. The skilled skier, for example, perceives a slope as offering passage down the mountainside because they can ski, are at the top of a slope suitable for skiing down, and are engaged in the project of skiing. The normal human agent takes on projects by forming an intention to do so. I take on the project of teaching my friend to knit, for example, by forming an intention to teach her. Since one's current task affects the course of absorbed coping, and one takes on a task by forming an intention, it seems that Merleau-Ponty can accommodate the fact that some actions are brought about by thought.

However, although this analysis explains how action generates thought in some cases, it does not account for all the ways in which thought can guide action. Consider this case. Lucy teaches kickboxing. She is showing her students a defensive move one employs if one's opponent attacks with a certain sort of kick. She tells her students to imagine an assailant kicks her with his right foot. She then demonstrates the defensive move to them. In this case, Lucy's action is initiated by her intention to demonstrate the move to her students. But it is problematic to suppose that this intention brings about her behaviour by shaping her perceptual experience. The difficulty is that the skill Lucy exercises is her skill at warding off a real assailant. It is because she can block a real kick that she can demonstrate how to do so in the absence of an opponent. The environment that is appropriate for exercising this skill is one where there is a real assailant – a person who is attacking Lucy and against whom she has to defend herself. It is a setting of this sort that will be perceived as offering an opportunity to perform the kick. A setting that does not contain a real opponent will not be perceived as offering an opportunity to exercise this skill. When Lucy demonstrates the move to her students, there is no real assailant, and so it cannot be the case that her intention brings about her action by leading her to perceive an opportunity to exercise her skill. A different account of this case is required.

The second issue is simply that Merleau-Ponty still owes us an account of Schneider's disability. His claim that one's grasp of one's bodily orientation depends on the exercise of one's motor skills sheds further light on Schneider's case. Schneider can easily perform actions required in the course of his daily living (concrete actions), but has difficulties doing such things as lifting an arm in response to a psychologist's order (abstract actions). To perform the latter, Schneider either has to watch the relevant limb – in this case, his arm – or engage in preparatory movements, which involve moving his whole body, then gradually confining the movement to certain body-parts. Merleau-Ponty claims that the purpose of these movements is to find the limb he has been asked to move and the body-part that symbolises the direction in which he has been asked to move it. Looking provides him with the same information. According to this interpretation, Schneider lacks the ordinary grasp of bodily orientation required for action, when the action is abstract. He does not lack it altogether, since he can perform concrete actions with ease. The idea that one is aware of how one's body is orientated by exercising one's motor skills suggests that, when it comes to abstract actions, Schneider is unable to exercise his motor skills properly. The next question is, of course, why is this so?

THE POWER 'TO RECKON WITH THE POSSIBLE'

Merleau-Ponty's answer to both of these problems lies with a capacity he takes the normal human agent to possess, and which is lacking in Schneider: the power 'to reckon with the possible' (Merleau-Ponty 1945: 127; 1962: 109; 2002: 125). It will help us to understand what this power is if we first consider the corresponding notion of the actual. Merleau-Ponty's account of absorbed coping provides us with this notion. In absorbed coping, the agent acts in immediate response to their perceived surroundings. Their actions are immediately driven by their perceptions – they perceive an opportunity to act and respond by acting, without the need for any conceptual thought. What the agent perceives is determined by their *actual* surroundings and their *actual* task – together with their motor skills. Thus, in absorbed coping, the subject reckons with the actual: their actual environment and actual task. We can therefore understand 'the possible', with which the normal person has the power to reckon, as encompassing possible environments in which they could be located and/or possible projects that they could undertake.

On Merleau-Ponty's account, both acting and perceiving involve the exercise of motor skills. An agent who possesses a motor skill is able to perform the bodily movements required to engage in some activity and to recognise environments that are suitable for doing so. The recognition of places as suitable for φ-ing is constituted by the perception of them as inviting one to φ. The content of perceptual experience is also shaped by the subject's environment and current task. Merleau-Ponty holds that where the subject is, and what they are currently doing, make certain of their motor skills available to them: those that are relevant to the pursuit of their project in their current environment. The subject, in other words, accesses their motor skills via their actual surroundings and current task. The presence of a piano, and the project of playing it, for example, make the pianist's ability to play available to them so that they can both perceive the piano as playable and actually play it. Since contending with 'the actual' involves accessing motor skills that are relevant to one's actual environment and current task, it follows that the power to reckon with 'the possible' should be understood as the power to access – and so use – motor skills that are relevant to merely possible tasks and environments.

One manifestation of this power is the perception of opportunities for action, over and above just those that relate to what one is currently doing. The discussion so far has claimed that it is the subject's environment, their motor skills and their current task that shape the content of their perceptions. However, this is not entirely correct. We can demonstrate this by comparing Schneider's pathological perceptual experience with what is perceived by the normal agent. One of the psychologists who worked extensively with Schneider was Kurt Goldstein. But Merleau-Ponty tells us that Schneider never recognises his house when he walks past it unless he set out with the intention of going there (Merleau-Ponty 1945: 157; 1962: 134–5; 2002: 155). This fact is striking because a normal perceiver will recognise a house that they know, even when they merely pass it on their way elsewhere.

Merleau-Ponty offers the following explanation. To recognise something is to perceive it as familiar, and things appear familiar when one is skilled at – or in the habit of – interacting with them. To perceive something as familiar is thus to perceive it as something for which a particular form of behaviour is appropriate. As the foregoing discussion has shown, to perceive something as offering an opportunity to engage in a certain form of behaviour is to exercise a motor skill. To recognise something on Merleau-Ponty's account is therefore to exercise a motor skill or set of motor skills. Schneider does not recognise Goldstein's house unless he is going there because he is unable to exercise those skills that *could* be used to interact with Goldstein's house, unless he is *actually* engaged in some task which involves interacting with it – for example, visiting Goldstein, posting a letter through his door, and so on. Schneider is only able to access those motor skills that are relevant to his actual surroundings and actual task. Thus he only perceives those opportunities for action that relate to what he is actually doing.

In contrast, the normal subject has access to more than just those motor skills that are made available by their actual environment and current task. They can also access motor skills that are relevant to merely possible projects they could undertake in their environment. The normal subject is thus able to recognise Goldstein's house, even if they merely pass it on their way to somewhere else. Recognising Goldstein's house involves perceiving it as offering opportunities for action, relative to the task of 'engaging' with it in some way. Thus to recognise it when one passes it on the way to somewhere else is to see the house in the light of a potential task. It is to perceive the house as offering an opportunity to act in relation to the possible project of, for example, visiting Goldstein. Schneider's case highlights the fact that the normal subject perceives more opportunities for action than just those that relate to what they are currently doing. They also perceive the world as requiring actions that relate to merely possible tasks. The perceived demands for action differ in their urgency. Those that correspond to what the subject is actually doing will be perceived as most urgent – and will therefore initiate action – whilst those that correspond to merely possible projects are perceived as less urgent.

The power to reckon with the possible also enables the agent to exercise motor skills that are relevant to merely possible environments. In the example given above, Lucy demonstrates a particular defensive move to her students during a kickboxing class. It seems that the skill Lucy exercises when she demonstrates the move to her class is her skill at defending herself against a real opponent. But since there is no real assailant, Lucy's exercise of her skill cannot be initiated and guided by her perception of an opportunity to exercise it. Merleau-Ponty explains cases like this by appealing to the human ability to access one's motor skills in relation to merely possible tasks and environments. In short, Lucy 'interacts' with an imaginary opponent. She can thus be understood as acting with respect to merely possible surroundings. Since her act of demonstrating the move to her students involves exercising her skill at fighting, to demonstrate the move Lucy must be able to access her fighting skill with respect to an imagined environment which contains an assailant.

Merleau-Ponty's analysis of cases where the agent acts with respect to a merely possible environment has the same form as his account of absorbed coping. It follows that to understand how action is brought about in these cases, we need to redescribe his account of absorbed coping in more general terms. Merleau-Ponty gives a very general statement of his account of human behaviour in the following passage:

> [F]or the normal person every movement has a *background*, and the movement and its background are 'moments of a unique totality'. The background to the movement is not a representation associated or linked externally with the movement itself, but is immanent in the movement inspiring and sustaining it at every moment.
>
> (Merleau-Ponty 1945: 128; 1962: 110; 2002: 127)

To uncover what he means here, let us consider the above passage with respect to absorbed coping. In absorbed coping, the agent perceives opportunities to act, which initiate and control their actions. What a subject perceives depends on what they can do. Their perception of their environment is also shaped by their current task or project, such that the most urgent demands for action are those that relate to what they are currently doing. It follows that one perceives one's surroundings primarily as a setting or backdrop for a particular sort of behaviour – activity that relates to one's current task. When playing football, for example, the agent perceives the goal lines as real boundaries, members of the opposing team as adversaries to be avoided, spaces between them as opportunities to progress towards goal, and so on. The player perceives ways to interact with the world that are relevant to the task of playing football, and so they perceive their environment primarily as a setting for this project. It is the agent's immediate environment, perceived as a setting for their current behaviour, that is the 'background' to action in cases of absorbed coping. When Merleau-Ponty talks about the movement and its background as being 'moments of a unique totality', he is referring to the way in which there is an intimate correspondence between the behaviour, and the subject's environment perceived as a setting for it. The claim that the background to the behaviour is what 'inspires and sustains' it simply refers to the way in which the agent's unreflective behaviour is brought about and controlled by their perception of their environment as 'requiring' the behaviour in question.

The background to absorbed coping is the subject's environment, perceived as a setting for that behaviour. We have seen above that to perceive, on Merleau-Ponty's account, is to exercise one's motor skills. Perception on this account is an activity of the perceiver. When the agent perceives a demand for action, they are not passively receiving data from the world. Rather, they actively 'summon' the invitations to behave from the world; they 'project' a situation around themself (Merleau-Ponty 1945: 158; 1962: 136; 2002: 157); they invest their environment with a bodily significance. In perception, the projection of a situation around oneself that calls for a particular kind of behaviour is constrained by the nature of one's environment. When I perceive a space-to-park, for example, providing that nothing goes wrong with the perceptual process, my 'summoning up' of this demand for action is in line with what my environment is really like – I am confronted with a space that is indeed suitable for parking, and the fact that it is suitable for parking guides my summoning up of the invitation to park there.

Just as absorbed coping is initiated and controlled by its background, which is brought into being by the subject's ability to summon up demands for action from their environment, so, too, behaviour such as that of Lucy takes place against a background which inspires and sustains it and is again constituted by the subject's capacity to project a situation around themself that calls for a certain kind of activity. Merleau-Ponty holds that, in a case such as that of Lucy, where the agent interacts with merely imagined surroundings, the agent represents those surroundings in thought. The agent then summons up the demands for action that this environment would make if it were real. Since the environment is not real, the demands for action that are summoned by the subject will not be perceived. Instead, they should be understood as imbuing their representation of the environment with a motor significance. The representation thus exerts a pull on the subject; it demands a certain kind of activity that is analogous to, but not the same as, the manner in which the subject *perceives* their environment as demanding action. The representation, imbued with motor significance, thus functions as the background to the action, pulling forth the agent's actions from them, and guiding their behaviour. The capacity to summon up demands for action from one's environment is conferred upon one by one's motor skills. When the agent perceives a rock-face as offering an opportunity to rock-climb, that is, when they summon up an invitation to climb from the rock-face, they are exercising their skill at climbing. Likewise, when the subject summons up demands for action with respect to an environment that is represented in thought, they are exercising their motor skills. Thus it can be seen that the agent is able to imbue a possible or imagined environment that they represent in thought with motor significance, because they are able to access their motor skills in relation to that represented environment – they are able to access those skills that they could use to perceive and act with respect to that environment if it were real.

The idea of imbuing a representation with motor significance may be *prima facie* rather puzzling, but in fact the phenomenon Merleau-Ponty has in mind is commonplace and easily recognisable. To see this, consider the following case. Bruce has read a lot about the British navy in the eighteenth century. He knows about the press gangs who forced men on to the ships, the dank, cramped conditions they endured onboard, the rampant disease and so on. However, his understanding of these facts is what might be called purely intellectual. One hot day, Bruce is on a crowded tube train when it breaks down. Stuck underground for an hour, in near total darkness, pressed up against his fellow passengers, Bruce has a sudden insight into eighteenth-century naval life. His conceptual understanding of the facts does not alter. But he now empathises with the sailors. He is able to imagine the claustrophobic feeling of being below deck, the gloomy light, being surrounded by other sweating bodies, and so on. In Merleau-Ponty's terms, Bruce's conceptual understanding of naval

life in the eighteenth century is now imbued with motor significance, as he has a bodily sense of the demands the situation
would make upon him if he were in it.

Cases such as that of Lucy are not particularly common. But
Merleau-Ponty's analysis allows us to see that the capacity it
involves is also at work in more common sorts of cases. In the case
of Lucy, she responds to perceived demands for action that are not
summoned up in accordance with the nature of her actual surroundings. Lucy summons these demands with respect to a
represented element of her environment: the imaginary assailant.
It follows that these demands for action imbue her representation
with a motor significance; they are not perceived. Merleau-Ponty
suggests that other cases should be analysed along similar lines. It
will be helpful for us to consider another such case: acting on the
basis of a moral judgement (Merleau-Ponty 1945: 130; 1962:
112; 2002: 129).

Suppose that I judge we all have a moral responsibility for
cleaning up our respective neighbourhoods and that I should pick
up the litter in my street. On this basis, I go outside and put the
litter in a bin. My action of litter-picking is generated by my
moral judgement, which is a thought representing what I should
do. The objects with which I interact – the pieces of litter and
the bin – are real rather than imagined. But Merleau-Ponty
nevertheless suggests that cases like this involve exercising the
power to reckon with a possible environment and should be
explained in a way analogous to that of Lucy. We have seen that
practice is required to acquire motor skills. It is these skills that
allow one to perceive an opportunity to act. Thus, to experience
one's environment as offering an opportunity for action, one must
have acted in that way in those (or similar) surroundings a sufficient number of times previously. If we suppose that I have never
collected litter in the street before, then I will not perceive my
situation as requiring litter-picking activity. The moral requirement to pick up the litter is only represented in thought.
I represent my environment as requiring litter-picking activity.
I then exercise my power to reckon with the possible to access
those motor skills that are relevant to the way in which I represent my environment, and thus imbue my moral judgement with

a motor significance. This then functions as the background to my behaviour, drawing forth my litter-picking activity. Once more, this illustrates how the power to reckon with the possible enables my thoughts to bring about action.

It should be clear from the foregoing remarks that the power to reckon with the possible is implicated in all of the normal human agent's behaviour. One always perceives more possibilities for action than those that correspond to one's current task. Often, one's actions will be initiated and controlled by both one's perceived environment and one's thoughts about one's situation. It follows that Goldstein and Gelb's distinction between concrete and abstract forms of behaviour ultimately has no application in the case of the normal human agent. Some actions may be more rooted in one's actual environment and current task, and some may involve reckoning with the possible to a greater extent, but for the normal human agent the abstract and the concrete are located on a continuum. They only become distinct forms of behaviour or types of actions in pathological cases such as that of Schneider.

Finally, we are now in a position to see how Merleau-Ponty accounts for Schneider's disability. Schneider can perform concrete actions with ease, but abstract actions present him with difficulties. The difference between the two sorts of action is that concrete actions correspond to perceived demands to act, whilst abstract actions do not. Schneider lacks the power to reckon with the possible, and so the only motor skills he can access are those that are relevant to his current project and actual environment. Verbal commands can be given a motor significance through habit. If one habitually goes line-dancing, then the commands of the caller will eventually gain a motor significance, so that one will immediately hear the commands as requiring one to perform a particular movement. But in other cases verbal commands must be imbued with significance using the power to reckon with the possible. Since Schneider lacks this power, he is unable to imbue the psychologist's order with motor significance and *experience* the demand to raise his arm. He understands the order conceptually, but he has no practical understanding of it. His lack of motor understanding affects his grasp of how his body is orientated. As we saw earlier, one's understanding of one's bodily orientation results from the exercise of one's motor skills. Since Schneider is unable to exercise his motor skills properly in the situation with his psychologist, his grasp of his bodily orientation is correspondingly deficient. He must thus perform the preparatory movements or watch his limb in order to obey the command.

CONCLUSION

Objective Thought conceives of the body as a mere object, whose behaviour can be explained by causal laws, and which does not differ significantly from other physical objects like cars and rocks. Empiricism takes consciousness to result from causal goings-on within the body. Intellectualism realises that consciousness cannot be explained in this way and conceives of consciousness as non-physical.

Through analysing the case of Schneider, Merleau-Ponty develops an alternative view of the body. His model incorporates new conceptions of action, understanding, knowledge and intelligence. Merleau-Ponty relies on the Gestalt discovery that one perceives one's surroundings as requiring one to perform certain actions or as being appropriate for certain forms of behaviour. The actions one sees one's environment as requiring are determined by what one can do in that environment, together with one's current task. Merleau-Ponty argues that one's bodily self is able to respond to a perceived demand for action by acting without the need for conscious thought to guide and control one's movements. This is made possible by the acquisition of motor skills or habits, which are twofold abilities to engage in a form of behaviour, and to see appropriate bits of the world as requiring one to act in this way. The normal human agent possesses the power to reckon with the possible, which can be thought of as a sort of bodily imagination. It enables one's bodily self to access motor skills over and above those which are made available by one's actual surroundings and current task. The power to reckon with the possible allows the agent to perceive opportunities for action that are not relevant to their current task. It also allows the agent to act in the absence of an appropriate environment – for example, where they interact with imagined surroundings. The same power also underlies the capacity to act on the basis of thought by imbuing the thought with a motor significance that can guide the agent's actions.

The bodily exercise of motor skills cannot be analysed causally. These actions are not mere causal responses to brute physical stimuli. Instead, one's bodily self copes with one's environment in ways that are appropriate to one's current task. One is able to unthinkingly adapt one's skills to physically dissimilar environments that share a common form. Motor skills can thus be considered a form of practical knowledge. One's bodily self knows how to act, and it has a motor understanding of one's surroundings that is not reducible to conceptual knowledge. Merleau-Ponty thus concludes that the body is a form of consciousness. Human subjects are what he calls 'being-in-the-world'.

4

THE WORLD AND ITS RELATION
TO CONSCIOUSNESS

The present chapter is concerned with Merleau-Ponty's account of
the world and its relation to consciousness. Merleau-Ponty takes
his conception of them to preserve the insights of Empiricism and
Intellectualism, whilst overcoming the difficulties inherent in
these views. Empiricism and Intellectualism conceive of the world
in the same way – as a collection of determinate, externally related entities – but differ in the ontological status they accord it.
Their respective claims about the ontological status of the world
are bound up with their conceptions of how the world is related
to consciousness. Empiricism claims that the world exists in-itself.
Its nature and existence do not depend on consciousness, which is
just one of many physical things within it. Intellectualism, in
contrast, takes the world to be constituted by – and so dependent
on – a Transcendental Ego, which lies beyond the world and is
wholly different from it. Merleau-Ponty holds that these two
extremes are the only positions available if the world is conceived
as a collection of determinate, externally related entities. He
claims that, by rejecting Objective Thought's conception of the

world, he is able to develop an alternative view of its ontological status and its relation to consciousness. Merleau-Ponty's aim is to show that consciousness and the world are mutually dependent – that is, internally related – parts of a single whole. Neither consciousness nor the world can exist without standing in this relation to the other. The claim that there is a Transcendental Ego which is independent from, and constitutes, the world, and the claim that there is a world-in-itself, which exists independently of consciousness, should both be rejected. He writes, '[t]he world is inseparable from the subject, but from a subject which is nothing but a project of the world, and the world is inseparable from the world, but from a world which the subject itself projects' (Merleau-Ponty 1945: 491; 1962: 430; 2002: 499–500).

THE STRUCTURE OF THE PHENOMENAL FIELD

One may think initially that Merleau-Ponty has already provided the account he is after with his analysis of the phenomenal field. The fundamental object of phenomenological investigation is the phenomenal field. The phenomenal field is that which is presented to consciousness. One might characterise it as experience. But there are different conceptions of experience. One might think of experience as an inner representation of the world, whose qualities are unaffected by whether or not it represents the world correctly. On the other hand, one might conceive of experience as immediately of things in the world, so that it cannot be characterised without referring to the worldly things it presents. Merleau-Ponty endorses the latter conception of experience. It follows that the phenomenal field is not an inner realm. It is that worldly region that is presented in experience. But that which is experienced can be considered from two perspectives. It can be considered as it is in-itself or it can be considered as it is presented to the subject. The phenomenal field is the worldly region that is presented in experience, considered as it appears to the perceiver. Thus the phenomenal field is neither something internal to consciousness, nor is it independent of consciousness.

It is clear from Merleau-Ponty's detailed descriptions of the phenomenal field that it is always articulated into consciousness and object. The phenomenal field contains both the worldly objects one perceives and one's own embodied self. But there are significant differences between the experience of one's own body on the one hand and one's awareness of everything else. One's own body is uniquely presented as the *subject* of one's perceptions. It is perhaps more accurate to say that I – the subject of my perceptions – am presented as embodied. I am not presented as having different sorts of properties from the other things I experience. Like other objects, I am presented as shaped, located and solid. Of course, inanimate objects like tables are not presented as conscious, but other people are, and – as we will see in the next chapter – my experience presents me as having the same sorts of properties as them. Instead, Merleau-Ponty holds that the difference lies in the structure of my awareness. My experience of things in the world has an act-object structure. It consists in acts of awareness that are directed at those things. My perception of my dog, for example, involves an act of awareness that is directed at my dog, which is the object of my perception. In contrast, my experience of my own body does not always have an act-object structure. Although I can perceive my body in the same way that I perceive other things – I can see it, touch it, taste it, etc. and, in these cases, it is the object at which some state of awareness is directed – there is another important form of bodily awareness. It is what can be called an 'adverbial' form of awareness. Rather than being aware of my body, I am simply aware *in* my body.

The idea is difficult to express, since grammar forces us to talk about awareness *of* things, which implies the act-object model. But further light can be shed on Merleau-Ponty's claim by considering awareness of one's own actions. Consider what it is like to lift an object – say, a box of chocolates – off the table. My experience presents the box and my arm differently. I experience the box as an object that I – the agent – move. But I do not experience my arm as an object that I move around. Instead, my arm is presented as that which does the moving. In other words, my arm is presented as (part of) me – the agent of my actions. Merleau-Ponty argues that the difference lies in the structure of experience in the two cases. Whilst my awareness of the box of chocolates has an act-object structure – it is constituted by an act of awareness that has the box as its object – my experience of my arm moving has an adverbial structure. It does not consist in an act of awareness that is directed at my arm. Instead, my moving my arm is a conscious activity, where 'conscious' does not denote a form of awareness that has my action as its object; it simply describes the kind of activity it is. Chapter 6 will consider this idea in more detail. The key point for present purposes is that whilst I can be aware of my own body in the same way that I am aware of other things, there is another form of bodily awareness that is radically different. Unlike my experience of other objects, it does not have an act-object structure. I am simply aware *in* my body. Or, if one prefers, my bodily activities are conscious. These differing modes of awareness mean that the phenomenal field is articulated into consciousness (my own body) and object (everything else I experience).

It seems that the manner in which consciousness and the world are presented in the phenomenal field establishes that they are mutually dependent parts of one whole. As we saw in Chapter 3, Merleau-Ponty holds that one experiences both the world and one's own body primarily in terms of one's capacities for action. One's surroundings are perceived as 'inviting' one to perform various activities so that chairs call one to sit on them, footballs appear kickable, food appears edible, and so forth. The perception of an opportunity to act is simultaneously an awareness of oneself as possessing the power to perform that action. The perception of, for example, a glass as reachable with my left hand is at the same time an awareness of myself as able to reach it with my left hand. It follows that in the phenomenal field, consciousness (one's bodily self) and the world surrounding one are presented as 'opposite poles' of the same phenomenon: the former is experienced as a power to perform certain actions, whilst the latter is experienced as a setting in which those actions can be performed. One's own body and the world are presented as complementary parts of one whole.

However, Merleau-Ponty cannot rest content with this analysis. The problem is that his descriptions of the phenomenal field merely show us that the properties of consciousness and the world complement one another. He has not shown us that consciousness and the world are *mutually dependent*. Consider again how experience presents the world. Merleau-Ponty argues that we perceive the world as a setting for certain actions. But the fact that some region of the world appears to us as, for example, a place to hide does not show that the existence or nature of that place depends in any way on the presence of a subject who can hide there. Moreover, experience presents the world as having spatial properties – things are presented as shaped, located and solid, and it seems *prima facie* that objects having those properties do not depend in any way on consciousness. Merleau-Ponty has shown us that experience presents the subject as having certain powers of action that correspond to the opportunities for action they perceive their surroundings as offering. But these are capacities they have in virtue of their physical structure and, as we have seen, experience presents the subject as embodied. Like the other things they experience, the subject is aware of themselves as having spatial properties, that is, they experience themself as shaped, located and solid. Experience therefore presents the subject as being part of the world. But, rather than suggesting that consciousness and the world are mutually dependent, experience seems to support the realist intuition that conscious beings are parts of a world that exists in-itself, whose nature remains fundamentally the same whether or not it contains any conscious beings.

THE NATURE OF THE EXPERIENCED WORLD

An answer to this worry lies with Merleau-Ponty's claim that all of the things we experience are constituted in our experience of them. We need to be careful how we understand this claim. One might read it as the idealist thesis that the world is reducible to experience of it, such that there is no transcendent world. But this is the Intellectualist stance that Merleau-Ponty rejects. He takes his arguments against Intellectualism to show that this notion of perceptual experience is untenable. It follows that perception must be thought of as a form of interaction between consciousness (the perceiver) and world (the perceived). The claim that all the things we experience are constituted in our experience of them should thus be understood as the claim that perceptual activity involves interacting with the world, and it is through this process of interaction that perceived things take shape or are constituted. Perception involves 'summoning' appropriate appearances in response to the promptings of the world.

Merleau-Ponty makes various remarks which suggest that this is his view. He states, for example,

> I start to focus my eyes on the table which is not yet there, I begin to look into the distance while there is as yet no depth, my body centres itself on an object which is still only potential, and so disposes its sensitive surfaces to make it a present reality.
>
> (Merleau-Ponty 1945: 276; 1962: 239; 2002: 278)

In this passage, Merleau-Ponty suggests that the table I see is constituted in my perceptual experience of it. Similarly, consider this passage,

> Apart from the probing of my eye or my hand, and before my body synchronizes with it, the sensible is nothing but a vague beckoning ... Thus a sensible datum which is on the point of being felt sets a kind of muddled problem for my body to solve. I must find the attitude which *will* provide it with the means of becoming determinate ... And yet I do so only when I am invited by it, my attitude is never sufficient to make me really see blue or really touch a hard surface.
>
> (Merleau-Ponty 1945: 248; 1962: 214; 2002: 248)

Here, Merleau-Ponty clearly states that 'the sensible' – that which we perceive – comes into being through perception of it. Moreover, we perceive the sensible in response to a 'vague beckoning' from the world. In other words, the sensible results from the interaction between the world and consciousness. A less general version of this thesis is familiar from the literature on colour. It is sometimes claimed that an object's *being* green is constituted by its *appearing* green to colour-perceiving subjects in suitable lighting conditions such as bright daylight. On this model, objects are not green in-themselves; their greenness is constituted in experience of them. But green appearances are the result of interaction between subjects with a certain sort of perceptual system and the spectral reflectance properties of the things they see. Merleau-Ponty's claim applies to the world more generally. He holds that *all* the properties we experience are constituted in experience of them.

Merleau-Ponty provides detailed arguments to show that the properties we experience are constituted in perception. It will not be possible to rehearse all of them in this limited space. Merleau-Ponty's thesis is perhaps most controversial with respect to spatial properties, since a great majority of theorists take these to be properties the world has in-itself. I will thus focus on his discussion of space, in particular his analysis of depth.

Merleau-Ponty states that depth is 'the most "existential" of all dimensions' (1945: 296; 1962: 256; 2002: 298). By this he means that it is the dimension that most obviously locates the perceiver in the world that they perceive. We can think of the matter like this. Suppose I look at a painting on the wall. The painting depicts a scene which is spread out across my visual field. However, the scene is only spread out in two dimensions – height and breadth. The scene does not extend out of the painting to include the space where I am standing. For the scene to encompass my spatial location, the painting would have to occupy three dimensions: height, breadth and depth. Since the scene in the painting does not include the space where I am standing, my experience does not present me as involved in the painting. I have a 'God's eye view' on the scene. Of course, it is impossible for me to be involved in the scene in the painting. I cannot converse with the people, eat the food, climb the trees, pick the flowers, and so on, because they are not real. There is only paint and canvas. But the example illustrates Merleau-Ponty's claim. To experience myself as located in the world I see, I must experience the world I perceive as including the place where I am. I must experience the world as extending in front of me, and behind me. This is the dimension of depth. Some writers, for example Casey (1991), read Merleau-Ponty as according depth a special status. However, it seems that the intuition that depth is 'the most "existential" of all dimensions' merely provides a starting-point for Merleau-Ponty's discussion. Nothing much hangs on depth's 'existentiality', since Merleau-Ponty's eventual conclusion is that the claims he makes about depth also apply to the other dimensions. He writes, 'Breadth and height ... viewed in their primary significance, they too are "existential dimensions"' (Merleau-Ponty 1945: 309; 1962: 267; 2002: 311).

Merleau-Ponty is interested in depth as a phenomenon, that is, the way it appears to a perceiving subject. I will examine his account of depth perception before explaining how he takes this to establish ontological conclusions about the nature of depth. Merleau-Ponty argues that Objective Thought cannot properly account for perception of depth. He presents his positive view by identifying problems with Objective Thought's analyses. For Objective Thought, depth is not literally visible. As Berkeley (2004) argues, all that we literally see is a flat, two-dimensional projection of the scene in front of our eyes. One might argue for this conclusion on the grounds that only those parts of objects that are facing the perceiver can cast an image on the retina. Thus only those surfaces of objects can be seen. Merleau-Ponty notes that the arguments against the Constancy Hypothesis show that we cannot reason from the images that are cast on the retina to what is seen. (The problems with the Constancy Hypothesis are discussed in Chapter 2.) But there is an alternative argument for the claim that depth is invisible. Depth is the distance between two points that are located in the same direction as my gaze. Thus the distance between the two points is hidden from me. Suppose, for example, that the two points are church steeples. They are both located directly in front of me, but one is fifteen miles behind the other. The steeple furthest from me, and the interval between the two, are both hidden behind the nearest steeple. Thus I cannot see the distance between them.

Merleau-Ponty argues that the claim that depth is invisible depends on the definition of depth as the distance between two points that are located in the same direction as my gaze. This definition of depth presupposes that depth is breadth viewed from the side. In other words, it presupposes that what appears to me as depth would appear as breadth to someone located at a different point in space. There is no essential difference between the two dimensions: they are interchangeable. Merleau-Ponty objects that this 'takes for granted the result of a constitutive process, the stages of which we must, in fact, trace back' (1945: 295; 1962: 255; 2002: 298). His thinking here is this. The assumption that depth and breadth are interchangeable is based on experience. Depth appears to me as breadth viewed from the side. But, for depth to appear in this way, it must be presented in my experience. Thus it cannot be invisible. One might object that it is geometry, not experience, which teaches me that depth and breadth are interchangeable. However, this requires that I experience the world as one to which geometry can be applied, that is, as three-dimensional. It follows that I must experience depth.

So how do we perceive depth? As stated above, Objective Thought holds that we do not perceive depth. Instead, depth is calculated on the basis of visual cues. Merleau-Ponty mentions two: the convergence of the eyes – one's eyes converge when one focuses on an object that is moving nearer – and the apparent size of objects. The phenomenon of apparent size is the way in which an object's size seems to vary with its distance so that it looks smaller when it is farther away. An object's apparent size should be distinguished from the real size one experiences it as being. One may experience a distant mountain as being large, even though its apparent size is small. Merleau-Ponty considers two ways that Objective Thought might appeal to these visual cues to explain the apprehension of depth. On the one hand, one might claim that the subject consciously judges the distance of objects, based on these visual cues. But Merleau-Ponty points out that, for the subject to judge the distance of an object based on these cues, the subject must have some reason to think that they indicate depth. It's unclear how they could know this without actually perceiving depth. Hence this suggestion presupposes what it is supposed to explain. Consider apparent size. The suggestion is that the subject reasons from the fact that an object appears a certain size to the conclusion that it is a certain distance away. But for the subject to know that a certain apparent size indicates a certain distance, they must *perceive* that the object appears to be that size when it is a certain distance away. Thus they must perceive depth. Merleau-Ponty then argues that, for a subject to judge the distance of an object from the convergence of their eyes, they must visualise their gaze as two sticks that touch an object and whose angle changes when the object is brought nearer. But this visualisation presupposes having had this experience. Again, this presupposes the perception of depth.

The second account of depth apprehension that Merleau-Ponty considers is an analysis offered by the Gestalt psychologists. They claim that these visual cues are not explicitly seen – the subject does not consciously notice them – but they are nevertheless processed by the subject's perceptual system to provide an apprehension of depth. The first thing to note about this analysis is that the perceptual system delivers perceptual experience. So the claim that certain cues are processed by the perceptual system to yield the apprehension of depth is the claim that, as a result of this processing, the subject *perceives* depth; it is not invisible. Second, perhaps more importantly, Merleau-Ponty points out that to identify the visual cues that are claimed to enter into depth perception, one must first consider how depth is perceived. It is only by noticing that we *perceive*, for example, the apparent size of an object as varying with its distance that apparent size can be identified as a visual cue. The Gestalt analysis therefore presupposes an account of the subject's *experience* of depth. Merleau-Ponty also objects to the suggestion that the visual cues *cause* the perception of depth. As we saw in Chapter 2, Merleau-Ponty shows that the arrangements of phenomena cannot be considered the causes of the perceptual meanings that emerge from them. He also provides further arguments, which we examined in Chapter 3, to show that the activities of consciousness – including perceptual activity – cannot be explained by appeal to causal laws.

The apparent size of objects, the convergence of one's eyes, and other alleged visual cues of depth cannot be reasons that license judgements about the distance of objects. Neither can they cause the perceiver to experience depth. Nevertheless, there is some important connection between these supposed visual cues and the experience of depth. The very fact that Objective Thought identifies apparent size, the convergence of the eyes, and so on, as the visual cues of depth is revealing. Merleau-Ponty holds that experience itself leads Objective Thought to this conclusion. Thus the visual cues and the perception of depth are linked in perception and we need to understand how these visual cues are connected with it. Merleau-Ponty begins by noting that the Gestalt psychologists are right to hold that the apparent size of objects and the convergence of the eyes are not explicitly perceived. However, they are wrong to conclude that these things do not feature in experience at all. He claims that the subject has a non-thetic awareness of them – they figure in the subject's experience, but their attention is focused elsewhere. We can see this because the subject can turn their attention to apparent size and convergence of their eyes, thus they must figure in their experience.

Merleau-Ponty appeals to the notion of motivation to explain the connection between the experience of depth and its visual cues. Motives bring about – that is, motivate – behaviour or states of mind. As we saw in Chapter 2, they have two defining characteristics. First, their motivating force is a result of their meaning. Second, the motive and the behaviour or mental state it motivates are internally related. Merleau-Ponty offers the example of a death motivating a journey. It is not the physical characteristics of the death – for example, the mere fact that a certain person has had a fatal heart attack – that motivates the journey, but the death as a meaningful situation. If the person who died was my friend, his death will have a meaning for me. It demands that I perform certain actions or behave in particular ways. It requires that I travel to his funeral to pay my last respects, to offer support to his family, and so forth. In this way, my friend's death summons me to make a journey. Merleau-Ponty claims that when I decide to make the journey, my decision 'affirms the validity of this significance and gives it its force and efficacy' (1945: 299; 1962: 259; 2002: 301). By deciding to undertake the journey, I give the summons a more central place in my life. I go about my daily affairs with this summons in sight – for example, I am mindful of the forthcoming journey when I book my dental appointment; I make a note to remind me to take pet food to feed my dog on the journey. In turn, this gives the summons more motivating force. Because I have decided to obey it, it makes more demands on me. It shapes my daily affairs in a way that it would not do if I had not decided to go. In this case, the motive and the motivated behaviour are internally related in that the motivated behaviour is brought about by the motive, but the motive acquires (some of) its motivating force from what it motivates. 'The relation between the motivating and the motivated is thus reciprocal' (Merleau-Ponty 1945: 299–300; 1962: 259; 2002: 302).

Merleau-Ponty's analysis focuses on the phenomenon of apparent size. He holds that the phenomenon of apparent size does not merely *indicate* depth; it *is* an experience of depth. 'Apparent size as experienced, instead of being the sign or indication of a depth invisible in itself, is nothing other than a way of expressing our vision of depth' (1945: 300; 1962: 259; 2002: 302). One might find this claim puzzling. It is unclear how the perceived size of something can be an experience of its distance from the perceiver. The worry can be brought out with the following example. There is an intuition that a real cow far away looks the same size as a toy cow close up. It is thus unclear how the two cows of the same apparent size can be *experienced* as different distances away from the perceiver. Of course, if one knows that real cows and toy cows are different sizes, then one will be able to *infer* from their apparent sizes that one is far away whilst the other is close up. But Merleau-Ponty has ruled out this explanation. To understand how the apparent size of an object can be an experience of depth, we need to examine the phenomenon of apparent size more carefully.

Merleau-Ponty observes that 'the apparent size [of an object] is not a measurable size' (1945: 301; 1962: 260; 2002: 303). He demonstrates this by considering how someone could reply to this question, 'How big is the apparent size of that ashtray?' Note that this is a question about the ashtray's *apparent* size, which, as we noted earlier, is different from the size the ashtray is perceived to really be. Merleau-Ponty points out that the perceiver cannot immediately reply to this question. To answer it, they must do something such as hold a pencil out in front of them and mark the apparent size of the ashtray against the pencil. The procedure is not just a more accurate way of gauging apparent size than simply estimating. Instead, there is no size capable of being estimated until the perceiver measures the apparent size of the ashtray against the pencil. The procedure 'cause[s] size to appear where hitherto it had no place' (Merleau-Ponty 1945: 301; 1962: 260; 2002: 303). Merleau-Ponty claims that this is because the procedure isolates the object from the context. The reason that apparent size is not measurable is because it is not merely an experience of size. It is the experience of real-size-seen-at-a-distance. What one sees is an object of a certain size (the size one perceives it to really be), which is located a certain distance from oneself. In other words, the ashtray always appears roughly four inches in diameter. One does not literally see it as being smaller when it is at a greater distance. One's experience presents 'the same [ashtray] seen from farther away' (1945: 302; 1962: 261; 2002: 304).

How is this perception of depth possible? Merleau-Ponty explains this by appealing to the notion of 'maximum grip'. He writes,

> For each object, as for each picture in an art gallery, there is an optimum distance from which it requires to be seen, a direction viewed from which it vouchsafes most of itself: at a shorter or greater distance we have merely a perception blurred through excess or deficiency. We therefore tend towards the maximum visibility, and seek a better focus as with a microscope.
>
> (Merleau-Ponty 1945: 348; 1962: 302; 2002: 352)

The subject has maximum grip on an object when they are in the best context for perceiving it. Merleau-Ponty claims that the properties we experience are constituted in perception, and perception involves summoning appearances in response to the promptings of the world. Thus the perceiver has maximum grip on some part of the world when they are in the best context for exercising their power of summoning. Merleau-Ponty claims that the perceiver senses when they do *not* have maximum grip on something – that is, when they are *not* in the best context for perceiving it. Their sense of deviating from maximum grip manifests as an experience of tension (1945: 349; 1962: 302; 2002: 352). The sense of tension enables the perceiver to get a better grip on the thing they are perceiving – they simply act to relieve tension, for example by moving closer to the object. Merleau-Ponty then claims that the experience of distance is the experience of having a greater or lesser perceptual grip on an object. In cases where one can discern less of its features, one has a looser grip on it. In cases where one can distinguish more of the object, one has a better grip on it. 'Distance is what distinguishes this loose and approximate grip from the complete grip which is proximity' (Merleau-Ponty 1945: 302; 1962: 261; 2002: 305).

Some care is needed here. Different properties are best perceived in different contexts. Maximum grip, in other words, varies depending on which property one is trying to perceive. In the case of colour, for example, maximum grip has to do with lighting context. The best light for viewing the colour of something is bright, natural daylight. Moreover, one may have a poor grip on the colour of an object that is close by (the object may be in shade) and a good grip on the colour of a thing that is farther away (it may be in bright sunlight). It follows that having maximum grip on an object is only to do with distance for certain properties. But Merleau-Ponty can deal with this worry. He holds that maximum grip has to do with distance when one is trying to discern an object's features, for example when one is trying to read the number of a bus.

We are now in a position to understand how apparent size is perceived as distance. When one sees an object at a distance, a component of this experience is the sense that one does not have maximum grip on the object. The subject's sense of deviation from maximum grip contributes to the overall content of experience so that one sees the object as a certain distance away. Although there is a sense in which an object looks smaller if it is in the distance – if one measures it by holding up a pencil to it, the object will appear smaller than it does close up – this is not literally a perception of the distant object as being small. The subject's sense of deviation from maximum grip allows them to perceive the object as always being the same size, but just seen from a greater or lesser distance. This is why the experience of apparent size is really the experience of an-object-of-a-certain-size-seen-a-particular-distance-away.

Merleau-Ponty's analysis so far has focused on the perception of depth. He has shown that the perception of distance is the experience of having a more or less tight perceptual grip on an object. However, he then draws conclusions about the nature of depth or distance. He suggests that distance should be *defined* 'in terms of the situation of an object in relation to our power of grasping it' (Merleau-Ponty 1945: 303; 1962: 261; 2002: 305). The distance of an object from the perceiver, in other words, is *constituted* by the 'tightness' of their perceptual grip on it. It follows that distance is not a property the world has in-itself. It is a property it acquires when perceivers of the right sort interact with it. But it is not clear how he reaches this ontological conclusion from his analysis of depth perception. There are (at least) three possibilities.

First, we have seen that Merleau-Ponty conceives of Objective Thought as a hypothesis that informs inquiry into the nature of the world and consciousness. In PhP, he presents data that conflict with this hypothesis, thus showing us that the hypothesis should be rejected. The rejection of Objective Thought means that we require a new framework for understanding the world, consciousness and their relation. Merleau-Ponty's aim is to develop an alternative model. To do this he observes consciousness and the world, and describes them as accurately as possible without assuming the perspective of Objective Thought. Proponents of Objective Thought also base their investigations on observation. But Merleau-Ponty accuses them – in particular, Empiricists – of failing to recognise that, if one describes one's observation of *x*, one is describing one's *experience* of it – that is, how *x* appears to one. Of course, Empiricists assume that the subjective, personal elements in experience can be sifted to leave information about an independently existing world. However, this is one of the assumptions of Objective Thought that must be rejected. It follows that Merleau-Ponty must proceed by describing lived experience of the world and consciousness – that is, how they appear to the perceiver. This is why he focuses on the *perception* of depth. Just as proponents of Objective Thought make claims about the nature of the things they observe, so too Merleau-Ponty draws conclusions about the nature of depth from his observations. But he does this without relying on the assumptions of Objective Thought. The question we have to ask now is: having set aside Objective Thought, does Merleau-Ponty's analysis of depth perception license the claim that distance is constituted in experience?

It is not immediately clear that it does. In fact, one might think that Merleau-Ponty's analysis gets things the wrong way round. Distance does not result from the tightness of the perceiver's grip. Instead, the tightness of the perceiver's grip results from distance. The fact that I can discern the number of the bus is not what makes the bus three metres away from me. Instead, the fact that the bus is three metres away results in my being easily able to discern its number. If this is so, then distance exists independently of perceivers. It does not come into being through perception. However, this objection does not defeat Merleau-Ponty's account. Merleau-Ponty does not deny that perception is explained (in part) by some fact(s) about the world. This is implied by his claim that perception involves interaction between the world and the perceiver. The perceiver exercises their perceptual powers in response to the promptings of the world. The nature of these worldly promptings explains *how* the perceiver exercises their perceptual powers. Thus, for Merleau-Ponty, some fact(s) about the world (partly) explains the tightness of their perceptual grip. What Merleau-Ponty denies is that the *distance* between the perceiver and the object is this fact. Instead, distance is the manner in which the perceiver experiences the tightness of their perceptual grip. However, although Merleau-Ponty can deal with this objection, he has yet to establish that distance is constituted in perception.

A slightly different argument is suggested by his remark that 'we have to rediscover ... primordial depth, which confers upon [objectified depth] its significance' (Merleau-Ponty 1945: 308; 1962: 266; 2002: 310). We might read him as arguing here that the objective conception of distance as the space between two points is an abstraction from the lived experience of depth. Since it is an abstraction from lived experience, it is lived experience that gives it its significance or meaning. In the same way one must experience a circle in order to understand what a circle is.

When we consider the experience of distance, what we find is that it is the experience of having a more or less tight perceptual grip on an object. Thus one might conclude that 'distance' *means* the tightness of a subject's perceptual grip on something they perceive. However, one might raise the following worry at this point. Merleau-Ponty holds that the 'objective' conception of distance as the space between two points, which remains the same regardless of how anyone perceives it, is an abstraction from the lived experience of distance as the tightness of one's perceptual grip. One might accept this claim but hold that the process of abstraction sifts out the subjective manner in which distance appears to perceivers like us, to leave information about what distance really is, independently of how anyone experiences it. This is the line taken by Objective Thought. A response might be that, to accept this claim, we need some grounds for accepting Objective Thought. Merleau-Ponty has shown that in fact Objective Thought is unable to accommodate various data and should be rejected. Since we have no reason to accept Objective Thought, we have no grounds for holding that the process of abstracting from the experience of distance yields information about distance in-itself.

There is a third way to read Merleau-Ponty's argument here. He has given us reasons to reject Objective Thought. Objective Thought provides two conceptions of the relation between consciousness and the world. For Empiricism, consciousness is just an incidental part of an independently existing world. For Intellectualism, consciousness constitutes the world. The failure of Objective Thought means that neither of these conceptions can be accepted. The only alternative is to take consciousness and the world to be mutually dependent parts of one whole. One might then read Merleau-Ponty as aiming to flesh out this conception with detailed accounts of various worldly properties. On this reading, Merleau-Ponty takes the rejection of Objective Thought to *establish* that consciousness and the world are mutually dependent. The goal of his discussion is to reconceive properties such as depth so that they are in line with this. It follows that the analysis of depth that we should accept is the one that accords with this model of the relation between consciousness and the world.

We thus have reason to accept Merleau-Ponty's analysis of depth as constituted in perception, since it is part of an account of consciousness and the world as mutually dependent parts of one whole.

The notion of maximum grip allows Merleau-Ponty to account for the normativity in perception. Perceivers sometimes *mis*perceive. Since one of Merleau-Ponty's aims is to understand perception, he must give an account of what misperception involves. It is usual to conceive of misperceptions as experiences whose content does not correctly 'match' the bit of the world experienced. This view presupposes that the world-in-itself has qualities, which veridical perception merely presents or – depending on how one thinks of perceptual experience – duplicates. Suppose, for example, that I misperceive a wooden desk as plastic. It is common to account for this by holding that the bit of the world I experience contains a desk, which is made of wood. My experience fails to match this by presenting the desk as plastic. But Merleau-Ponty takes the qualities of perceived things to be constituted in perception of them. It thus makes no sense, on his picture, to talk of the content of perception 'matching' perception-independent qualities of the world. It follows that he must give a different account of misperception. His notion of maximum grip allows him to do this.

The qualities a perceived thing 'really' has are those one perceives it as having when one has maximum grip on it. Bearing in mind what was said earlier, maximum grip differs for different properties. Thus one may not be able to get maximum grip on an object all at once. A perception of something will be correct if it is consistent with how that thing appears at maximum grip. It will be incorrect – that is, it will be a misperception – if it is inconsistent with it. '*Consistent*' with how something appears at maximum grip does not mean *matching* how something looks when one has maximum grip on it. As the phenomenon of apparent size illustrates, there is a sense in which the appearance of a thing varies with context, even though it simultaneously appears the same across different contexts. Thus a blue shirt will be perceived as a uniform blue, even though it looks darker in dim light or where shadows fall across it. The text on a page always appears a certain size, thickness and crispness, even though it appears fuzzy from farther away when it is out of focus. This is generally referred to in the literature as 'perceptual constancy'. Merleau-Ponty accounts for perceptual constancy in the same way that he deals with apparent size. He holds that one's sense of deviating from maximum grip is a component of one's perceptual experience, so that one perceives the thing's qualities as the-same-but-viewed-in-a-different-context. Just as a distant mountain does not literally appear small, but large-seen-in-the-distance, so too the blue shirt does not literally appear dark blue, but mid-blue-seen-in-shadow. Similarly, the text on a page does not literally look fuzzy; it appears as crisply-printed-but-out-of-focus.

I have only discussed Merleau-Ponty's account of depth. However, he offers other arguments to show that all other experienced properties are brought into existence by perception. Suppose we accept these arguments, and endorse Merleau-Ponty's thesis that the things the subject perceives are constituted in their perception of them. A question that this raises is whether different subjects share the same world. Perhaps each of us perceives the world completely differently so that each of us lives in a different world – one that contains different things and has different properties – from those inhabited by others. Notice that this possibility remains, even when it is recognised that, on Merleau-Ponty's account, one perceives in response to the beckoning of the world, and that there are appropriate and inappropriate ways to exercise one's perceptual powers. It might be that the appropriate way for each of us to exercise our perceptual powers is different, so that the things that emerge from perceptual interaction with the world are different for each subject. In other words, maximum grip might be different for all of us.

Merleau-Ponty allows that there is a certain amount of variation in the way that different people perceive the world. We saw in Chapter 3 that what one sees is partly determined by one's motor skills. Thus people who have different motor skills will see the world differently. Moreover, Merleau-Ponty recognises that different cultures have different ways of seeing the world. This is because their habitual ways of interacting with it differ, and this leads to a difference in the way that they perceive it. In certain cultures, for example, people habitually drive cars, whereas in others they do not. People who have acquired the skill of coping with cars will see them as affording driving, whilst people who have not acquired this skill will not. Yet despite this variation, there is a commonality to the way that we each see the world, which results from the fact that our bodies have more or less the same physical structure. The structure of our bodies confers certain motor skills on us – for example, the ability to walk, the capacity to hold small objects in our hands, etc. Since these are skills that the majority of us share, we will all see the world as offering us similar opportunities for action. Merleau-Ponty writes, 'these mountains appear high to me, because they exceed my body's power to take them in its stride, and, even if I have just read *Micromégas*,[1] I cannot so contrive it that they are small for me' (1945: 502; 1962: 440; 2002: 511). The things that take shape in my perception of the world are thus the same as those that others perceive. Merleau-Ponty alludes to this common core of human experience when he describes one's body as the 'trace' of an 'anonymous existence' (1945: 406; 1962: 354; 2002: 412), and when he claims that sense experience is 'anonymous' (1945: 250; 1962: 216; 2002: 251). The body and sense experience are anonymous insofar as their character is shared by the majority of human beings. The result is that we live in a world that has the same basic structure for all of us.

Merleau-Ponty holds that the properties we experience the world as possessing are not ones that it has in-itself. They are instead properties that arise through our perceptual interaction with the world. The discussion so far has focused on the things perceived. Merleau-Ponty holds that these are constituted in perceptions of them. But the same is also true of the embodied perceiver. One experiences oneself as possessing the same sort of properties as perceived things. One is aware of oneself as taking up a certain amount of space, being a certain colour, having a certain shape, making particular noises, etc. It follows that the embodied subject must also be constituted through perceptual interaction with the world.

THE SUBJECT AND THE WORLD THAT PRECEDE PERCEPTION

On Merleau-Ponty's account, perceived things and the embodied subject are constituted through the activity of perceiving. But there is now a problem. Throughout the foregoing discussion, I have emphasised that the perceiver does not create perceived things or their own embodied self out of nothing. Instead, the perceptual activity that brings experienced properties into existence involves interaction between the subject and the world. But, for perception to be interaction between a subject and a world, there must be a subject and a world that interact. Moreover, these must precede perception for it to be an interaction between them. For Merleau-Ponty to maintain that the world and consciousness are mutually dependent parts of one whole, he must therefore show that this is the case for the subject and world that precede perception. He now seems to be in rather a bind. His commitment to phenomenology means that he must establish this on the basis of experience. But surely the subject and the world that interact in perception and which give rise to perceived things cannot themselves figure in experience.

One might be tempted by the following response to this problem. The observant reader will have noticed that I have spoken interchangeably of perceived *properties* and perceived *things* being constituted in experience of them. I have spoken this way because Merleau-Ponty holds that things are fully constituted by their perceived properties. His claim rests on two premises. First, he thinks that we are only justified in claiming that something exists if we have evidence for this claim. This is surely uncontroversial. Evidence for the existence of some worldly item has to include experience of it. It follows that the only properties we can justifiably claim to exist are those we can experience. Second, he endorses what is known as a bundle theory of objects – the view that objects are just bundles of properties. It follows from these two claims that perceived things are constituted by their perceived properties. One might then suppose that the problem identified above is the traditional difficulty that faces bundle theorists. Some philosophers, for example Locke (1997), argue that objects cannot be merely bundles of properties; the properties must inhere in something else that holds them together – a substance. Even if all of an object's properties are perceivable, the substance in which they inhere is not. Analogous points apply in the case of the relation between the embodied perceiver and their properties.

It might be supposed that Merleau-Ponty's account of how properties are united as things is sufficient to answer the worry raised above. His account appeals to his views on the nature of properties. Properties are sometimes thought of as universals. According to this view, a property is an entity, which is shared by all the particular items that possess it – for example, all aquamarine things share the property 'aquamarine-ness'.[2] But the claim that all aquamarine things have a common component – the colour-property aquamarine-ness – assumes that a thing's colour can be abstracted from the rest of its properties. It assumes, in other words, that a thing's colour is related externally to the rest of its properties; it does not modify, nor is it modified by them. The same is true of the thing's other properties. Merleau-Ponty rejects this view. He also holds that a thing's properties are internally related to one another. By this he means that the identity of each of a thing's properties is dependent on its being related to the other properties. Merleau-Ponty's claim is based on his observation that each property of a thing is modified by, and implies, its other properties. The quality of a thing's colour, for example, is affected by its texture, so that the red of a woolly carpet is not *literally* the same as the red sheen of a flower's petals, even if we can legitimately *talk* about them as being the same shade. If a thing's properties cannot be abstracted from one another, then there is not literally one universal property, say aquamarine-ness, which all aquamarine things have in common. Instead, properties are the internally related, particular qualities of actual things.

The claim that a thing's properties are internally related to one another provides a way for Merleau-Ponty to account for a thing's unity without positing an underlying substance. There is nothing more to the carpet than its woolly redness, its springiness underfoot, the soft scrunching noise it makes as one walks over it, and so on. But the carpet's qualities are not like so many separate pieces that somehow need to be strung together by some external means. Instead, the internal relations between the qualities mean that each one implies the others, thus uniting them as a single item. This seems to provide a response to the worry outlined above. Merleau-Ponty has shown that perceived things are entirely constituted by their perceived properties. There is no underlying, unperceived substance. The same holds for the embodied subject. Thus it appears that there is no unexperienced world and subject for which Merleau-Ponty must account. However, it is hopefully clear that this response will not suffice. The worry does not rest on the charge that Merleau-Ponty cannot account for the unity of perceived things/the embodied subject. Its source is the claim that perception involves interaction between the subject and the world. The thesis that a thing's properties are internally related does nothing to relieve this difficulty.

The problem is that Merleau-Ponty takes perceived things and the embodied subject to be constituted in perception, which he conceives as interaction between the subject and the world. The subject and the world that interact in perception must precede it. For him to defend the view that the world and consciousness are mutually dependent parts of one whole, he must show that this is the case for the world and subject that precede perception. Moreover, he must do this on the basis of our experience of them. However, it seems that, since what is perceived is constituted in perception, the subject and the world that precede perception cannot themselves be perceived.

Merleau-Ponty's way out of this conundrum is ingenious. He argues that the world and the subject that precede perception can figure in our experience without being perceived. Indeed, they figure in *all* our experience. Consider, again, what Merleau-Ponty has shown us about perception. Perceiving is an ongoing process of making the indeterminate and ambiguous determinate. The perceiver is presented with vague something-or-others that invite further exploration. They suggest to the perceiver how they should be perceived. The subject responds to these suggestions by summoning the appropriate appearances, and the vague something-or-others take shape as things. But this process is not cumulative like painting a picture, where the more one paints, the more picture there is. Perception is necessarily of a figure on a background, which means that the whole scene cannot be made determinate all at once. The figure is the focus of one's attention; it is seen clearly and in detail. It stands out from the background, which is perceived indistinctly, as indeterminate. Merleau-Ponty observes that one experiences the background as continuing indefinitely beyond one's field of vision – one does not perceive it as simply stopping at the limits of one's perceptual reach. One experiences the area surrounding the figure as populated by vague presences. The further they are from the figure, the more ambiguous they become. The indeterminacy of what is seen increases with the distance to such an extent that one's awareness of the furthest region of the background is simply the experience of a vast presence, continuing indefinitely into the distance. The ambiguity is so great that one does not experience the vast presence as possessing any qualities whatsoever. One is simply aware that it is there. This, for Merleau-Ponty, is the world that precedes perception. It forms the background to all one's experience; it is that indeterminate, massive presence against which things are seen.

There is, nevertheless, something more that can be said about this vast presence. It 'pulls' us in a certain direction. The 'pull' is felt by the subject and is what initiates the activity of perceiving. Merleau-Ponty describes it as a sort of tension that the subject feels which is resolved when they perceive the world in a certain way – that is, they perceive it as having certain qualities. Elsewhere, he describes the world as arousing vague expectations in the subject, which are then satisfied when they perceive it in a certain way. He offers one such example in the following passage:

> If I walk along a shore towards a ship which has run aground, and the funnel or masts merge into the forest bordering on the sand dune, there will be a moment when these details suddenly become part of the ship, and indissolubly fused with it. As I approached, I did not perceive resemblances or proximities which finally came together to form a continuous picture of the upper part of the ship. I merely felt

> that the look of the object was on the point of altering ... Suddenly the sight before me was recast in a manner satisfying to my vague expectation.
>
> (Merleau-Ponty 1945: 24; 1962: 17; 2002: 20)

The 'pull' we experience is not a tangible characteristic that we perceive the world as having. It is not a property that we apprehend using our senses. It is instead a feeling of tension, which stands right at the outset of perception. Insofar as perception is the activity of bringing perceived properties into being, the awareness of the presence that we have at the limits of our perceptual reach is awareness of that bit of the world *before* perception of it takes place. One has not yet started coping with the presence. This is why it appears so indeterminate that it has no properties, so that all it offers us is the experience of a 'pull'. In this way, Merleau-Ponty holds that the world that precedes perception can be experienced, even though it cannot be perceived.

I have so far analysed the experience of the 'pull' as awareness of the world that precedes perception. But it is clear that it is also the experience of the subject who precedes perception. A pull involves something that draws and something that is drawn. To experience the world as pulling is to simultaneously experience oneself as pulled. The experience of the pull is not awareness of any tangible characteristic or property. The same is true of the experience of being pulled. To experience oneself as pulled, in other words, is not yet to experience oneself as having any particular properties or power for action. Since these arise through the activity of perceiving, the experience of being pulled is an experience of the subject (oneself) that precedes perception.

Does this provide a conception of the world and consciousness as mutually dependent parts of one whole? One might worry that it does not. The fact that one thing (the world) pulls whilst the other (the subject) is pulled does nothing to establish the nature of the relation between them. They could be entirely independent of one another, rather like mismatched teams in a tug-of-war – one team pulls and the weaker team is pulled, but after the game is finished, both teams go their separate ways. Merleau-Ponty certainly became dissatisfied with the conception he reached in

PhP. He later wrote, '[t]he problems posed in PhP are insoluble because I start there from the "consciousness"–"object" distinction' (Merleau-Ponty 1969: 200). One can see his later notion of the *Flesh* as a new attempt to conceive the world and consciousness as mutually dependent. However, there is another way to view the account he offers in PhP. Sean Kelly[3] suggests that the subject and the world that precede perception cannot be thought of as separate entities. The only sensible notion of individual things conceives them as the sorts of items that we perceive, and these only come into being through our perception of them. Thus the subject and the world cannot be thought of as separate items, one of which incidentally pulls the other. Instead, Merleau-Ponty's view is that, prior to perception, there is simply a system of forces. The subject and the world are 'opposite poles' of these forces. There is nothing more that can be said about them. But there cannot be a force that does not have opposite poles. This is what a force is. It follows that the subject and the world are mutually dependent parts of one whole. Although Merleau-Ponty himself perhaps did not realise it, he *does* succeed in accounting for consciousness and the world in the way he wants in PhP.

CONCLUSION

Merleau-Ponty aims to show that the world and consciousness are mutually dependent parts of one whole. He takes this conception of their relation to be implied by the failure of Objective Thought. Empiricism takes the world to be one that exists in-itself, independently of consciousness, which is just one of the many things contained in it. Intellectualism, in contrast, holds that the world is constituted by a Transcendental Ego that is wholly different from the world and lies outside it. Merleau-Ponty holds that, if we reject Objective Thought, then we must reject both of these positions. The remaining alternative is to view consciousness and the world as mutually dependent. He sets out to develop such a conception of them. Part of his project involves showing that the properties we experience both ourselves and things in the world as having are constituted in our perception of them. The perceiver summons appropriate appearances in response to the summonings of the world. In this chapter, I have examined the argument he provides in the case of depth. Merleau-Ponty first provides an account of how depth or distance is perceived by the subject. On this basis, he then defines the distance between the subject and a thing the subject perceives as the 'tightness' of their perceptual grip on it. A thing is near when the subject has a 'tight' grip on it and can discern more of its features. It is further away when their grip on it is 'loose' and 'approximate' and they can discern less of its features. It is clear that on this account, distance is a property the world has only in relation to embodied perceivers. He offers similar arguments for the other properties we experience. Merleau-Ponty uses his notion of perceptual 'grip' to account for normativity in perception. For every type of property, there is a best context in which to perceive it. In other words, there is a context in which the perceiver is best able to exercise their perceptual power of summoning in response to the promptings of the world. When the perceiver is in this context, they have 'maximum grip' on the thing they perceive. A perceived thing's *real* properties are those the subject perceives it as having when they have maximum grip on it. A subject perceives something correctly when their perception of it is consistent with how it appears at maximum grip.

The subject and the world that interact in perception cannot themselves be perceived. Merleau-Ponty must show that they are mutually dependent parts of one whole, and he must somehow do this on the basis of experience. He does this by pointing to a way of experiencing the world which allows it to figure in one's experience without being perceived. This is the awareness one has of it as the background to all one's explicit perceptions. It presents the world as an indeterminate, massive presence that lacks any determinate properties. One experiences this massive presence as exerting a 'pull' on one to perceive it in a certain way. The experience of the pull is, at the same time, an experience of being pulled. It is thus an experience of oneself as the subject that precedes perception. Merleau-Ponty's description of this experience allows us to account for the subject and the world as opposite poles of a system of forces. As such, they are mutually dependent parts of one whole.

5

OTHER SELVES AND THE HUMAN WORLD

Merleau-Ponty has given an account of our existence as physical creatures, situated in the world. But there is a further dimension of our existence that he has yet to address: the social. Each of us inhabits a world that we share with other people. Moreover, the vast majority of us live with and encounter others on a daily basis. A full analysis of our existence therefore requires an account of other selves. Merleau-Ponty's thoughts on this issue will be the focus of the current chapter.

CULTURAL OBJECTS

For Merleau-Ponty, the social dimension of our existence encompasses more than just other people. It also includes cultural objects, or artefacts: things habitually used or produced by humans, such as cars, paintings and spoons. Merleau-Ponty holds that cultural objects are perceived differently to natural objects.

He claims that unlike natural objects, 'each [cultural object] spreads around it an atmosphere of humanity' (Merleau-Ponty 1945: 400; 1962: 347; 2002: 405). When one perceives an artefact, one immediately sees it as something that has a place in some form of human behaviour. They appear as 'behavioural sediments', deposited in the world as things. Consequently, perceiving a cultural object gives one a sense of other people. One feels the presence of other selves when one perceives an artefact – even though one may be aware that those others have long since gone. The difference between the experience of natural objects and the experience of artefacts is illustrated by the following case. When walking through a forest, I feel alone. Surrounded by natural objects, I have a sense of having escaped from human society. I then see a thermos flask under a tree. The sight of the flask gives me a slight jolt as I feel the presence of another human being in the flask. Even if I can see that the flask is covered in lichen and has not been used for some time, it still looks like a distinctively human object, which gives me a sense of other people having passed this way.

Cultural objects can appear indeterminate or ambiguous in various ways. In some cases, one's perception of a cultural object gives one a sense of another person without providing much detail about who that person is. Merleau-Ponty gives the example of seeing footprints in the sand. One senses another self without seeing whether they are male or female, young or old, and so on. In other cases, one has a much more determinate sense of the other – for example, if one goes into a house whose occupants have been recently evacuated, one will get a strong sense of who they are and what kind of life they lead. Similarly, the artefacts of my culture, such as hairbrushes and staplers, appear as 'sediments' of highly determinate activities such as brushing one's hair and stapling pieces of paper together. But the implements of an unknown civilisation are perceived ambiguously – the ancient pot looks distinctively human, but I have no determinate perception of its use (Merleau-Ponty 1945: 400; 1962: 347; 2002: 405). An account of social existence must also explain how it is possible to see cultural objects in this way.

Merleau-Ponty takes cultural objects and other people to raise essentially the same problem:

> Whether it be a question of vestiges or the body of another person, we need to know how an object in space can become the eloquent relic of an existence; how, conversely, an intention, a thought or a project can detach themselves from the personal subject and become visible outside him in the shape of his body, and in the environment which he builds for himself.
>
> (Merleau-Ponty 1945: 401; 1962: 348–9; 2002: 406)

Both artefacts and other human bodies raise the question of how it is possible to see human thoughts and projects by looking at a physical object. Nevertheless, there are important differences between the two cases. To see an artefact is to feel the presence of other humans, but, as we saw above, the others may not actually be present. To see another living human body, in contrast, is to experience the actual presence of another self. Moreover, other people are the *subjects* of thoughts and projects, whilst artefacts are not. Merleau-Ponty also notes that the problem of other selves is more fundamental than that of cultural objects. Plausibly, one first comes to see cultural objects as distinctively human by perceiving the human behaviour in which they are used or produced. After time, the artefacts appear as the sediments of such activity. Cultural objects that one has never seen in use will also appear as behavioural sediments in virtue of their similarity to those one has seen used. However, this explanation presupposes an analysis of how one sees behaviour as manifesting another's thoughts and projects. It follows that an account of other selves is prior to an account of cultural objects.

THE PROBLEM OF OTHERS

The analytic literature dealing with the problem of other selves tends to focus on three issues:

(1) a conceptual problem that asks how I should conceive of other selves;

(2) an epistemological problem that concerns how I know that there are other selves; and

(3) a phenomenological problem that asks what experience of another self is like.

The problems are clearly related. One needs a conception of another self before one can say how one knows that there are other selves or what one's experience of another self is like. Moreover, an account of one's experience of others may explain how one knows that there are other selves, since experience can ground knowledge.

Traditional attempts to solve these three problems have encountered difficulties, and solipsism – the doctrine that I am alone – has been an ever-present threat. Merleau-Ponty holds that these problems largely result from Objective Thinking. He argues that 'the existence of other people is a difficulty and an outrage for Objective Thought' (Merleau-Ponty 1945: 401; 1962: 349; 2002: 406). Difficulties arise in the first instance because neither Empiricism nor Intellectualism is able to offer a satisfactory conception of other selves. Subsequently, Objective Thought cannot provide solutions to the other two issues – knowledge and experience of others – either. The problem for Empiricism is that it has only one category of being at its disposal: physical matter, or being-in-itself, which it takes to be atomistic and causally determined. On this picture, consciousness is a physical thing and is identical with the body or a part of the body such as the brain and possibly the nervous system. Conscious activities are causal processes; conscious states are physical states. Merleau-Ponty objects that one cannot conceive of consciousness at all on this view, because it is impossible to give a reductive physiological account of features that he takes to be definitive of consciousness, such as intentionality and meaning. He writes, 'how significance and intentionality could come to dwell in molecular edifices or masses of cells is a thing which can never be made comprehensible' (Merleau-Ponty 1945: 403; 1962: 351; 2002: 409).

Intellectualism develops out of the problems faced by Empiricism. The Intellectualist realises that consciousness cannot be understood on the Empiricist view, and so introduces a second category of being: consciousness, or being-for-itself, which is not identical with physical matter and is not causally determined. Intellectualism fares slightly better than Empiricism, since it can at least offer some conception of consciousness – although it is a conception that Merleau-Ponty rejects – but there are still insurmountable difficulties. Knowledge and experience of my own mind are straightforward. I am aware of – and so come to know – my own states by introspection, for example I feel pain and thus know that I hurt. But it is impossible for me to be aware of anyone else's conscious states in this way. I can only experience another self through awareness of their body. However, Intellectualism retains the notion of the body as a mere object. People – the physical creatures I see around me – are thus puppets, 'merely pieces of mechanism worked by springs' (Merleau-Ponty 1945: 401; 1962: 349; 2002: 407) – and to see another body is not to be aware of another self. It is completely unclear how I could come by the idea of another mind from this perspective, and there are notorious problems with explaining how I can know that there are other selves if consciousness is conceived as non-physical. The difficulties are further compounded by Intellectualism's claim that consciousness constitutes the world. Another consciousness would also have to be a constituting agent. But, for me to be aware of the other, they would have to appear as part of the world that I constitute, and so be constituted by me. If they are constituted by me, then it is wholly unclear how they can also be a constituting agent. Thus no account of other selves can be given, and Intellectualism leads inevitably to solipsism, forcing me to conclude that there is only one self, me.

The problems encountered by Objective Thought's attempts to account for other selves are diffused by Merleau-Ponty's conception of bodily subjectivity. He rejects Objective Thought's ideas of both the body and consciousness. On his view, the body is not a mere physical object, which simply obeys the laws of causation. It is intelligent and possesses its own forms of knowledge and understanding, which are manifest in its grip on the world. As we will see in Chapters 6 and 7, he also argues for the corresponding claim – namely, that consciousness is not independent from the body. It is essentially embodied. Since consciousness is bodily and bodies are conscious, there is no great obstacle to explaining how I experience and come to know other selves – they are embodied beings, and thus perceivable elements of the world that I inhabit. One may think at this point that Merleau-Ponty has completely solved the problems of other selves and removed the threat of solipsism, since he has provided solutions to (1)–(3). One may be subsequently puzzled to find that this is only the beginning of his discussion. There is, of course, a further problem connected with the issues of other selves – (4) a developmental problem of explaining how the child develops an understanding of others. Merleau-Ponty is interested in this issue, but his discussion in PhP is by no means solely or even centrally concerned with this empirical question. Instead, Merleau-Ponty focuses on what might be called (5) the problem of intersubjectivity. Each of us ordinarily experiences ourself as one of many selves, to whom we relate in various ways, and with whom we share a common world. The problem of intersubjectivity, as Merleau-Ponty understands it, is the problem of giving a phenomenological account of this experience – that is, of making its structure explicit.

He draws our attention to two central features of intersubjectivity. First, intersubjective experience involves being aware of others *as* subjects, at least some of the time. The thought here is this. Even if consciousness is conceived as essentially embodied and so perceivable, we can still distinguish between two modes of awareness one might have of another self: awareness of the other self as a subject, and awareness of them as an object. When I am aware of someone as an object, I am aware of what is in fact another person, but my experience of them does not present them as significantly different from inanimate items like tables and rocks. We can get some intuitive purchase on this mode of awareness by reflecting on the experience I can have of someone's brain activity using an MRI scanner. In this case, the object of my awareness is what is in fact another self – the person whose brain I am scanning. But it seems the experience I have of them using the MRI scanner is on a par with my awareness of things such as cars and coffee cups, even if I *know* that what I am experiencing is in fact another conscious being. In contrast, to be aware of another as a subject is for one's experience to present them as someone who perceives, acts, thinks and so on. Ordinarily, each of us is aware of others as subjects: one *experiences* oneself as being in the company of other conscious beings; one does not merely *believe* that this is so. An account of intersubjectivity must capture this aspect of experience by analysing one's awareness of others as subjects. Second, Merleau-Ponty notes that intersubjectivity involves the experience of reciprocity – in short, the experience of others as being aware of oneself in the same ways that one is aware of them. This in turn means that my experience must present me as something experience-able by others, and something that others can experience as a subject. A full analysis of intersubjectivity must also show how my experience presents me as something that others can experience as a subject in the same way that I experience them.

One might suppose that for experience to exhibit these features, my experience of myself and my awareness of others must be 'symmetrical'. My experience of myself and my awareness of others must be, in some sense, the same. The two features of intersubjective experience seem to require symmetry for the following reasons. It seems obvious that one experiences oneself as a subject. (This is not to say that one always experiences oneself in this way. It seems plausible to suppose that I may experience what is in fact myself without being presented to myself as a subject – for example, by seeing an MRI scan of my own brain activity.) It thus seems that to experience another as a subject, one must therefore experience the other in the same or sufficiently similar ways to the manner in which one experiences oneself. Similarly, it seems that to experience oneself as something that others can experience in the same way that one experiences them requires one's experience to present oneself and the other in the same or sufficiently similar ways.

We can read the symmetry requirement in different ways. It could, for example, be read as requiring that my experience of myself is qualitatively identical with my awareness of another. But it is completely implausible to suppose that my experience could ever satisfy this requirement, and it surely does not need to for it to present others as subjects, and me as something that others can experience in the same way that I experience them. We can identify further ways of reading the symmetry requirement by considering various ways in which experience of two items may be *a*symmetrical. Experience may present them as having different types of property – for example, one might appear to have feathers, whilst the other appears to have fur. Or the structure of one's awareness might be different in both cases – for example, perception is of a figure against a background, and my awareness of the figure has a different structure to my awareness of the background. The former is the focus of attention, whilst the latter is perceived implicitly. Or one might be aware of the two items using different faculties – for example, I might perceive one, but have some extrasensory intuition of the other. Merleau-Ponty seems to understand symmetry to require that I experience myself and others as being the same sort of beings, and that my experience does not present either of us as privileged. What this amounts to will be discussed below.

There is radical asymmetry between my awareness of my own mind and my experience of another consciousness on the Intellectualist account. I experience my own mind using introspection, but I cannot introspect another consciousness. Any knowledge I have of another self must be based on inference from what I *can* observe – another body. The radical asymmetry in my experience is an inevitable consequence of the way in which Intellectualism conceives of the mind. Merleau-Ponty's account of consciousness as bodily means that such radical asymmetry is not inevitable – since both of us are embodied creatures, it might turn out that I perceive the other in exactly the same way that I perceive myself. But it does not guarantee that my experience of myself and others will be symmetrical.

Merleau-Ponty also takes solipsism to be a difficulty for him, in spite of his conception of consciousness as essentially embodied. He holds that to fully eradicate solipsism requires a satisfactory account of intersubjectivity – the experience of being one of many selves sharing a common world. As we have seen, this experience has two important features: it involves being aware of others as subjects, and experiencing oneself as something that others can experience in the same way that one experiences them. If experience did not satisfy these two conditions, then it would present one as alone in some sense. If I was only ever aware of others as objects, then I would have no experience of being in the company of other conscious beings. My experience would present me as the only subject. Similarly, if I was not aware of myself as something that others could experience in the same way that I experience them, then my experience would present me as somehow having a special view of others which they could not have of me. My experience would therefore present me as not being truly one of them, and so it would not be awareness of being one of many selves. By presenting me as having a special view of others, my experience would also present me as a different sort of being. In this way, my experience would present me as being alone. Both kinds of experience are solipsistic insofar as they present me as being alone, albeit in different ways. Thus both are experiences of solitude. Although these solipsistic experiences do not entail ontological solipsism – the claim that I am the only self in existence – they give the position some appeal. Experience is an important source of knowledge. If my experience never presents me with others as subjects or presents me as being a special kind of entity that has a special view of others that they cannot have of me, then I lack one important source for the knowledge that there *are* other subjects or that I am one of many selves who share a common world.

SYMMETRICAL EXPERIENCE

Merleau-Ponty begins his discussion by considering the perception of another's body. He argues that I do not perceive another bodily self as a mere object. I experience them as a power to perform various kinds of action. Moreover, I am never just presented with another body. I always perceive another body as it is situated in its environment, interacting with it. The basic unit of experience is thus the other as being-in-the-world. Merleau-Ponty holds that one's perception of anything is affected by the context in which it is perceived. This is true of my experience of another's body and my awareness of their surroundings. My perception of the other's body informs my experience of their surroundings, and my perception of their environment informs my experience of their body. By seeing them interact with the world, I see it as having a value for their behaviour. When I watch a football match, for example, I see the football flying towards the goal as to-be-intercepted by the goalkeeper, and I see that it requires them to jump to the left and stretch out their hands to reach it. My perception of the world as requiring the other to behave in certain ways informs my experience of the other. The powers of action I perceive them as possessing are those I experience their environment as requiring from them. Thus I am aware of the other's body and environment as complementary parts of one whole.

The first thing to note about this experience is that I am aware of the other as an agent, that is, as a subject, since I see their activity as behaviour, not the mechanical workings of a mere object. Second, it gives me an awareness of the world as shared. Merleau-Ponty has so far described me as perceiving things as requiring me to act in various ways. I thus experience the world as having a value for *me* in terms of *my* potential for action. Seeing someone else act transforms the appearance of the world. Instead of seeing it as simply offering *me* opportunities for action, I see the world around the other person as having a value for *their* behaviour. But the things with which they interact are objects that *I* can also use. Merleau-Ponty writes, 'There is taking place over there a certain manipulation of things hitherto my property. Someone is making use of my familiar objects. But who can it be? I say that it is another, a second self' (1945: 406; 1962: 353; 2002: 412). In this way, I experience us as inhabiting a common world.

Third, it is clear from Merleau-Ponty's description that my awareness of another bodily self is much the same as my experience of my own body. As we saw in Chapter 3, I am not aware of my body as an object. Instead, I experience it as the power to perform various kinds of actions. My awareness of my body is bound up with my awareness of the world around me. I am never just presented with my body. I always experience it as it is situated in my environment, engaged in activity. The basic unit of experience, in other words, is my being-in-the-world. Just like my perception of the other's body, my experience of my own body is affected by my perception of my environment, and vice versa. I experience my environment as requiring certain actions – footballs appear kickable, chairs invite me to sit on them, kittens invite me to stroke them, and so on. The actions I perceive my surroundings as requiring are those that I can perform. The powers of action I experience my body as possessing are those I perceive to be demanded by my environment. In this way, I am aware of my body and my environment as two complementary parts of one whole. I perceive my surroundings as demanding certain actions, and I experience my body as the power to perform the actions my environment requires.

Merleau-Ponty claims that the other thus appears to me as 'a miraculous prolongation of my own intentions ... [our bodies are presented as] one whole, two sides of one and the same phenomenon' (1945: 406; 1962: 354; 2002: 412). He is not claiming here that my experience presents the other's body as somehow belonging to me so that I experience myself as possessing two bodies. Instead, he suggests that I am aware of the other's body in the same ways that I am aware of my own. I am aware that the two bodies are numerically distinct – that they are indeed two bodies – but my experience does not present either of them as 'special' or 'privileged'. My awareness of the other bodily self and my experience of my own body are thus symmetrical. Both my body and the body of the other appear as 'manifestations of behaviour' (1945: 405; 1962: 352; 2002: 411).

Merleau-Ponty argues that it is possible to perceive the other bodily self in this way because the other's body is similar to one's own. One might suppose that this involves reasoning by analogy. The argument from analogy is traditionally offered as an explanation of how I know that there are other minds. The argument involves reasoning from observed similarities between my body and the body of someone else to the conclusion that since my body is associated with my consciousness, so too the other's body must be inhabited by a mind. There are notorious difficulties with this argument. It also presupposes the Intellectualist view of consciousness as separate from the body and unobservable.

Needless to say, it would be disastrous for Merleau-Ponty if his solution to the problem of intersubjectivity relied on the argument from analogy. His response is that the way in which the similarity of our bodies allows me to perceive the other body as an embodied subject does not involve any reasoning by analogy. He points out that even very young infants are able to imitate others' behaviour, for example, if one playfully bites the hand of a very young infant, it will open and close its own mouth. To do this, they must perceive others' bodies as similar to their own. To copy the adult's biting action, the infant must be aware of its own mouth as similar to the adult's in that both can be used to bite. But the infant's imitation cannot be based on reasoning from analogy. The infant is too young to think and, in any case, it has never seen its mouth in a mirror, so does not know that it looks the same as the adult's. Instead, the infant immediately experiences the adult's mouth and its own as being for the same purpose (Merleau-Ponty 1945: 404; 1962: 352; 2002: 410).

More recent research perhaps sheds light on this phenomenon. Experiments conducted on monkeys establish that the same neurons in the motor cortex – 'mirror' neurons – fire whether the animal is performing a particular action itself or watching another animal perform the same action (Rizzolatti et al. 1995). Experiments provide evidence for an analogous human mirror system, although mirror neurons are not found in humans (Rizzolatti et al. 1996). It is hypothesised that the mirror system underpins our ability to perceive each other's bodily movements as actions. When I see you acting, the mirror system fires as if it was me performing the action, thus generating a perception of you as an agent engaged in behaviour, rather than a mere object moving. Clearly, the functioning of the mirror system depends on the similarities between our bodies and the fact that I could perform the action I see you performing. Moreover, theorists have argued that, since the same neurons fire whether I watch someone else act or prepare to act myself, the firing of those neurons will bring about action in my own case, unless they are prevented from doing so by a 'containing mechanism'.[1] We can therefore surmise that the infant's imitative biting action results from watching the adult's action because the containing mechanism is not yet in place.

I do not simply watch others, I also communicate with them. Merleau-Ponty holds that, when I communicate with another, there is no radical asymmetry between my awareness of myself and my experience of the other. He describes what it is like to converse with another. When I have a conversation with someone, I do not know in advance exactly what I am going to say. Instead, my words – and those of my partner – are drawn forth by the discussion, in much the same way that my actions can be initiated and controlled by my environment. Just as the air of formality at the dinner party regulates my behaviour so that I do not swear and eat with my mouth open, so too my partner's doubting response to what I tell them immediately calls forth a vigorous defence of my point from me, even though I did not plan in advance to defend what I say so vehemently, and I may not even be entirely convinced that it is right. Likewise, my partner hears that I am upset by their doubt, and this prompts them to speak more gently as they try to placate me. But it is not just my words and tone that are drawn from me by discussion. Merleau-Ponty also notes that conversation brings forth thought. The things I express during a conversation will sometimes be opinions I formed before talking to the other. But often – and this is particularly true as the conversation progresses – talking to someone prompts me to think things that I might otherwise never have thought.

Moreover, it is not just that I am inspired to think new thoughts by conversing. Merely observing an object, for example a painting, can provoke new reflections, but the experience of being inspired by an object one sees is different from the experience of thought arising through communication. The difference between the two scenarios is captured by Merleau-Ponty's observation that dialogue 'draws from me thoughts which I had no idea I possessed' (1945: 407; 1962: 354; 2002: 413). Merleau-Ponty is not suggesting here that I am literally surprised by my thoughts in the same way that I may find what someone else says surprising. This is a description that more properly fits the pathological experience of thought insertion. Instead, he is referring to the following phenomenon. Sometimes in conversation, one thinks in speech. Rather than having fully formed thoughts that one then expresses in words, the act of thinking is constituted by speaking. We will investigate this idea further in Chapter 7, but for now it can be motivated by reflecting on the fact that thinking can sometimes involve talking to oneself 'in one's head'. Furthermore, an inner monologue can be replaced by spoken words – as is aptly illustrated by those occasions when one is deep in thought and suddenly realises that one has been talking aloud to oneself (much to the consternation of passers-by). Thus, when my verbal response to the other is drawn forth from me by the discussion, it does not express a thought I had prior to the conversation, it constitutes a new thought.

It follows that there is a sense in which the other is partly responsible for my thinking. Indeed, Merleau-Ponty claims that, in these cases, there is just one train of thought for which both conversational participants are responsible. He writes, 'my thought and his are inter-woven into a single fabric ... they are inserted into a shared operation of which neither of us is the creator' (1945: 407; 1962: 354; 2002: 413). The claim that in certain conversations I talk by thinking helps to make sense of this remark. What I say constitutes my thought. The other's verbal response to me also constitutes their thinking. The train of thought constituted by what is said in the discussion thus comprises both my thinking and my partner's. Moreover, it is this train of thought – what has previously been said in the discussion – that calls forth our responses. My conversational partner and I thus think together. We are both the subjects of a single stream of thought. We are 'collaborators', not independent subjects (1945: 407; 1962: 354; 2002: 413). It follows that my experience of conversing with another is not asymmetrical awareness of myself as a subject of thought, and the other as a mere object. I experience both of us as subjects, jointly thinking about the topics we discuss.

THE PROBLEM OF SELF-CONSCIOUSNESS

Merleau-Ponty has so far analysed my experience of another as being symmetrical with my awareness of myself. But Merleau-Ponty notes that there is a difficulty with the account he has given. He writes,

> But is it indeed other people we arrive at in this way? What we do in effect is to iron out the I and the Thou in an experience shared by a plurality, thus introducing the impersonal into the heart of subjectivity and eliminating the individuality of perspectives. But have we not, in the general confusion, done away with the Alter Ego as well as the Ego?
>
> (Merleau-Ponty 1945: 408; 1962: 355–6; 2002: 414)

The problem he identifies here is this. An essential part of what it is to be a person in the full sense of the term – an *I* – is to be self-conscious. It is to be aware of oneself as *the* subject of one's own experiences. Whatever that might involve, it is, at the very least, to be aware of oneself in a way that one cannot be aware of anyone else, that is, to have privileged awareness of oneself. There are different ways that this requirement might be fulfilled, but, on any account, it follows that self-consciousness essentially involves an asymmetry between experience of oneself and experience of another. However, there is now a serious problem. It seems that an account of intersubjectivity must show that there is symmetry between my experience of myself and my awareness of others for it to capture the experience of being one of many selves who share a common world. But this is incompatible with self-conscious experience, which requires asymmetry between my awareness of myself and my experience of others.

Of course, Merleau-Ponty is interested in making our actual experience explicit. Although Merleau-Ponty has emphasised the ways in which my experience of others is symmetrical to my awareness of myself, there are many ways in which it differs, and can thus meet the asymmetry demanded of it by self-consciousness. Perceptual experience is egocentric – I see things from a point of view in space, which is the place where my body is situated. My perceptual experience of my own body is thus different from my perception of another bodily self. I can, for example, view another's body from any angle, but I can only see my own body from one perspective. My experience of another's behaviour also differs from my experience of my own. I merely observe the other acting, but my awareness of my own actions includes the experience of being their agent. (The experience of agency will be examined further in Chapter 6.) Merleau-Ponty also notes that, although I can experience another's emotions and do not need to *infer* that he feels a certain way, my experience of their emotions is different from my awareness of my own. I observe the other's emotions as they are manifest in their inter-actions with the world. But one's own emotions are lived through – they colour one's perception of the world, and influence one's behaviour. There is a genuine sense in which I can share the emotions of another. But, even in such a case, there is still asymmetry between my experience of their emotions and their awareness of them. I can, for example, share another's grief and anger, but our perspectives are different. *I* am saddened by my friend's grief, but *he* grieves for his wife. In the same way, *he* is angry because his watch has been stolen, but *I* am angered because he is angry (Merleau-Ponty 1945: 409; 1962: 356; 2002: 415). Even communication does not eliminate the asymmetry between my experience of myself and my awareness of another. Each participant in a conversation has their own perspective on it.

Does this then mean that my actual experience is not inter-subjective? Merleau-Ponty thinks not. He holds that each of us does in fact experience themself as one self amongst many who share a common world. The question is how to give an account of this experience, given that there is asymmetry between my experience of myself and my awareness of others.

One might suppose at this point that Sartre's (1958) account of experiencing others can solve the problem. His account analyses my experience of others as subjects, and shows how I am aware of myself as something that others can experience in the same way that I experience them. However, Sartre does this without giving up the asymmetry which is crucial to self-conscious experience. Sartre appeals to a phenomenon which he calls 'the gaze' – the experience of being perceived by another person. Sartre claims that I experience the gaze of another as threatening. My awareness of someone else watching me results in feelings of discomfort and shame. He gives the example of being caught peeping through a keyhole. Before I become aware that someone is watching me, I feel no shame or embarrassment. I am absorbed in watching the person undressing on the other side of the door. But as soon as I realise that I am being watched, I feel ashamed and embarrassed. Sartre analyses shame as experiencing myself as another sees me. In the example above, I suddenly realise how I must look to the other person who has caught me peeping through the keyhole. The realisation is manifest in the feeling of shame. Sartre observes that to experience myself as another sees me is to experience that other as a subject – a perceiver, a thinker, a subject of emotional states.

He continues his analysis by claiming that to experience another as a subject is to simultaneously experience myself as an object. Not only am I aware of myself as something that the other can see, that is, something that is an object of perception; under the gaze of another, I also experience my freedom as curtailed. Like Merleau-Ponty, Sartre claims that an essential feature of consciousness is that it is free. I can choose (within certain limits) what to be and do. I can, for example, choose whether to be a lecturer or a gardener. I can choose whether to sit here writing this book or to walk my dog in the sunshine. Moreover, I am always free to change my mind. Having decided to become a lecturer, I can later choose to resign and take up gardening. In this sense, my identity is not fixed and so I am not compelled to act by being a particular kind of person. However, others see me as a person of a certain sort, one who engages in particular kinds of activity. My awareness of how another sees me congeals my nature as a particular kind of person who does certain kinds of things. The person who is caught peeping through the keyhole, for example, is suddenly aware of themselves as a Peeping Tom. Thus they experience their freedom as curtailed. They are no longer a free being with no fixed identity. They are the kind of person who peeps through keyholes, and this compels them to engage in certain kinds of behaviour. This is another way in which I experience myself as an object in the gaze of another. I experience it as robbing me of the freedom that is essential to being a subject.

Sartre's account of the gaze explains how I experience another as a subject, and experience myself as something that others can experience in the same way that I experience them. These two forms of awareness occur simultaneously when I experience the gaze of another. The experience is asymmetrical, since I am aware of the other as a subject, whilst being aware of myself as an object. The experience also accounts for reciprocity: I experience myself in the same way that I experience others, but not at the same time. However, Sartre's analysis is problematic. He claims that I am aware of myself as an object when I experience the gaze of another. In other words, I experience the other's gaze as objectifying me. But there are various different senses in which I may experience myself as an object or as being objectified. One sense has already been outlined in the earlier discussion – it seems possible to experience what is in fact myself but be presented with myself in such a way that I appear no different from inanimate items like tables and chairs. Such experience presents me as a mere object – something that has no subjective life. A second sense of 'object' means an object of awareness or thought. To be an object in this sense is to be the thing at which some act of awareness is directed or the thing some thought is about. Something can be an object in this sense without being a mere object – we can perceive and think about subjects. To experience oneself as an object in this sense is to be aware of oneself as perceivable and so as the sort of thing that others can see and think about. A further sense in which one might experience oneself as an object is more properly described as the experience of being objectified. There is dispute over what it means to objectify someone. Nussbaum (1995) identifies different senses in which this can be understood. However, the basic idea is that it involves treating someone in a way that does not fully acknowledge their status as a subject, for example by failing to properly recognise someone's autonomy. Correlatively, I might experience myself as being objectified by experiencing someone as treating me in a way that does not fully acknowledge my status as a subject, for example by experiencing that person as failing to fully recognise that I am an autonomous being.

Sartre's analysis seems to run together different senses of experiencing oneself as an object. It seems right to claim that shame – at least on some occasions – is awareness of how one appears to another person. Shame therefore involves experiencing oneself as perceivable. It is awareness of oneself as something that can be an object of perception and thought. Sartre's claim that one experiences the other as robbing one of one's freedom could be read as the claim that one experiences oneself as a mere object – something inanimate. This is implausible. Although certain forms of awareness might count as experiencing oneself as a mere object – for example, seeing an MRI scan of one's brain activity – the experience of shame cannot be analysed in this way. Alternatively, it might be read as the claim that I experience someone as denying my autonomy and so failing to fully acknowledge my status as a subject. This does seem to fit Sartre's claim that the gaze robs me of my freedom. It follows that shame can be thought of as awareness of oneself as an object of perception and thought, and the experience of being objectified by someone who fails to properly recognise one's status as a subject, by robbing me of my freedom. However, it does not follow that, when I feel shame, I do not experience myself as a subject. Merleau-Ponty holds that awareness of any sort is necessarily accompanied by consciousness of oneself as the subject who is aware. This will be considered in more detail in Chapter 6. It follows that even though shame is the awareness of oneself as an object in the two senses outlined above, it is accompanied by awareness of oneself as the subject of one's own experiences. Thus it still involves privileged awareness of oneself.

There are also further difficulties. Sartre is correct in claiming that an experience such as shame has to be analysed as awareness of how one appears to another person. Shame is therefore awareness of the other as a subject, even if it cannot literally involve experiencing oneself as a mere object. However, the real presence of another self is not required for me to experience shame. The Peeping Tom might suddenly see themself as another *might* see them and feel ashamed, even though no other is actually present and observing them. One might therefore conclude that Sartre's account is inadequate as an analysis of experiencing another as a subject. Finally, Sartre's account implies that I must always find others threatening and feel shame in their presence. Although it is true that one sometimes feels uncomfortable under the gaze of another, this experience does not characterise all human relations. Sartre's account of how one may respond to another's gaze deepens this objection. He claims that I may respond to another's gaze by submitting to it and taking on the role of an object – a mere thing with no freedom, will, desires and so on. This response is masochistic. Alternatively, I can respond by gazing back at the other, as it were, and trying to turn them into an object for me. This response is sadistic. The result is that all human relations either involve sadomasochism, as one person continually submits to the gaze of another who seeks to turn them into an object, or conflict, as both parties try to turn the other into an object and retain the status as subject. Again, this fails to capture the nature of many – if not most – human relations. Merleau-Ponty thus rejects Sartre's account as inadequate.

The problem that Merleau-Ponty faces is this. The experience of intersubjectivity is the experience of being one of many selves who share a world. The experience has two important features: it involves awareness of others as subjects; and experience of oneself as something that others can experience in the same way that one experiences them. If my experience does not have these two features, then it will be the experience of solitude, which opens up the threat of solipsism. For experience to have these features, it seems that one's awareness of oneself and one's experience of others must be symmetrical. It cannot present me as 'special' in any way. However, part of what it is to be a self-conscious creature is to have experience of oneself that one cannot have of any other being. Thus self-conscious experience is essentially asymmetrical. Merleau-Ponty thus seems to be faced with a dilemma. Either my experience is self-conscious, in which case it is not truly intersubjective. Or my experience is intersubjective, in which case it is not the experience of a self-conscious being. My experience is undoubtedly self-conscious – we have seen above some of the ways in which my experience of myself differs from my experience of others. In this sense, my experience is solipsistic. However, it is also intersubjective. I am ordinarily aware of myself as being one of many selves who share a common world. Merleau-Ponty thus observes that '[c]onsciousnesses present themselves with the absurdity of a multiple solipsism, such is the situation which has to be understood' (Merleau-Ponty 1945: 412; 1962: 359; 2002: 418).

Merleau-Ponty's solution is that 'solitude and communication cannot be the two horns of a dilemma, but must be two "moments" of one phenomenon' (1945: 412; 1962: 359; 2002: 418). He continues, 'the central phenomenon consists in my being given to myself ... that is, I find myself already situated in a physical and social world' (1945: 413; 1962: 360; 2002: 419). The first part of his solution echoes claims he has made about our experience of the natural world. The subject always finds themself already in the world. At no point does experience present them as entering the world from some oblivion. The situation in which the subject finds themself has various dimensions. One of these is social. I find myself already situated in a world that contains other selves, to whom I am related in various ways. Thus I find myself already in communication with others. I will return to this claim shortly.

The next part of Merleau-Ponty's solution concerns what it is to be situated in the world. He claims that 'my insertion into the world ... is not distinct from my freedom, the fundamental power which I enjoy being the subject of all my experiences' (1945: 413; 1962: 360; 2002: 419). We saw in Chapter 3 that the human subject experiences themself as located in space by exercising their motor skills in response to their situation. Their awareness of the position of objects in space around them is constituted by perceiving those objects as reachable in certain ways, that is, as requiring certain actions for them to reach them. The subject's awareness of how they must move to reach the objects around them is simultaneously an awareness of how they are situated with respect to those objects. To perceive one's surroundings as requiring certain actions is to exercise one's motor skills. One's experience of being located in a certain place is thus the result of exercising one's skills for interacting with that environment. An important component of the normal human subject's capacity to interact with their surroundings includes what Merleau-Ponty calls 'the power to reckon with the possible'. This is the ability to situate oneself with respect to merely possible situations. It allows the subject to perceive the world in the light of possible tasks they could undertake. It also allows the subject to exercise motor skills that are relevant to merely possible environments.

The power to reckon with the possible confers a sort of freedom upon the subject. Rather than being constrained to act in ways that are required by their actual situation, they are able to act with respect to merely possible situations. Suppose, for example, that I have decided to walk my dog. I see the world in the light of this task so that I perceive his lead as requiring me to pick it up and clip it on to his collar, my boots as requiring me to put them on, the front door as requiring me to walk through it, and so on. As well as seeing opportunities to act in ways that are relevant to my current task, I also perceive my surroundings in relation to things that I could be doing. Thus as I walk into the kitchen gathering various dog-walking implements, I see my kettle as for-tea-making. My perception of my kettle as requiring tea-making behaviour allows me to turn aside from my current dog-walking task, and make a cup of tea instead. The power to reckon with the possible thus allows the subject to turn aside from their current situation and enter a new one. The human capacity to cope with the world thus involves 'a faculty of withdrawal' (Merleau-Ponty 1945: 413; 1962: 360; 2002: 419).

Merleau-Ponty uses these ideas to give a deeper analysis of solitude. The subject finds themself already situated in a world that has a social dimension. They find themself already in communication with other selves who share their world. The faculty of withdrawal that they possess means that they can turn away from the situation, and so withdraw from communal life. This is what solitude is: it consists in turning aside from the social world. But this means that embracing solitude involves simultaneously acknowledging the fact that I am in communication with others and so affirming that I am one of many selves who share a common world. In this sense, solitude and communication are two sides of one phenomenon. It follows that the fact of solitude does not bring with it the threat of solipsism. But Merleau-Ponty's proposed solution is puzzling. The problem that emerged from our earlier discussion was that, since one's awareness of oneself is essentially different from one's awareness of others, solitude – the experience of being in some sense alone – is unavoidable. Solitude accompanies one's experience of others. This fact seems to bring with it the threat of solipsism. Merleau-Ponty's later analysis of solitude conceives of it as withdrawal from communal life. His aim is to show that solitude and communication are two sides of the same phenomenon. But his later analysis simply offers a different notion of solitude. Whilst it is true that solitude conceived in this way goes hand-in-hand with communication, this fact does nothing to dispel the threat posed by the first sort of solitude.

The way out of these difficulties lies with Merleau-Ponty's account of the manner in which each of us is already situated with respect to the social world. The problem of solitude arises because perceiving brings with it an experience of oneself as privileged. It follows that to perceive is to have asymmetric experience of oneself and others. To block the move from asymmetry to solipsism, Merleau-Ponty needs to show that there is an experience of the social which does not involve *perceiving* others. He takes the problem that faces him here to be roughly analogous to a difficulty that confronts him when he accounts for the world. As we saw in Chapter 4, for Merleau-Ponty to provide an account of the world and consciousness as mutually dependent parts of one whole, he needs to show that the world that precedes perception can somehow figure in experience. He does this by pointing to the fact that perception has indeterminate aspects. One perceives a figure on a background. Whilst the figure is perceived indistinctly, the background appears as indeterminate and ambiguous. The further the background is from the figure, the more ambiguous one's experience of it. One's awareness of the furthest region of the background is simply the awareness of a vast, indeterminate presence. Merleau-Ponty identifies this massive presence with the world that precedes perception. It is not yet perceived as having any determinate qualities, but it draws us to perceive it in certain ways. Merleau-Ponty appeals to these ideas to explain how each of us is already situated with respect to the social world. One dimension of the 'pull' is social – before we perceive other people, we are drawn into social situations. The experience of the pull towards a social world is an experience of the social world that precedes perception of others. Since it precedes perception of the other, there is not yet an experience of oneself as privileged with respect to the other. The upshot for Merleau-Ponty is that the privileged awareness of oneself that is a necessary component of self-conscious experience does not bring with it the threat of solipsism. As McGinn (1998) puts it, my experience presents me as *separate* from others, but this separateness is not grounds for supposing that I am the only self. The background to every experience of separateness is the awareness of being already situated with respect to a social world.

CONCLUSION

Merleau-Ponty aims to give an account of the experience of intersubjectivity. He begins by noting two facts about such experience: it involves awareness of others as subjects, and it involves experiencing myself as something that others can experience in the same way that I experience them. He suggests that, for experience to satisfy these two constraints, my awareness of myself and others must be symmetrical. However, although certain forms of experience do involve a degree of symmetry, my awareness is never entirely symmetrical. I am self-conscious, and this means that my awareness of myself presents me as privileged. Merleau-Ponty worries that there is a route from here to solipsism. If my experience presents me as privileged, then it seems to show that I am special, and this implies that I am the only one of my kind. I might then be tempted to conclude that I am the only self; or I am the only one of a special kind of self. I am not properly part of the world of others that I perceive. Merleau-Ponty's solution to this problem is to show that there is a way of experiencing the social world that does not involve the awareness of myself as privileged. Since perception involves a privileged experience of myself, he must show that there is a way to experience the social world without perceiving it. He does this by appealing to the background awareness we have of a vast indeterminate presence that pulls us to interact with it in various ways. The vast presence draws us into social situations. Thus it is an experience of the social world that precedes perception of others. In this way, Merleau-Ponty dissolves the threat of solipsism whilst retaining the asymmetry that is essential to self-consciousness. The result is an account of my experience which presents me as privileged and so separate from others, but as already partaking in social existence.

6

THE MIND 1
PERCEPTION, ACTION AND EMOTION

Merleau-Ponty's discussion of the cogito in PhP is concerned with
the nature of the mind. This chapter and the next will consider
his view. He aims to show us that the mind is essentially embodied and embedded in its environment. The Cartesian conception
of it as an inner realm is untenable. Unsurprisingly, Descartes
looms large in Merleau-Ponty's discussion. Burnyeat (1982) cred-
its Descartes with being the first to claim that one can have a
special kind of knowledge of one's mental goings-on. I can know
the contents of my own mind with certainty, and only *I* can
know my own mind in this way. This is usually referred to as
'self-knowledge'. To make sense of this claim requires a conception of how my experiences and thoughts can be *objects* for me, in
a way that allows me to have indubitable knowledge of them.
Descartes was thus led to conceive of the mind as an inner realm,
populated by one's own mental states, and to claim that each of
us has a faculty of introspection – a kind of inner vision – with
which one's mental states are inspected. The inner realm is distinct and independent from the external world. Unlike sensory

awareness of the external world, which is subject to illusion, introspective awareness of one's own mind provides one with incorrigible knowledge of one's own mental states.

Merleau-Ponty sees Descartes's view as inextricably linked to an account of intentionality. A defining feature of consciousness is the way in which it can be directed at things beyond itself – for example, I can have thoughts about my dog, I can have experiences of the Eiffel Tower, etc. The feature of 'ofness' or 'aboutness' is intentionality. The traditional way to account for the mind's intentional directedness at the world is in terms of representation. On this view, an intentional state is of or about some worldly item in virtue of representing it. A thought of mine is, for example, about my dog because it has a component (a concept, a notion, an idea) that stands for or represents my dog. These mental representations are what populate the inner realm on Descartes's view. If Merleau-Ponty is to replace the Cartesian model, he must provide an alternative notion of intentionality. He must also explain how I can have special knowledge of my own mental life that does not appeal to introspection of a private inner realm.

Merleau-Ponty's strategy in PhP is twofold. He tries to show that, although there is something right about Descartes's claim that we each have a special knowledge of our own mental life, he is wrong to hold that self-knowledge is incorrigible. In this way, Merleau-Ponty aims to weaken a central consideration in favour of the Cartesian conception of mind. He also offers us an alternative notion of intentionality, which is encapsulated by his slogan 'empty heads turned towards the world' (Merleau-Ponty 1945: 407; 1962: 355; 2002: 413). For Merleau-Ponty, the fundamental form of intentionality is an unmediated, direct, embodied relation to the world. When, for example, I hold a cup in my hands, I – a particular bodily being – am in direct contact with it. This basic kind of embodied contact with the world is at the heart of what Merleau-Ponty calls 'motor intentionality'. Conscious activities and states that involve motor intentional directedness at the world are not representations, neither are they the sort of thing that could populate Descartes's inner realm. Consequently, they cannot be inspected using some kind of inner perception. It follows that the Cartesian picture of subjectivity must be rejected for those forms of consciousness that have motor intentionality. Merleau-Ponty first develops the idea of motor intentionality via his discussion of perception and action. But he holds that other conscious activities also involve motor intentional directedness at the world. He then offers an alternative notion of the self-awareness that grounds knowledge of one's mental life. This chapter will begin by examining the notion of motor intentionality. After this, I will consider three different aspects of mental life – perception, action and emotion – showing how Merleau-Ponty reconceives them to develop a radically anti-Cartesian view of the mind. Chapter 7 will examine Merleau-Ponty's account of thought and his conception of self-knowledge.

MOTOR INTENTIONALITY

Motor intentionality involves direct, unmediated, intentional contact between the subject and the world.[1] Merleau-Ponty first develops this notion in his discussion of perception and action.[2]

The claim that perception involves direct contact with the world will be familiar to analytic philosophers. In the analytic literature about perception, direct theories are contrasted with indirect accounts, which claim that perception involves intermediaries and is therefore *not* directly of the world. However, whilst it is easy to make sense of the idea that perception is direct with respect to tactile perception – there is a clear sense in which touching an object involves direct contact between me and the object – it is not so obvious what it means to claim that visual perception is direct. For one thing, it seems that there are always 'intermediaries' involved in visual perception, for example light waves and one's retinas mediate between things in the world and one's perceptions of them. Moreover, looking at an object does not involve literal contact between one's eyeballs and that thing. Of course, Merleau-Ponty holds that the senses are integrated so that sight and touch are just two components of one sensory system. But the fact that vision and touch are integrated with one another is not sufficient to explain what it means to claim that visual perception is direct. An alternative reading of the distinction takes direct theories to hold that the worldly objects of perception are constituents of experiences of them. In contrast, indirect theories claim that the worldly objects of perception are *not* constituents of experiences of them. Instead, a perceptual experience is related to its worldly object in virtue of having a constituent which stands for, or represents, that worldly object. On this view, indirect theories of perception take perceptual experiences to involve representations of their objects, whilst direct accounts do not. This understanding of the direct/indirect distinction offers a nice gloss on Merleau-Ponty's claim that perception is directly of the world and unmediated by representations. Thus I will understand Merleau-Ponty as claiming that the worldly objects perceived are constituents of perceptual experiences of them.

Theorists agree that at least some actions are intentional. But, generally speaking, they account for the intentionality of action by appealing to representational states. Actions are defined as bodily movements that are brought about in the appropriate manner by mental states such as intentions. An action will be directed at some worldly item, insofar as it is brought about by an intention that represents that object. My dog is the intentional object of my stroking him, for example, because my stroking action is appropriately initiated by an intention that represents me stroking my dog. On this view, the intentionality of action derives entirely from the intentionality of the mental states that initiate and guide it. Those states are intentionally directed at the world in virtue of representing it. In this sense, the intentional relation between the agent and the world is *not* direct, and is mediated by representations. Since Merleau-Ponty holds that action involves direct, intentional engagement with the world – that is, intentional contact that is not mediated by representations – he must give some alternative account of what it is for an action to be directed at the world.

One may be puzzled at this point. Acting involves manipulating the world with one's body, which involves direct contact between one's body and worldly things. Drinking a cup of tea, for example, involves holding a cup in my hand; dancing involves direct contact between my feet and the floor. One might think this surely means that to act is to directly engage with worldly things in a way that is unmediated by representations. However, this is insufficient as an account of the intentionality of action. Notice first that not just any bodily contact with the world constitutes an intentional relation between the world and the subject. If, for example, I am unconscious, there is direct bodily contact between my body and the hospital bed in which I am lying. But it is implausible to claim that the bed is the intentional object of some conscious activity – I'm unconscious, so there is no conscious activity which could be directed at the bed. Suppose now that I am conscious. Insofar as I have tactile experience of the bed, it is the intentional object of my tactile experience. In this case, the contact between my body and the bed is intentional, but the intentionality is that of perception. But we are interested in the intentionality of *action*. Thus we need to know what more is required for contact between my body and the world to constitute the kind of intentional relation involved in action.

Merleau-Ponty allows that the subject's intentions may *sometimes* play a role in what they do. I may, for example, consciously consider whether I have time to walk my dog, decide that I do have time, and so form an intention to walk him, which brings about my dog-walking. But Merleau-Ponty denies that intentions are essential. He holds instead that action can be – and most often is – immediately initiated and guided by perception, without the need for any intervening mental states. His account of absorbed coping allows him to analyse the intentionality of action in the following way. Action involves intentional directedness at the world. The objects at which an action is directed are those perceived things which initiate and guide the action. The contact between my body and worldly things will have action intentionality if that contact was brought about by my perception of those things as 'requiring' the action that I perform. On this account, action involves direct intentional contact with the worldly objects at which it is directed. It is not mediated by representations.

PERCEPTION

Merleau-Ponty takes his account of motor intentionality to be incompatible with Descartes's view of the mind as a distinct inner realm, populated by one's own mental goings-on, which the subject can inspect by 'turning their gaze inwards'. He writes, 'the acts of the *I* are of such a nature that they outstrip themselves, leaving no interiority of consciousness' (Merleau-Ponty 1945: 431; 1962: 376; 2002: 438).

Merleau-Ponty's claim has *prima facie* plausibility – if neither perception nor action involves representations, then there seems to be nothing capable of populating the inner realm. However, Descartes's view is entrenched in our thinking, particularly about perception. Thus more careful consideration of the issues is required. It is very tempting to reason as follows. There is undeniably a distinction between appearance and reality. Appearance does not always correctly inform us about reality – we sometimes have perceptual illusions where the world's appearance does not tally with how it really is. Moreover, experiences and their worldly objects are different categories of things which means that they cannot be numerically identical – my dog, for example, is not one and the same thing as my experience of him. It is natural to think that I can have certain knowledge of appearances, but not worldly things. Thus it seems that the appearances are distinct from worldly objects and capable of being objects of knowledge for me. It follows that they must be inner items, which are available to introspection. Thus it seems that the Cartesian position is vindicated. Merleau-Ponty must resist this tempting line of reasoning if he is to reject Descartes's position.

One option would be to embrace idealism and give up the distinction between reality and appearance, but this is not the path Merleau-Ponty takes. Instead, he aims to block the move, from accepting that there is a distinction between appearance and reality, to claiming that we can be certain about how things appear, whilst being uncertain about how they really are. He writes,

> Perception is precisely that kind of act in which there can be no question of setting the act itself apart from the end to which it is directed. Perception and the perceived necessarily have the same existential modality, since perception is inseparable from the consciousness which it has, or rather is, of reaching the thing itself ...

If I see an ashtray, *in the full sense of the word see*, there must be an ashtray there, and I cannot forego this assertion. [italics in original]

(Merleau-Ponty 1945: 429; 1962: 374; 2002: 435–6)

One might suppose that Merleau-Ponty is simply arguing here that 'perception' is a success-term – 'to perceive' means to have veridical experience, whilst non-veridical experiences are called 'illusions'. This implies that if I am certain that I am having a perception that *p*, then I am certain that *p*. However, it is clear that this point does not threaten Descartes's view. He can maintain that I have infallible knowledge of how things seem to me, but not whether my experience presents the world correctly. Since perceptions are veridical experiences whilst illusions are non-veridical, it follows that I cannot know of any particular experience whether it is a perception or an illusion. But this reading of Merleau-Ponty is incorrect. He is not merely disagreeing with Descartes over what we should *call* veridical and non-veridical experiences. Instead, he claims that, given his account of perception as direct, knowledge of one's perceptual experience and knowledge of the worldly things presented in such experience stand or fall together. Descartes's claim that one can have certainty about experience whilst being uncertain about the world is untenable.

To understand why this is so, we need to consider the Cartesian position in more detail. We can understand Descartes's claim that I can be certain how things seem to me whilst unsure if the world is as my experience presents it as the claim that I can have infallible knowledge of the 'seeming objects' of my experience – the things that my experience appears to be of – but not of its worldly objects. To see what Descartes's position commits him to, let us begin by making two obvious claims. First, for me to have knowledge of a thing, there has to be a thing about which I know. I cannot know, for example, about the present King of England if there is no present King of England. Of course, I can have knowledge of merely fictional entities – I can know, for example, that Sherlock Holmes has an assistant named Watson. Nevertheless, there still has to *be* a fictional character for me to have knowledge of it, even though such entities do not exist in the same way that I do. Second, if a and b are numerically identical, then what I know about a I will also know about b. This is so, even if I do not know that a and b are the same thing, and thus do not know that since I know that a is F, I also know that b is F. Descartes claims that I can know about the seeming objects of my experience without knowing about its worldly objects. His claim thus presupposes that there *are* seeming objects of experience, and that these are not identical with perception's worldly objects.

For Descartes to maintain this thesis, he must endorse an indirect theory of perception. Such theories claim that worldly objects are not constituents of experience of them. Instead, a perceptual experience is related to its worldly object in virtue of having a constituent which stands for or represents that worldly object. It should be clear how an indirect theory of perception allows for the claim that there are seeming objects of perception, which are not identical with its worldly objects. The seeming object of a perceptual experience will be the component that stands for, or represents, a worldly object. Merleau-Ponty's contrasting view is that perception is direct – that is, the worldly things perceived *are* constituents of one's perceptions of them. A perceptual experience is not of something in the world in virtue of having a component that stands for or represents that thing. Since this component is lacking, there is no room on this picture to distinguish between the seeming and the worldly objects of experience. Thus the Cartesian thesis that one can have infallible knowledge of the seeming objects of experience whilst knowing nothing about its worldly objects cannot be maintained.

Merleau-Ponty continues by arguing that in cases where the subject misperceives, there is simply unsuccessful apprehension of the world – rather than error about the world together with successful apprehension of one's own experience. We can understand him as giving a deflationary account of 'appearance' talk. To clarify his position, consider his treatment of cases such as the following. Whilst looking at birds in the garden, I say to my friend, 'It certainly *seems* to me that there is a canary over there, although I'm not sure if there *really* is.' It is perhaps natural to read such a statement in line with the Cartesian view that one can be certain about the seeming objects of one's experience (I am certain that my experience is 'as of' a canary in the garden), but not about its worldly objects (I am not certain whether my 'as of' a canary experience correctly matches the world). But Merleau-Ponty suggests that rather than understanding them as expressing certainty about the seeming objects of experience together with uncertainty about its worldly objects, they should be understood as expressing 'the certainty of a possibility' (1945: 430; 1962: 375; 2002: 436). To say that I am certain it *seems* there is a canary over there is just to say I am certain it is possible there *is* a canary over there – and this is just to say there is a real possibility that that corner of the garden contains a canary. Reflection on the use of statements such as 'it certainly seems to me that there is a canary in the garden' provides a certain amount of support for this position. The meaning of such a statement varies depending on context. It might mean '*I* am sure there is a canary, even though *you* doubt', or 'I am *fairly* sure there is a canary, but not completely certain', or some variation thereof. But, in ordinary use, this statement does not pick out something – a seeming object of experience – about which the utterer claims to have certain knowledge. Instead, the statement simply expresses some degree of certainty about the real world.

We can compare what Merleau-Ponty says about perception with what we ordinarily say about another sort of case. Suppose that I am trying to calculate the sum of 2 + 2. There is a correct answer – 4 – and it is this that I aim for when I perform the calculation. I am not infallible and I may make a mistake. But when I mistakenly conclude that 2 + 2 = 5 we simply say that I am wrong about the real sum of 2 + 2. There is very little (if any) temptation to say that, although I am wrong about the sum of 2 + 2, there is something I am right about – namely, the *seeming* sum of 2 + 2. We would not, for example, read a statement such as 'It certainly seems to me that 2 + 2 = 5, although that might not be the correct answer' as expressing the fact that I am certain about one thing (the seeming sum of 2 + 2) and uncertain about another (the real sum of 2 + 2). We would simply read it as saying something like 'I am fairly sure that the real sum of 2 + 2 = 5'. Merleau-Ponty makes an analogous claim about perception.

An objection can be raised at this point. One may accept that Merleau-Ponty's account of perception as direct – that is, as having motor intentional content – means that no distinction can be drawn between the seeming and the real objects of experience. However, the direct model of perception still allows us to talk of experiences as individual items that can be identified and differentiated from one another. It makes perfect sense to talk about *the* experience I had of my dog last Tuesday, and to distinguish it from a numerically distinct experience I have of him today. Moreover, my experience of my dog is not one and the same thing as my dog – the former is an experience whilst the latter is that canine being who shares my home. Thus it seems that the direct theory of perception posits items that are distinct from worldly objects: namely, the experiences. Surely, then, my experiences can be objects of knowledge (I can know about them). Since they are not identical with worldly items, they must be inner objects, which I know about by using introspection.

However, this suggestion is problematic. The fact that we can *talk* about experiences as individual items that are distinct from their worldly objects does not mean that those experiences are inner items that can be introspected. To reason in this manner is to be beguiled by language. For Merleau-Ponty, to perceive is to be directly aware of a worldly item – that is, worldly items are constituents of perception of them. A perception is thus constituted by a worldly object and an act of awareness. But Merleau-Ponty holds that 'perception is precisely that kind of act in which there can be no question of setting the act itself apart from the end to which it is directed' (1945: 429; 1962: 374; 2002: 435). His thought here is that the relation between the two components of a perception is internal, that is, the whole is not reducible to the mere sum of its parts. To put the matter another way, if an act of awareness is 'added' to a worldly object to produce a perception, the result is not the worldly object plus another item – the act of awareness. Instead, the result is simply the-worldly-object-viewed-in-a-certain-way or, if one prefers, a view-of-the-object. But a view-of-an-object is not itself capable of being an object of knowledge. The only thing here that one can know about is the worldly object on which one has a view.

Similarly, this leaves us with nothing in perception that could be an object of introspection. On the contrary, to be aware of a perception is to be aware of a-worldly-object-viewed-in-a-certain-way (or to be aware of a view-on-an-object). This consists in nothing more than viewing the worldly object in that way. In other words, it just *is* to perceive or to be conscious of the worldly object. It follows that, if perception is directly of the world, then experiences are not inner items and they are not available to introspection. Experiences, considered as distinct from their worldly objects, cannot be objects of knowledge. It is only the things perceived that the subject can come to know.

The foregoing picture has implications for what it is to be conscious of one's own experience. Perception involves (at the very least) registering the presence of things in one's perceptual field. However, we can distinguish between being *aware* of those things and *merely* registering their presence. In the first case, the way in which the subject registers the presence of things contributes to 'what it is like' for them; they are conscious of them. Note that there are different ways in which the subject can be conscious of the things in their perceptual field. As we have seen, perception has a figure-background structure. The figure is the focus of attention and is perceived distinctly and in detail, whilst the background is perceived with varying degrees of indistinctness and indeterminacy. The subject is conscious of both the figure and the background – they both contribute to 'what it is like' for them – even though their awareness of them is different. In contrast, *merely* registering the presence of things does not contribute to 'what it is like' for the subject. People with certain kinds of brain damage, for example, have no visual experience, but they can nevertheless respond accurately to visual stimuli. They merely register the presence of objects in their visual field without being aware of them. This is known as blindsight. In normal perception, one is *conscious* of the things one perceives; one does not merely register their presence. Merleau-Ponty must account for the difference between the two kinds of case. The Cartesian, of course, can appeal to introspection. In both cases, the subject is in a state which represents the presence of the object. The difference is that, in the former case, the subject is also introspectively aware of the state, whereas in the latter case they are not. But perceptions cannot be introspected on Merleau-Ponty's view, so he must offer an alternative account of the difference between the two cases.

Merleau-Ponty is not entirely clear on this issue. However, certain remarks he makes are suggestive of the following position. It is tempting to suppose that to be aware of something is for that thing to be an object at which some state or act of awareness is directed. Indeed, this act-object model of awareness is implied by grammar – language forces us to describe awareness or consciousness as always being *of* something. It is thus very natural to assume that *conscious* perception – where one is *aware* of objects, rather than merely registering their presence – must involve consciousness *of* one's perceptions. One is then led to posit some faculty of awareness – introspection – that is directed at one's own experiences. Conscious perception, on this account, involves two acts of awareness. One that is directed at a worldly object, and a second which is directed at the experience itself. However, we have seen that, for Merleau-Ponty, perceptions are not the kinds of things that may be introspected. It is not, in other words, possible to be aware *of* one's perceptions – the only potential objects of awareness in perception are the worldly things perceived. It follows that accounting for what is conscious about conscious perception requires an alternative conception of awareness that does not construe it as an act directed at an object. The perception is an act of awareness directed at an object, but the consciousness of conscious perception is not.

Merleau-Ponty's various references to our relationship with things being 'lived through' can be read as alluding to a different construal of awareness. Perception is an activity which involves sensing things in one's environment. Rather than thinking of conscious perception as consciousness *of* perceiving, we should think of it as a conscious activity. In other words, 'conscious' should not be understood as denoting a form of awareness that has one's perceptions as its objects. Instead, it should be understood as describing the kind of activity that perceiving is. One may say that the subject is conscious *in* perceiving, rather than conscious *of* her perceptions. This idea can be difficult to grasp.

Part of the problem, as indicated above, is that language forces us to talk about awareness being *of* something. But the following example may help clarify what is being suggested. Suppose I am annoyed with my partner for not cleaning the kitchen and so I wash the dishes angrily. It does not seem correct to claim in this case that I am in a state of anger that has the dishwashing as its object. A more accurate description understands 'angrily' as describing the way in which I wash the dishes. It describes the kind of activity that my dishwashing is: angry dishwashing activity.[3] We can understand Merleau-Ponty as making a similar claim about conscious perception. Perception is an activity that is directed at worldly objects. To claim that perception is conscious is simply to describe what kind of activity perceiving is. The subject consciously perceives; they are not conscious *of* their perceptions. Merely registering the presence of objects without being aware of them – as happens in blindsight – is a different activity, in the same way that meditative dishwashing is different from washing the dishes angrily.

ACTION

Two important claims have emerged from Merleau-Ponty's discussion of perception. The first is that there is nothing in perception that could be an inner item, something that populates the Cartesian inner realm. The second claim concerns what it is to be aware of one's perceptions. As we have seen, one is not, strictly speaking, aware *of* one's perceptions at all. Awareness of one's perception is not an act-object form of awareness. Instead, to be aware of one's perceptions is a conscious activity. It is to consciously perceive. Merleau-Ponty develops this idea after showing that perceptions are not objects of any sort. They are not inner items, neither are they worldly objects, situated in the world amongst other worldly items like tables and chairs. Since they are not objects of any sort, they cannot be things at which some state of awareness is directed. It follows that consciousness of one's own perceptions cannot be explained on an act-object model of awareness. Merleau-Ponty takes both of these claims to also apply to action.

Like perception, action – on his account – has motor intentionality. It involves direct, unmediated, embodied contact with the world. As we saw above, this understanding of action's intentional directedness at the world goes hand-in-hand with a rejection of the idea that actions are essentially bodily movements brought about in the appropriate manner by representations. The traditional account holds that the objects at which an action is directed are those that are represented in the intention that guides the action. Merleau-Ponty's contrasting view is that action is directed at those perceived things that initiate and guide action. The contact between my body and things in the world will have action intentionality if that contact was brought about by my perception of those things as 'requiring' the action I perform. Given this account of action, it is easy to see how the first thesis – action involves no inner items – applies to it. Bodies are physical things that inhabit the 'external' world. They cannot be denizens of an inner, Cartesian realm. The only potential candidate is the intention that brings about action on the traditional view. Since Merleau-Ponty denies that actions are always brought about by intentions, there is nothing on his view of action that could be an inner item. Actions, for Merleau-Ponty, are all out in the world.[4]

However, one may be initially puzzled by my claim that Merleau-Ponty's second thesis also applies to actions. The second thesis is that I do not observe my own perceptions. My consciousness of them is not an act-object form of awareness. Instead, it is to consciously perceive. He reaches this view because my perceptions are not inner or outer items. They are not things that I could come across in either inner or outer space. Thus I cannot observe them. But matters are different when it comes to action. There is an obvious candidate for observation: my own body. My body is a physical thing, a part of the world, and as such it can be observed. It is then tempting to think that it can be an object of awareness for me like any other worldly item. It follows that there is no reason why my awareness of my own actions cannot be construed as an act-object form of awareness. In other words, consciousness of my own actions consists in states of awareness that are directed at my own body.

But this view of what it is to be aware of one's own actions is radically mistaken. We can bring out what is wrong with it by considering what it is to be aware of one's own actions on the Cartesian view. This account claims that actions are essentially bodily movements brought about in the appropriate manner by intentions. Intentions are mental states and so denizens of the inner realm. The body is a physical thing, and so something that belongs to the outer realm – that is, the external world. Awareness of one's own actions thus has two components: introspective awareness of an intention, together with external, sensory awareness of one's own body and its movements. Notice that this picture assimilates awareness of one's own actions to the experience of telekinesis. Telekinesis is acting on objects at a distance – for example, lifting a chair on the other side of the room – using some kind of mental energy. If telekinesis exists, then presumably the experience of performing telekinetic acts involves awareness of one's mental effort (one's intention to move the chair), together with perception of a worldly object moving (in this case, the chair). This seems to be how I experience my own actions on the Cartesian model. When I act, I am both aware of a mental event (an intention, a trying, a willing), and I perceive an object moving (my own body).

It is obvious that this account of what it is to be aware of one's own actions is woefully inadequate. The peculiarity of this description highlights the fact that there is a vast difference between moving a worldly object and moving my body. When, for example, I raise my arm to lift a glass, the glass is an object that I – the agent – move. But my arm is not an object that *I* move about. Instead, my arm is the agent of the moving – my arm is the mover. Of course, this way of putting things is apt to sound very odd. It implies that my arm has a mind of its own and moves independently from what I want it to do, like some errant body-part possessed by a restless spirit. But this is not what is meant by the claim that the arm is the agent of the moving. Instead, the thought is that the body is presented in experience as the subject of action – rather than an object which the subject moves about – or, better still, experience presents me, the subject of action, as embodied. An account of what it is to be conscious of one's own actions must capture this aspect of experience.

Notice that simply removing intentions from the picture does not help. The traditional model takes awareness of one's own actions to have two components: introspective awareness of one's intentions, and observation of one's body. If we take away introspection of intentions, all that we are left with is perception of one's body and its movements, and this is insufficient as an account of what it is to experience my own actions. Compare the situation again to the experience of telekinesis. Remove the experience of mental effort and all that remains is perception of an object moving. The account remains hopeless. One might suppose that what is missing is the fact that my body is experienced as located where *I* seem to be, whilst the chair is not. But the appeal to location makes little, if any, difference. The chair could be located right next to me – I could even be sitting on the chair – yet I would not experience it as the subject of action. The fact that I experience my body as being where I seem to be is not enough to explain how it is that I am aware of myself qua agent as embodied.

One might think that the account can be remedied by appealing to proprioception – the so-called 'internal' sense each of us has of our own body. In cases where there is no disability or damage to the nervous system, each of us is immediately aware of such things as the position of our limbs relative to each other; our active and passive bodily movements; whether or not our body is in contact with other surfaces; whether our limbs are hot or cold; whether parts of our bodies itch, tickle, hurt, and so on. Moreover, it seems I can only be proprioceptively aware of my own body – I cannot feel pains in your leg, nor can I feel pains in the table. Thus one might suppose that we can distinguish between the experience of my own body and the experience of the table, and account for the fact that I experience my own body as the subject of my actions (that is, I experience myself qua agent as embodied) by appealing to the fact that I have proprioceptive awareness of my body. However, if proprioception is simply understood as an extra sense, which differs from sight, touch, hearing and so on, only insofar as it has one's own body as its sole object, then the appeal to proprioception gets us nowhere. Simply claiming that I have an extra way of perceiving my body does not capture what it is to experience my body as the agent of my actions. Suppose, for example, that I have a microscope which I can only use to view one chair. The fact that I have an extra means of sensing the chair does not miraculously mean that I experience the chair as the subject of my actions. It's not clear why matters should be any different if the extra means of sensing is proprioception and the object I sense is my own body.

What this reveals is that the problem lies with claiming that the experience of my own actions is an act-object form of awareness. The claim that my own doings are an object for me, something at which my awareness is directed, something that I observe, means that I experience myself – the subject of that experience – as a spectator of my actions, rather than their agent. The way out of this conundrum is to construe awareness of one's own actions differently. Instead of involving an act or state of awareness that is directed at one's own body and its doings, to be aware of one's own actions is simply to consciously act, or to be aware *in* acting. 'Conscious' does not denote a form of awareness that has one's doings as its objects; it simply describes what kind of activity acting is. In other words, one is not literally aware *of* one's actions at all. Instead, to experience one's own actions is to engage in a conscious activity. In the same way that to be aware of one's perceptions is to consciously perceive.

The claim that Merleau-Ponty takes awareness of one's own actions to involve consciously acting sheds light on some claims he makes about bodily experience in PhP. He describes various ways in which the experience of one's own body differs from the experience of other things. My body, for example, can never be absent from my experience – if I am perceiving, then my body is experienced; it is a permanent feature of my perceptual field (Merleau-Ponty 1945: 106–9; 1962: 90–92; 2002: 103–6). I cannot take up different perspectives on my own body like I can with other objects. Other physical things are open to exploration. I can move round them in space or turn them over in my hands. But I can only experience my own body from one perspective (1945: 106–7; 1962: 90–91; 2002: 103–5). My body is presented as the subject of sensation. Pains are always felt as located in my body. Moreover, one does not experience the parts of one's body as the *cause* of pain. Instead, it is the parts of one's body that hurt (1945: 109–10; 1962: 93; 2002: 107). Merleau-Ponty notes many other differences between the experience of my own body and the experience of other things.

These differences lead him to conclude that 'the body [is not] an object of the world' (1945: 109; 1962: 92; 2002: 106). This remark may appear hyperbolic. After all, objects are solid physical items with size, shape and location, and my body is presented as sized, shaped and located. Thus experience *does* present my body as being an object in this sense, even though my awareness of it is different from my experience of other physical things. However, it seems to me that this is not the sense of 'object' which is at issue here. Merleau-Ponty does not mean to claim that I do not experience my body as physical. His claim instead is that the primary form of bodily awareness does not have an act-object structure. It does not consist in observation *of* my body. To be aware of one's body is simply to engage in conscious bodily activities. This is not to say that I cannot observe my body at all. I can touch it, see it, smell it and hear it, and, when I do, it is an object for me – something at which my awareness is directed. But this is not the primary form of bodily awareness – experience of myself, qua subject, as embodied. Merleau-Ponty writes, 'I observe external objects with my body, I handle them, examine them, walk round them, but my body itself is a thing which I do not observe' (Merleau-Ponty 1945: 107; 1962: 91; 2002: 104).

EMOTION

Merleau-Ponty turns next to what he calls 'affective intentionality' (1945: 531)[5] – that is, emotions and moods. Contemporary theorists often treat these as different in kind, but Merleau-Ponty does not distinguish between them. His discussion focuses on love, but he intends his claims to apply to other emotions and moods as well. Merleau-Ponty holds that love is intentional: one loves worldly entities such as other people, dogs and cars. He argues that, like perception and action, love – and other moods and emotions – have motor intentionality and involve direct, unmediated, embodied contact with the world. If this is so, then they cannot be items that dwell in an inner Cartesian realm, and awareness of one's own moods and emotions cannot involve introspection of them.

Merleau-Ponty begins by considering an initial argument in favour of Descartes's analysis. One might suppose that *feeling* love for something and *really* loving it coincide, and that one cannot be mistaken about whether or not one loves someone or something. One might then argue that Descartes's analysis best captures these facts: introspective awareness of love (feeling love for something) provides one with incorrigible knowledge that one loves. Merleau-Ponty responds by arguing that, contrary to what Descartes claims, one *can* be mistaken about whether or not one loves someone. Indeed, it is not unusual for someone to think that they love another, but to realise later that this is not so. One might initially suppose that such cases can be understood as cases of misinterpretation. According to this suggestion, one's mistake consists in applying the wrong concept to what one feels – for example, categorising lust as love. An error of this sort can have various sources. It may be that one has not fully understood how the concept 'love' should be applied. Or one's judgement may be swayed by the fact that one greatly desires to be in love. It seems that this kind of error can be accommodated on the Cartesian model. Descartes can maintain that *feeling* lust and *really* lusting coincide so that it is impossible for a person's introspective awareness of their lustful states to be subject to illusion. However, when the subject comes to make a *judgement* categorising their feeling, their judgement may be mistaken for reasons such as those cited above – the subject may not have a complete grasp of the concepts involved in their judgement, or their judgement may be clouded by desires and so forth. It follows that Descartes can acknowledge this kind of error without giving up his conception of love as an inner item, which can be introspected, and which can be the object of infallible knowledge.

Merleau-Ponty allows that people may sometimes misinterpret how they feel, where this involves applying the wrong concept to their feeling. However, he denies that all cases of mistaken love can be treated in this way. Sometimes, he claims, one's *feelings* of love are false or illusory so that on some occasions, one feels love for someone without actually loving them. Merleau-Ponty intends this to be a commonplace observation about human lives. Indeed, it is not unusual for someone to say, 'I thought I loved him/her, but I came to realise that I did not'. On Descartes's account, feeling love constitutes introspective awareness of one's love. Introspection is supposed to provide one with incorrigible knowledge of whatever one introspects. The claim that one can have false feelings of love therefore threatens Descartes's view, since it means that introspection does not provide the subject with incorrigible knowledge of their mental state – at least in the case of emotions and moods. Descartes has two options at this point. Either he can retain the claim that love is an inner item, which means he has to explain how introspective awareness of an inner item can be subject to illusion. Or he can hold on to the idea that introspective awareness of the inner realm is infallible, but give up the claim that love is a purely inner object. Both of these options are problematic.

The problem with the first option is that it is wholly unclear how one could account for introspective illusions. In the case of sensory awareness of the external world, illusions can be explained by appealing to such things as the conditions required for one's sense organs to function properly, and what it is for a sense organ to be healthy. We can explain why I misperceive a tree as a person, for example, by appealing to the fact that it is too far away for me to see it properly. Likewise, my experience of a black hole in the centre of my visual field can be understood as the result of damage to my optic nerve. But there seems to be no comparable explanation in the case of introspection. We have yet to discover an organ responsible for introspective awareness, and it is wholly unclear what the conditions might be for the faculty of introspection to function properly. The second option is problematic for Descartes because it entails giving up the claim that one's mental goings-on populate an inner realm, which is distinct from the external world. Rather than taking love to be an inner object, one might hold, for example, that love involves not just loving feelings, but also ways of interacting with the world (this is Merleau-Ponty's view and I will say more about this shortly). One strategy would be for Descartes to claim that, even if love is partially constituted by ways of interacting with the world, there is still a component – the 'feeling' component – that can be thought of as an inner item that is available to introspection, and which can be an object of infallible knowledge. However, taking this line still involves admitting that conscious life is not restricted to just inner goings-on. Moreover, it may lead one to wonder what value there is in conceiving of love, and other emotions, as having an inner component which one can know about for certain, since it has been conceded that one no longer has infallible knowledge of one's love. These difficulties may not be insurmountable. Nevertheless, they suggest that Descartes's account of love may not fit the facts as well as it first seemed, and they motivate the search for an alternative.

Merleau-Ponty begins by offering an alternative account of feelings. On the Cartesian model, feelings are denizens of the inner, mental realm, capable of being introspected. Whilst Merleau-Ponty does not deny that there are such things as feelings – clearly we feel happy, bored, sad, ecstatic, grumpy, loving, etc. – he argues that the Cartesian conception of them is incorrect. Feelings, for Merleau-Ponty, are aspects of how the world is perceived. On his account, perception has an affective dimension – a dog can look scary, I can see an armchair as homely, an old church can appear foreboding, and so forth. Sometimes, the situation as a whole can be experienced as having an affective value, for example, I can experience a dinner party as permeated by an air of formality, whilst a family party is experienced as a relaxed affair. Merleau-Ponty claims that feelings infuse the content of perception, and are not separable from it. To see what he means in more detail, consider the experience of familiarity.

Things of various sorts can look familiar. Moreover, the phenomenology of 'looking familiar' cannot be adequately captured by claiming that one *sees* properties such as the particular configuration of someone's face, then *judges* that one is acquainted with that person. Two not-so-ordinary cases provide support for this claim: the Capgras Delusion and déjà vu experiences. A person suffering from the Capgras Delusion believes that someone they know – usually a close relative – has been replaced with an imposter who looks very similar. An accepted explanation of the

Capgras Delusion claims that it involves a defective emotional response (Ellis and Young 1990). Although there is a sense in which the relative looks the same insofar as his or her facial features have the same configuration, they are the same height and build, their hair is the same colour, and so forth, there is a sense in which they appear different – they do not look familiar.[6] Phenomenologically speaking, cases of déjà vu involve the opposite experience where a person (or thing or place) that one does not know looks familiar. Moreover, one can see from the person's facial configuration, height, build and so on that one does not know them. Nevertheless, the stranger looks familiar. It follows that something's looking familiar is not a matter of judgement, but part of the content of experience. Merleau-Ponty continues by claiming that for something to look familiar is essentially for it to feel familiar – where the feeling of familiarity infuses one's perception of the thing, thereby altering the way it looks. The flip side of this claim is that having a *feeling* of familiarity just is for something to *look* familiar. Indeed, it is hard to see what it might be to have a 'free-floating' feeling of familiarity that was not manifest in the perception of things, places or people as familiar. Thus the feeling of familiarity is inseparable from the perception of something, someplace or someone as familiar.

Merleau-Ponty argues that the same is true in the case of other feelings, such as love. Feelings of love infuse the content of one's perceptions and are not separable from its content. They alter the appearance of the beloved so that, for example, I perceive her as lovable. Her face looks beautiful and full of warmth. But they also affect the content of my perceptions more globally. Objects associated with the loved one take on an extra felt significance – I perceive the cushion where she sits when she visits as somehow important. The otherwise ordinary café where we meet looks homely and inviting. I experience noisy children as vibrant and full of life rather than annoying. I perceive my everyday tasks as less urgent. Events in my house are permeated by an air of boredom as I wait for her to arrive. There are many other ways in which feelings of love manifest in one's perception of the world.

We saw above that Merleau-Ponty conceives of perception and action as integrated components of a single capacity to engage with the world. Perception presents its subject with opportunities for action. The affective content of perception contributes to the experience of one's surroundings as requiring certain forms of behaviour. The perception of a shark as menacing, for example, contributes to my perception of my environment as offering me an opportunity to flee. My loving experience of the world likewise contributes to my sense of which actions are required by my surroundings. To perceive someone as lovable is to perceive them as requiring certain forms of loving, attentive behaviour. The 'important' appearance of the cushion the beloved sits on invites me to take care of it and clean it, to prevent my dog from playing with it. My perception of the noisy children as vibrant and full of life solicits smiles from me rather than grumpy swearing. The café invites me to go inside. My everyday tasks invite me to relax, insofar as they are no longer perceived as urgent. Nothing in my house solicits enthusiastic action as I wait for her to arrive. Thus we can see that certain forms of behaviour correspond to my loving experience of the world.

Merleau-Ponty's analysis of loving feelings as aspects of the way we perceive the world, which call forth particular kinds of behaviour, allows him to claim that love is 'the way in which [the lover] establishes his relations with the world; it is an existential signification' (1945: 437; 1962: 381; 2002: 444). Love, in other words, is a certain kind of bodily engagement with the world, a certain way (or cluster of ways) of perceiving and acting. However, Merleau-Ponty motivated the search for an alternative to Descartes's model by observing that there are cases of illusory love, where one feels love for someone but does not actually love them. The identification of love with ways of perceiving and acting does not yet provide a means of distinguishing between real and illusory love.

Merleau-Ponty offers two ways of drawing the distinction, neither of which is sufficient on its own. The first appeals to the idea of 'situational values'. Merleau-Ponty holds that certain situations have an affective value, which is independent of the perceiver. We can see this from the fact that I can perceive situations as having an affective value without feeling it. I can, for example, see a landscape as gloomy without feeling gloomy myself (Merleau-Ponty

1945: 31–2; 1962: 23; 2002: 27). Similarly, I can experience a funeral as a sombre affair without feeling sombre. (One might suppose that this conflicts with Merleau-Ponty's analysis of feelings as aspects of the affective content of perception. But this is not so. Although feelings are inseparable from the affective values of perceived things, the affective dimension of perception is not exhausted by the feel of what one sees.) Sometimes the affective value of a situation may induce feelings in someone, but it is implausible to claim that it is a real emotion the person feels. A sad film about a dying princess, for example, may induce feelings of grief in someone who watches it. But it is implausible to claim that the viewer is *really* grieving. Thus Merleau-Ponty holds that a feeling is false or illusory if it has been induced by a situational value.

Merleau-Ponty's distinction between affective values that result from the perceiver and those that do not is an intuitively appealing one. But it requires further examination. It appears to be in *prima facie* tension with what Merleau-Ponty says about perception. Perceiving, for Merleau-Ponty, is not the passive registering of information about the world. Instead, the perceiver plays an active role in constituting what they see. Perceived things, for Merleau-Ponty, result from interaction between the perceiver and the world. The world prompts the subject to exercise their perceptual skills in certain ways. It 'tells' the subject how to perceive it. Through this process, perceived things take shape. Thus the nature of everything we perceive depends in part on our nature as perceivers and partly on the nature of the world. It follows that all perceived affective values – the gloominess of the landscape, the lovability of my dog – issue both from the perceiving subject and the thing perceived.

Although it is true that all perceived affective values issue from both the perceiving subject and the thing perceived, we can still distinguish between different kinds of affective value. There is a difference between seeing someone as the *subject* of an emotion and seeing someone or something as the *object* of an emotion. Merleau-Ponty holds that we can see other people's emotions manifest in their bodily engagement with the world. I can, for example, see someone's love for their puppy in the tender expression on their face, the way they gently brush its fur and prepare its dinner. Like all perceived qualities, the appearance of the other results from the interaction between the perceived and the perceiver. In this case, I see that that person is loving. I perceive that person as the *subject* of love, the author of the emotion. The perception of affective value in this case is different from seeing my dog as lovable. In the latter case, I perceive my dog as the *object* of emotion. I perceive him as requiring certain forms of loving behaviour from me. Of course, I may both see the other as loving *and* as requiring certain kinds of loving behaviour from me. To put the matter more simply, by seeing that someone loves their dog, I may thereby see them as lovable. But this fact does not threaten the distinction between seeing someone as the author of an emotion and seeing them as the 'object' of emotion, that is, as someone with whom I should interact in a certain kind of 'emotive' way.

The analysis can also accommodate cases such as the gloomy landscape. One may at first find this claim puzzling, since it is extremely implausible to hold that the landscape feels gloomy, interacts with the world gloomily, or sees the world as gloom-inducing. It is also implausible to hold that anyone who perceives the landscape as gloomy sees it as capable of being a subject of gloom in these ways. Nevertheless, it seems that the landscape is perceived as a quasi-subject of gloominess. This claim may initially seem odd. However, the phenomenon in hand is actually commonplace. It includes, for example, the anthropomorphising of inanimate things. A teddy bear can appear contented. A lone tree growing in the middle of a building site can look forlorn. A squat coffee mug can appear jolly. In all of these examples, the inanimate thing is perceived as something capable of having emotions, that is, as a subject. Similarly, a figure in a painting can appear happy. Although we would not ordinarily describe this as a case of anthropomorphising, it also involves perceiving something as a subject of emotion, in spite of the fact that one also perceives it as incapable of perception and action.

We can also distinguish between seeing something as an object of emotion, and *vicariously* seeing it as an object of emotion. Merleau-Ponty points out that part and parcel of seeing another as the subject of an emotion is seeing the world 'through their eyes'. In some cases, this means perceiving as objects of emotion the things that elicit the other's emotions from them. This is basically a form of empathy. In the above example, seeing that the other loves their dog may also involve vicariously seeing their dog as lovable. Similarly, my perception of a shopkeeper as angry may involve vicariously seeing the customer who has upset her as angering (that is, as an object of anger).

Merleau-Ponty also argues that one's cultural, historical and social 'upbringing' affects how one perceives the world. As we saw earlier, this is because what one sees is determined in part by one's motor skills – the habitual ways that one interacts with things in the world. Different cultures have different ways of interacting with the world. In certain cultures, for example, people habitually use post boxes, whereas in others they do not. People who have acquired the skill of coping with post boxes will see them as affording letter-posting, whilst people who have not acquired this skill will not. Unsurprisingly, the community to which one belongs also influences the affective dimension of the things one perceives. Objects are given a cultural significance by different societies. Presents, for example, are considered a good thing to receive in many cultures. Black cats, on the other hand, are claimed to be unlucky by many communities. People literally learn to see objects as manifesting the value placed on them by their culture. Presents are seen as good, as soliciting pleased forms of behaviour. Black cats are perceived as bad luck, as to-be-feared.

These ideas allow Merleau-Ponty to account for situational values, whilst maintaining that all perceived properties result from the interaction between the perceiver and what is perceived. A perceived value will be situational if it is perceived as the emotion of another subject, if it results from the vicarious per-ception of something as the object of some emotion, or if it is a conventional value. Sometimes, a situational value may induce feelings in the perceiver. The perception of a gloomy landscape may give rise to feelings of gloominess in the perceiver. Seeing another's fear may make the perceiver feel afraid. The vicarious perception of another's surroundings as objects of emotion may elicit feelings from the perceiver. I may, for example, feel angered by the customer who has upset the shopkeeper. Or I may feel love towards the other's dog.[7] Likewise, the perceiver may feel pleased when they receive a present or scared when they see a black cat because of the value placed on these items by their culture. However, as suggested above, the fact that some feeling of mine results from a situational value is insufficient for it to be classed as false or illusory. I may, for example, be genuinely pleased to receive a present. A gloomy landscape may induce genuine feelings of gloom in me. Likewise, sometimes seeing someone or something 'through another's eyes' leads to genuine emotions about that thing. My friend, for example, may not like dogs very much. But through perceiving my loving behaviour towards my dog, my friend sees my dog as lovable and then comes to love my dog.

Merleau-Ponty offers a second way to distinguish between real and false love. He holds that, whilst real love 'concerns [the subject] in his entire being' (1945: 434; 1962: 379; 2002: 441), if my love is illusory 'I was not wholly myself in thrall ... I maintained within me corners set aside for other things' (1945: 434; 1962: 378; 2002: 440). He claims, in other words, that real love is constantly manifest in one's perceptions and actions. It colours one's entire engagement with the world. When I am out shopping, for example, odd things I encounter remind me of the loved person. The mug in which I am served tea may be the same colour as the mugs in her house, and the sight of it immediately brings her to mind. My day is given shape by the fact that I will see her at the end of it. I start to feel excited as the end of work approaches. Tasks I would ordinarily enjoy doing seem less important, they do not require me to perform them urgently, and so on. Illusory love, on the other hand, may be manifest in the same ways as real love, but it does not colour one's entire engagement with the world. Instead, it is confined to only one part of one's life. I may, for example, feel love towards someone I met at a grand party. I see her as beautiful and lovable. I am drawn to behave in loving ways towards her. However, as soon as I leave the mansion, she is gone from my mind. My engagement with the world continues as it would have done if I had never met her.

Again, this way of distinguishing between real and false love is intuitively appealing. It is implausible to claim that I really love the woman from the grand mansion in the example above, since she plays no part in my life when I am away from her. But it is clear that this way of distinguishing between real and false love is insufficient on its own. Certain situations place such high demands on the subject that there is no 'room' for love to be manifest in the subject's perceptions and actions. Imagine, for example, a soldier caught up in the midst of battle. They have to break through enemy lines, plant a bomb in enemy territory, then return to base. The soldier must fully concentrate on the task in hand. The demands for action they perceive their environment as making are all urgent. The soldier's love for their partner is not manifest in their perceptions and actions in this situation. They do not, for example, pass some roses growing in a garden and see them as inviting them to pick them to give to their beloved. But the fact that the soldier's engagement with the world in this situation does not manifest their love for their partner does not count against their love being genuine.

This is why both ways of distinguishing between real and false emotion are important. To return to the viewer who feels grief for the dying princess in the film, it is the fact that their feeling of grief is induced by a situational value, *and* the fact that it will rapidly vanish once the film is over, that marks it out as a false feeling of grief. If the feeling of grief were to persist once the film was over, and manifest in the viewer's engagement with the world, so that, for example, they stayed in bed when they should have gone to work, experienced their usual pleasures as hollow and empty, was constantly reminded about the princess as they wandered around the world, then there would be grounds for saying that the viewer is genuinely grieving. But this grief would be inappropriate and irrational, since the grieved one is a mere character in a film. Similarly, someone might have a feeling of grief towards an appropriate object, for example, their dead brother, but if the grief were to rapidly vanish after a couple of hours and play no role in that person's subsequent engagement with the world, we would have grounds for saying that they are not really grieving – even though the feeling of grief was not induced by a situational value.

A further feature of Merleau-Ponty's analysis of the difference between real and false love is that there will be cases where it is indeterminate whether someone's love is real or illusory. I may, for example, have come to love someone by first seeing them as lovable in the eyes of someone else. Love for that person may then be a fairly constant feature of my engagement with the world, but without touching all of my life. Merleau-Ponty's account tells us in this case that there is no answer to the question of whether my love is genuine. It is ambiguous. This accords with our intuitions.

In summary, love, for Merleau-Ponty, is a way of engaging with the world – a way of seeing it and interacting with it. Real love touches every aspect of one's life and is not just momentarily induced by the values of the situations in which one finds oneself. But some cases of love are ambiguous. The love is neither real nor illusory, but has aspects of both. As we have seen, Merleau-Ponty takes perception and action to have motor intentionality. They involve direct, unmediated contact with things in the world. His analysis of emotions and moods accounts for them as ways of perceiving and interacting with the world. It follows that emotions and moods have motor intentionality too. They are not inner items that populate a Cartesian mental realm.

CONCLUSION

Merleau-Ponty has shown that the Cartesian model of the mind as an inner realm populated by one's own mental goings-on must be rejected for perception, action and emotion. None of these can be construed as involving mental representations. Instead, they are all motor intentional and involve direct, embodied contact with the world. It follows that one's knowledge of one's perceptions, actions and emotions cannot be based on introspection – there is no inner item to introspect. Instead, one's awareness of these states is adverbial: one consciously perceives and engages with the world. This adverbial awareness of one's perceptions, actions and emotions grounds one's knowledge of them. It follows that, as far as these states are involved, there is no inner realm of consciousness. As Merleau-Ponty remarks, 'I am wholly outside myself' (1945: 467; 1962: 407; 2002: 474).

7

THE MIND 2
THOUGHT

Merleau-Ponty rejects the Cartesian picture of the mind as an inner realm populated by one's own mental states. Instead, he aims to reconceive consciousness as essentially embodied. We saw in Chapter 6 that one source of support for the Cartesian picture is self-knowledge: the special knowledge each of us has of our own mental life. Such knowledge is first-personal – each of us can only have such knowledge of our own mental life. Descartes also claims that it is indubitable. Descartes's conception of self-knowledge leads him to posit a private mental realm where one's mental states reside. Each of us can inspect our own mind using introspection – a kind of infallible inner vision – which provides us with indubitable knowledge of our own mental life. The Cartesian picture also implies a view of intentionality as representation. Intentional states represent the worldly things they are about. These mental representations are the denizens of the Cartesian inner realm. For Merleau-Ponty to reject this view of the mind, he must provide an alternative account of self-knowledge and he must explain intentionality in a way that does not commit him to items that are capable of populating a Cartesian interior. An important aspect of our mental lives that we have yet to examine is thought. Merleau-Ponty's account of thought and self-knowledge will be the focus of the present chapter.

One may initially suppose that thought creates problems for Merleau-Ponty. The central difficulty is the fact that thoughts have content. Moreover, at least some thoughts involve attributing states and properties to entities that are not currently perceived. For a thought's content to float free from context in this way, it looks as though it must be representational. The reason that I can have a thought about Weston when he is not in sight is because a component of my thought represents him. It is natural to then assume that thoughts are mental representations contained within the mind and that the subject knows their own thoughts on the basis of introspection. Moreover, it implies that thinking is only contingently related to embodiment.

The latter claim needs to be clarified, since it is not obviously true. For one thing, the subject's bodily senses provide input for their thoughts – I *hear* Weston barking and wonder if someone is at the door; I *see* that there is no one there and infer that he is barking at next-door's cat. If I did not sense the world, it's not clear that I would have anything to think about. More importantly, the claim that thoughts are mental representations is compatible with a rejection of the Cartesian view of the mind as non-physical. One might hold that mental states and processes are identical with brain states and processes. On this view, the brain is essential to thought and, since the rest of the body is what keeps the brain alive, it is also required for thinking. However, notice that, on this picture, bodily activities are different in kind from thinking. The former involve moving the body around and interacting with one's environment, whilst thoughts are representations that are realised in the brain. Bodily movements provide input to the mind in the form of information gathered by the senses, and they are the mind's output in cases where thought brings about action. But, in principle, the mind could be removed from the body. All that is required is some way of sustaining the brain and providing input for it to think about. In short, the thinking subject does not need to have a body; they could be a brain in a vat. It is in this sense that thinking is only contingently related to embodiment. Merleau-Ponty must resist this line of reasoning if he is to overthrow the Cartesian picture and provide a conception of consciousness as essentially embodied.

Merleau-Ponty's discussion of thought in PhP is quite compressed and incomplete. However, he can be read as adopting the following strategy. He accepts that certain thoughts have representational content, but he denies that they are 'inner' items. He argues instead that to think a thought is to express it. Expressions can have representational content, but they are not the sort of thing that can populate a private, inner realm. Moreover, only embodied beings are capable of expression. It follows that to be a thinker one must be embodied. The mind cannot be simply identified with the brain. Merleau-Ponty makes his case by advancing two related theses. The first concerns the relation between thought and its expression. The second concerns the relation between an expression and its meaning. In both cases, Merleau-Ponty holds that the relation between the two relata is internal. It is not always clear from his discussion that there are *two* claims at issue, but it is fruitful to see him as advancing distinct theses. These two claims imply a further thesis about episodes of thinking: namely that these are bodily activities. Finally, Merleau-Ponty gives an alternative account of how the subject knows their own mental life, which does not involve introspection of an inner realm.

Merleau-Ponty takes the Cartesian model to have been discredited by the failure of Objective Thought. He is thus primarily concerned with developing an alternative, rather than providing a full defence of it. I will examine his four theses in turn.

THOUGHTS AND THEIR EXPRESSION

Merleau-Ponty's aim is to develop a notion of thought as essentially connected with embodiment. On his model, only embodied beings will be capable of thinking. He will also construe thoughts in such a way that they cannot be denizens of a Cartesian interior. He does this by conceiving of thought as dependent on its expression in such a way that to think a thought just *is* to express it. In other words, expression is not a contingent accompaniment to a thought that would have existed whether or not its subject expressed it. Expression constitutes or performs thought. He then conceives of expression as a bodily activity.

It is clear that we ordinarily take certain bodily activities to express thought. On Merleau-Ponty's view, these include (but are not limited to) language, music, painting and physical gestures. He claims that 'there is no fundamental difference between modes of expression' (1945: 448; 1962: 391; 2002: 455). Since he takes thought to be performed by its expression, it follows that to engage in one of these bodily activities just is to think. He writes, 'speech in the speaker does not translate ready-made thought, but accomplishes it' (1945: 207; 1962: 178; 2002: 207). Similarly, 'the orator does not think before speaking, nor even while speaking; his speech is his thought' (1945: 209; 1962: 180; 2002: 209). Again, 'the word and speech must [be] the presence of thought in the phenomenal world, and moreover, not its clothing but its token or body' (1945: 212; 1962: 182; 2002: 211). Since Merleau-Ponty holds that all modes of expression are fundamentally the same, these claims should be understood as applying not just to language, but to music, painting, physical gestures and so on. Only embodied beings can engage in these forms of expression because they are bodily activities. The thoughts that result from these activities are public items – utterances, inscriptions, artworks, hand gestures and so on. They are available to the senses. They are not inner items capable of being introspected.

However, even if one allows that these bodily activities constitute thinking – and I will return to this issue below – it is far from obvious that all thought is like this. Indeed, it seems undeniable that there is a form of thought which is private and which does not involve moving one's body. It is not expressed in any of the ways mentioned above. Moreover, we are inclined to think of this as the central form of thought. For Merleau-Ponty's model to be plausible, it must accommodate such private thinking. He must show that it is not unexpressed; he must somehow conceive of its expression as a bodily activity; and he must account for its privacy without construing it as the sort of thing that is capable of inhabiting an inner realm. Merleau-Ponty does this by conceiving of private thinking as silent speech. To engage in such thinking consists in silently saying sentences of public language to oneself. On this view, my private thoughts are not unexpressed. Their expression takes the form of silent utterances. He conceives of silent speech as parasitic on public speech. Its dependency is twofold. First, it is only subjects that are capable of coping with the world – perceiving and interacting with it – that can have a language. Since coping is a bodily activity, to have a language requires one to be embodied. I will say more about this below. Second, Merleau-Ponty holds that the production of silent utterances is itself a bodily activity.

One might read his latter claim as identifying all silent speech with what is known as 'subvocal' speech. This is speech that is produced without drawing air across one's vocal cords. Some of the muscles that are used in speaking are also utilised in the production of subvocal speech. It is thus the product of bodily activity. Furthermore, the identification of silent utterances with subvocal speech provides a way of explaining the privacy of such thoughts without construing them as capable of inhabiting a Cartesian interior. Subvocal speech cannot be heard, thus it cannot ordinarily be detected by others. However, technology is currently being developed to recognise subvocal speech, by reading the patterns of muscle movement that are involved in its production. The eventual aim is for people to be able to communicate with one another without speaking aloud.[1] It follows that one's subvocal utterances are not private as a matter of principle. They are public items that are contingently undetectable. They are thus comparable to secret notes, hidden so well that no one finds and reads them, but which are nevertheless public items that others could detect.

But private speech of the sort we are considering here cannot plausibly be identified with subvocal speech. Scientists developing the technology to recognise subvocal speech emphasise that it is not a 'mind-reading device' capable of detecting thought in general. There is a difference between speaking without drawing air across one's vocal cords and the sort of silent speech that constitutes certain episodes of thinking, which precisely does *not* involve moving any of the muscles one uses when speaking aloud. In fact, Merleau-Ponty's claim that silent speech is a bodily activity should not be read as an identification of all silent uttering with subvocal speech. Instead, Merleau-Ponty's view is that silent utterances are *imagined* speech. To silently say things to oneself is to imagine utterances. A certain amount of support for this claim comes from the fact that we ordinarily talk of having a *voice* 'in one's head'. Moreover, the voice that silently expresses one's private thoughts tends to be one's own. My private thoughts are not expressed in a male voice. Neither are they expressed in the voice of Barbara Cartland. If I try to express my private thoughts in a different voice, I end up imagining someone else saying them. This suggests that when I make a silent utterance, I imagine myself saying it. Also, it's wholly unclear how else to make sense of the fact that my silent utterances are expressed in my own voice. What else could this mean, except that I imagine my own voice saying them?

Merleau-Ponty then argues that imaginings in general are not inner items. Instead, they take place in the world. He makes this point by considering Sartre's (1972) example of imagining one's friend Peter. He writes,

> When I imagine Peter absent, I am not aware of contemplating an image of Peter numerically distinct from Peter himself. However far away he is, I visualize him in the world, and my power of imagining is nothing but the persistence of my world around me. To say that I imagine Peter is to say that I bring about the pseudo-presence of Peter by putting into operation the 'Peter-behaviour-pattern'. Just as Peter in imagination is only one of the modalities of my being in the world, so the verbal image is only one of the modalities of my phonetic gesticulation.
>
> (Merleau-Ponty 1945: 210–11; 1962: 181; 2002: 210)

Here, Merleau-Ponty points out that imagining Peter does not involve contemplating an inner image of him. Instead, one imagines Peter as in the world somewhere. Merleau-Ponty describes this as bringing about the pseudo-presence of Peter.

His analysis refers to his account of reckoning with the possible. As we saw in Chapter 3, the human subject possesses motor skills. These are exercised in perception and action. Possessing a motor skill enables one to perform certain actions and perceive appropriate environments as offering an opportunity to perform them. One's motor skills allow one to invest one's surroundings with bodily significance. In perception, one exercises one's motor skills in response to the promptings of the world to summon the appropriate appearances. In the perceptual case, investing one's surroundings with bodily significance involves perceiving them as requiring one to engage in certain forms of behaviour. However, human subjects also possess a capacity that Merleau-Ponty calls 'the power to reckon with the possible'. This is the capacity to access and so use motor skills over and above those that are relevant to one's actual surroundings and current task. One thing this capacity allows the subject to do is access their skills of coping with things that are absent, to summon the demands for action that they would make on them if they were present.

Merleau-Ponty claims in the above passage that imagining Peter involves the power to reckon with the possible. One is skilled at coping with Peter – that is, one has spent time with him, getting to know and like him, so that one has built up habits of interacting with him. Like all habits, one's 'Peter-skills' have two components: a behavioural component (one behaves in a friendly, relaxed manner towards Peter), and a perceptual component (one perceives him as familiar, likeable and so on). The power to reckon with the possible enables one to access these Peter-skills when he is absent and thus summon up the demands he would make on one if he were present. In this way, one brings about the 'pseudo-presence' of Peter. It is clear on this account that imagining Peter is a bodily ability – it involves exercising certain physical skills – those for coping with Peter. Merleau-Ponty holds that the pseudo-presence of Peter is not an image or any other item contained 'within the mind'. It is a part of the world. But it is a subjective element of it, rather than a worldly entity that is publicly accessible. He takes the same points to apply to imagined speech. To imagine speech is to exercise one's skills at talking and hearing utterances. One exercises these skills to summon up the demands made by speaking and hearing an utterance. In this way, one brings about the pseudo-presence of the utterance. As in the case of imagining Peter, the pseudo-presence of an utterance is not an inner item. It is a part of the world, albeit a subjective entity that is not publicly accessible.

I stated earlier that Merleau-Ponty's primary aim is to develop an alternative model to the Cartesian account of the mind by reconceiving thought and thinking. He is less concerned with defending this alternative. Nevertheless, he does offer some arguments in favour of it.

It is uncontroversial that some episodes of thinking involve saying sentences to oneself. This phenomenon provides some support for Merleau-Ponty's claim that expression does not translate an independently existing thought, but constitutes it. It is implausible in such cases to suppose that the subject first has a thought – for example, that it is raining – which they then translate with a sentence that has the same content, 'It's raining'. If this were so, then it would be wholly unclear why the subject says the sentences to themself – they simply duplicate their thoughts and serve no apparent purpose. A better explanation holds that saying sentences to oneself simply constitutes thinking – the silent utterances just are one's thoughts. Furthermore, there seems to be no essential difference between saying sentences silently to oneself and speaking aloud – as is aptly illustrated by those occasions when one is deep in thought and suddenly realises that one has started talking aloud. Neither does there appear to be any significant difference between speaking and writing. Since silently saying sentences is to think, it follows that talking and writing must constitute thought as Merleau-Ponty claims. This is not to say that speaking and writing *never* translate a ready-made thought. I might, for example, look in the cupboard, think to myself that we need to go shopping, then say to my partner, 'We need to go shopping.' Here it seems that I have expressed my thought that we need to go shopping by uttering a sentence with the same content. It also seems that I would have had this thought whether or not I uttered the sentence to my partner. But given the discussion above, we can see that for Merleau-Ponty this thought consists in my saying to myself, 'We need to go shopping' – that is, it is constituted by its silent linguistic expression.

Merleau-Ponty also points to other phenomena that provide support for his claim that thought is constituted by its expression. He notes that

> thought tends towards its expression as towards its completion ... [and] the thinking subject himself is in a kind of ignorance of his thoughts so long as he has not formulated them for himself, or even spoken or written them, as is shown by the example of so many writers who begin a book without knowing exactly what they are going to put in it.
>
> (Merleau-Ponty 1945: 206; 1962: 177; 2002: 206)

What he has in mind here is the fact that people are moved to express their thoughts – either to others or to themselves in a diary or an inner monologue – and the act of articulating one's thoughts is what gives shape to them. It is, for example, a common experience to move from inchoate feelings about some issue to a view on the matter through talking about the issue with a friend. Moreover, expressing one's thoughts often involves mental effort – as is the case in writing this book. The effort results from the fact that the subject is thinking 'on the page' or 'in their speech'. They are not just recording thoughts that have already been fully worked out.

Merleau-Ponty also argues that certain aspects of pre-scientific thinking are best explained by supposing that thought is inseparable from its expression. He writes, 'For pre-scientific thinking, naming an object is causing it to exist or changing it: God creates beings by naming them and magic operates on them by speaking of them' (1945: 207; 1962: 178; 2002: 206). For Merleau-Ponty, when one names an object, one does not start with a prior idea of the object as a particular entity of a certain sort, to which one simply assigns a noise. It is in the act of naming an object that one forms an idea of it – to name an object is to conceive of it. The experience of naming an object is thus of introducing it into one's conceptual landscape, setting it amongst the other things of which one conceives and giving shape to it as an entity of some particular sort. Given this, it is unsurprising that pre-scientific thought held that naming an object causes it to exist, and talking of it changes or fixes its nature. In contrast, if one supposes that thought is independent from its linguistic expression, then it is the act of conceiving an object that introduces it into one's conceptual landscape as a thing of a certain sort. The act of naming it is simply to assign a noise to it. On this picture, it is unclear why naming an object should be attributed any creative or magical powers. It follows that the model of thought as expression is best able to make sense of this pre-scientific thinking.

Merleau-Ponty has argued that thought and its expression are internally related. By this he means that thinking is performed or constituted by its expression. However, at this point the following objection can be raised. Many of the activities that Merleau-Ponty classifies as expressions of thought are rule-governed. Moreover, one has to be following the rules that govern the activity for one to count as engaging in it at all. Of course, this does not mean that one must always follow the rules correctly for one to count as engaging in some rule-governed activity. It is possible to make mistakes. However, to make a mistake, one has to be following the rules. Merleau-Ponty's example of the geometer illustrates these points (1945: 440–5; 1962: 383–8; 2002: 446–51). A geometer draws a diagram to prove various truths about triangles, such as the fact that the sum of angles in a triangle is always 180 degrees. The geometer's activity differs from that of a young child sketching, where the shape they draw changes its meaning as they add to it, looking first like a house, then like a boat, and so on (1945: 440; 1962: 384; 2002: 446). The geometer's drawing can be classed as a proof, whilst the young child's cannot because the geometer – unlike the child – is following the rules for constructing proofs. The proof may contain mistakes, that is, it may deviate from how the rules state that the proof should be constructed. The child's drawing also differs from what these rules prescribe. But the child cannot be thought of as making a mistake – he or she is just engaging in a different activity. The reason the geometer's deviation from the rules can be classed as a mistake is because the child is following (or attempting to follow) them.

The problem for Merleau-Ponty is that it looks as though following a rule involves using the rule as an instruction, which tells one how to proceed. In other words, it looks as though following a rule involves having it 'before one's mind' and using it to guide one's activity. Let us call this 'explicitly following a rule'. Since it is natural to think of a rule as representing the way that something should be done, it seems that following a rule involves mentally representing the content of the rule. It follows that to express thought requires the subject to mentally represent the rules governing the relevant form of expression. Of course, mental representations are thoughts. Merleau-Ponty thus faces a dilemma. Either these mental representations are unexpressed – in which case it is possible for there to be thought without expression – or they are expressed. But, if this is so, then the subject must have further thoughts which represent the rules governing the relevant form of expression, and so on ad infinitum.

The above objection relies on the claim that, to engage in rule-governed behaviour, one has to have the rule before one's mind and use it as an instruction to guide one's activity. In other words, to engage in rule-governed behaviour one has to explicitly follow rules. But this conception of rule-following is notoriously problematic. There is a right way and a wrong way to follow a rule. To follow a rule one must know how it should be applied. On the picture we are considering, applying a rule involves explicitly following it. Thus, to apply the first rule, the subject must explicitly follow a second rule, which states how the first rule should be applied. However, to follow the second rule, the subject must explicitly follow a third rule, stating how to apply the second rule. Clearly, if one claims that the subject always applies a rule by explicitly following another one, a vicious infinite regress ensues and no rule-governed activity can take place. To avoid the regress, there must be a way of applying a rule without *explicitly* following it. If Merleau-Ponty can provide an account of what is involved in *implicitly* following a rule, where this does not involve mentally representing it, then he will have dissolved the dilemma that faces him.

Merleau-Ponty's account of perception and action provides a partial solution to this problem. He conceives of perception and action as two interdependent aspects of a single capacity – the ability to 'cope' with the world. The subject becomes skilled at a certain activity, or builds up a behavioural habit, through practising the activity in question. Once they have practised sufficiently to acquire the skill, they are both able to perform the relevant bodily movements with ease and see appropriate parts of the world as requiring those bodily movements. The skilled snowboarder, for example, can keep their balance on the snowboard as they descend a snowy slope, and see certain slopes as offering them opportunities to snowboard. The proficient agent can then respond to their perception of opportunities to act by acting, without the need for any intervening thought. The subject can become skilled at engaging in rule-governed activities. Once they are proficient, they will see appropriate parts of the world as requiring the actions prescribed by the rule and disallowing those actions the rule prohibits. Dreyfus and Dreyfus (1999) discuss the example of a chess player. Once someone has become proficient at chess, their grasp of the rules is manifest in their perception of the chessboard. They simply perceive the pieces as offering certain possibilities for action and disallowing others – for example, they see a bishop as offering diagonal movement across the board and prohibiting non-diagonal movement. In this way, the subject is able to apply rules without explicitly following them. The rules become perceived demands for action to which the subject can respond by immediately acting.

Clearly, not all rule-following takes this form. It is only after one has acquired a skill that one is able to perceive the world in the light of that skill, and acquiring a skill requires practice. One's grasp of a rule will therefore only manifest in one's perception of the world when one has followed that rule a sufficient number of times. Dreyfus and Dreyfus (1999) and Wrathall (2007) point out that the novice follows rules explicitly. But, to avoid regress, the subject's explicit rule-following must, at some point, rest on the non-explicit application of rules. When learning to play chess, for example, one has to think about the rules governing the movement of the pieces; one must have those rules before one's mind, and use them to guide one's chess playing. Thus one may explicitly identify the knight as the piece that looks like a horse. There are rules for identifying things that look like horses. These rules set out criteria that something must satisfy in order for that thing to look like a horse. However, the novice need not explicitly follow these rules to identify the chess piece that looks like a horse. Providing they have seen a sufficient number of horse-like entities, certain chess pieces will simply appear horse-like to them.

In the example described above, the subject explicitly follows a rule by non-explicitly applying rules they have already learnt. They have acquired the skill of identifying horse-like entities, and are thus able to immediately perceive certain entities as horse-like. This capacity then allows them to explicitly follow the rule for identifying the knight, which states that it is the chess piece that looks like a horse. However, one may wonder how someone learns to follow a rule in the first place. On Merleau-Ponty's account, one can learn to follow a rule by copying another person. Each of us has an innate capacity to copy others. We are able to do this immediately and unreflectively. Even babies are able to copy others around them, well before they are capable of thought. This capacity to copy others allows for training. The subject is able to copy what they see someone else doing. They can then practise the activity until they have acquired it as a habit or motor skill that affects their perception of the world. It follows that someone can learn to follow a rule without ever explicitly following it. They can be trained to follow it by copying another's behaviour.

The upshot is that Merleau-Ponty's claim that thought is performed by its expression is not threatened by the fact that various ways of expressing thought are rule-governed. The subject does not need to *explicitly* follow rules in order to engage in rule-governed behaviour. In other words, they do not need to mentally represent a rule in order to follow it.

MEANING AND EXPRESSION

Merleau-Ponty's claim that the relation between thoughts and their expression is internal goes hand-in-hand with his second thesis: namely, that an expression and its meaning are also internally related. This is a claim about how expressions – such as the sentence 'Weston is hungry' – get their meanings. It will be easier to understand Merleau-Ponty's claim if we first consider the alternative position which he rejects.

The alternative view is, of course, that expressions and their meanings are *externally* related. An expression gets its meaning by being associated with it. The word 'dog', for example, gains its meaning in virtue of being associated with a particular sort of canine animal. Importantly, this account presupposes that expressions and their meanings exist independently from one another. Merleau-Ponty denies that this is the case for the following reasons. Consider what kind of entity an independently existing meaning might be. There are two options. On the one hand, meanings might be subjective entities – that is, they might exist within consciousness. This option is ruled out by Merleau-Ponty's claim that thoughts and their expression are internally related. To claim that meanings exist within consciousness is to identify them with ideas or concepts. In other words, it is to identify meanings with thoughts (or parts of thoughts). An expression, on this view, gets its meaning by being associated with a thought (or a component of a thought). This, of course, requires the thought (or component) to exist independently of its expression. Since Merleau-Ponty argues that thought is *not* independent of its expression, meanings cannot be identified with ideas or concepts that exist independently of their expression.

The second option is to think of meanings as objective entities – objects that exist independently of consciousness. Meanings are clearly not physical objects like tables and dogs that exist in particular regions of space at particular times – I cannot touch a meaning with my hands, or stub my toe against one. Thus, if meanings are objective entities, they must be abstract objects. The claim that meanings are objective entities is therefore a form of Platonism. Merleau-Ponty denies that meanings exist independently of consciousness. He does not offer any conclusive argument for this denial. Moreover, since there is a vast literature on Platonism with compelling reasons offered both for and against the position, I will not attempt to settle the matter here. One may nevertheless reject the claim that expressions are meaningful in virtue of being associated with independently existing meanings on the following grounds. If one holds that meanings are abstract objects and expressions gain their meanings by being associated with them, one must explain *how* this association comes about. It is not very clear what one might say about this issue. Perhaps the most obvious line to take is to claim that humans (or other conscious subjects) associate meanings with expressions. The word 'dog', for example, has the meaning 'canine animal' because people have associated the expression with this meaning. But, in order to associate a meaning with an expression, a subject has to have that meaning 'before their mind' – they have to entertain it in thought. Moreover, their entertaining of that meaning – their thinking of it – must be independent of the expression they then associate with it. Thus this account presupposes that thought is independent of its expression. Since Merleau-Ponty has argued that thought is *not* independent of its expression, he can reject this view. It may be possible to provide an account of how meanings, conceived as abstract objects, become associated with expressions without appealing to a conscious subject who does the associating. The considerations offered above do not, therefore, entirely settle the matter. However, it is hard to see what form such an account could take. Thus, if one claims that thought is internally related to its expression, one has good reason for also holding that expressions are internally related to their meanings – which is Merleau-Ponty's view.

Merleau-Ponty has rejected the view that expressions are associated with independently existing meanings. His alternative account holds that the relation between an expression and its meaning is internal. In other words, meanings do not exist independently of their expression. There are different ways of developing this claim. Merleau-Ponty offers two proposals. He makes his first suggestion in connection with language, but, since he thinks that there is no fundamental difference between the various forms of expression, he presumably takes similar points to apply in the case of music, painting and so on. Consider again the account that he rejects, which claims that expressions are merely associated with their meanings. The view implies that the expressions themselves – the noises that constitute words, the shapes, colours, textures that constitute paintings, the physical movements that constitute gestures, and so on – are meaningless. On this view the sound 'dog' is just a meaningless noise until the idea 'canine animal' is associated with it. Since expressions themselves have no meaning, there is nothing about an expression that determines which meaning is assigned to it. The idea 'canine animal' could just as easily have been associated with the noise 'cat'. Merleau-Ponty's first proposal denies that expressions themselves are meaningless and that the assignment of meaning to them is arbitrary.

Some care is required here. Merleau-Ponty seems to be suggesting that the sounds that constitute words (the shapes, textures, and colours which constitute paintings, etc.) have some kind of intrinsic meaning – a meaning they have in-themselves, whether or not anyone ever grasps it or apprehends it. The problem is that this is in conflict with another of his claims – namely, that meaning does not exist independently from consciousness. However, there is a way of understanding Merleau-Ponty's proposal without jeopardising the idea that there is only meaning for consciousness. The sounds that constitute words only have meaning for conscious beings. But it does not follow that conscious beings must assign meanings to those sounds arbitrarily. Instead, given the properties of the sounds and the nature of the conscious beings that hear them, those beings cannot help but find those sounds meaningful in certain ways. There is an obvious parallel with what theorists often say about colour. Objects in-themselves are not coloured. They only appear coloured to perceivers like us. But this does not mean that we assign colours to those objects at random. Given our perceptual systems and the nature of those objects, we cannot help but see them as having certain colours.

However, although Merleau-Ponty's first proposal is not in conflict with his claim that meaning is dependent on consciousness, there are other problems with it. It is extremely counterintuitive to suppose that we cannot help but hear certain sounds as having particular meanings. This would mean, for example, that the sound 'dog' could only mean canine animal for us and could not have meant feline creature. Merleau-Ponty anticipates this objection and asks 'is not the link between the verbal sign and its meaning quite accidental, a fact demonstrated by the existence of a number of languages?' (1945: 217; 1962: 187; 2002: 217). He responds as follows:

> If we consider only the conceptual and delimiting meaning of words, it is true that the verbal form ... appears arbitrary. But it would no longer appear so if we took into account the emotional content of the word, which we called its 'gestural' sense, which is all-important in poetry, for example.
>
> (Merleau-Ponty 1945: 218; 1962: 187; 2002: 217)

Here, Merleau-Ponty distinguishes between the conceptual meaning of a word and what he calls its 'gestural' meaning.[2] He claims that sounds have an emotional impact on us so that they are able to convey some indeterminate meaning. This is what he refers to as 'gestural' meaning. The conceptual meaning of a word is the concept or idea that it expresses. It is the gestural meaning that grounds a word's conceptual meaning. Since the emotional impact of a sound expresses an ambiguous meaning, it does not determine which conceptual meaning the sound later comes to express. Instead, the gestural meaning sets boundaries to the kinds of conceptual meanings the sound may later accrue. It follows that the conceptual meaning of words is not entirely arbitrary, even though it is not entirely determined by the sounds that constitute those words.

Merleau-Ponty appeals to pathological evidence to support his claim that words have a gestural meaning. He observes that

> Certain patients can read a text 'putting expression into it', without, however, understanding it. This is because the spoken or written words carry a top coating of meaning which sticks to them and which presents the thought as a style, an affective value, a piece of existential mimicry, rather than as a conceptual statement.
>
> (Merleau-Ponty 1945: 212; 1962: 182; 2002: 212)

There are also examples of language use that seem to provide some support for the notion of gestural meaning. Consider, for example, the first verse of Lewis Carroll's *Jabberwocky*:

Twas brillig, and the slithy toves
Did gyre and gimble in the wabe:
All mimsy were the borogoves,
And the mome raths outgrabe.
(Carroll 2003: 132)

'Words' such as 'brillig' are not part of a language and have no conceptual meaning. Yet they nevertheless manage to convey something – albeit something rather ambiguous. Passages from James Joyce's masterpiece *Finnegans Wake* similarly lend some support to the idea of gestural meaning. Consider, for example, this remark: 'Rot a peck of pa's malt had Jhem or Shen brewed by arclight and rory end to the regginbrow was to be seen ringsome on the aquaface' (Joyce 1939: 3). Again, many of the 'words' have no conceptual meaning but still manage to convey something to the reader. However, although these examples lend *some* support to the idea that sounds have a gestural meaning, they do not entirely vindicate it. The language used by Joyce, for example, is based on English and also contains words of other languages. Thus one could argue that the words he invents gain their meaning from their connection with public languages. Similarly, one could argue that Carroll's nonsense derives its meaning from its affinities with English. 'Slithy toves', for example, sounds similar to 'slimy toads', and it is perhaps in virtue of this resemblance that the former conveys something. It is thus difficult to assess Merleau-Ponty's claim that sounds (colours, textures and so on) have a gestural meaning. Perhaps more importantly, even if one could establish that sounds have a gestural sense, we still require an account of how words gain their conceptual meaning.

Merleau-Ponty develops his second proposal by considering physical gestures. These include beckoning with a hand to call a friend, shrugging one's shoulders in response to a question, and angrily shaking one's fist at someone. Merleau-Ponty holds that gestures can express thought – for example, beckoning with my hand expresses the desire that my friend come over here. Gestures are meaningful – for example, shrugging one's shoulders in answer to a question means that one does not know the answer. There is a question concerning how gestures gain their meanings. Most, if not all, gestures have conventional meanings. There is, for example, a convention which dictates that shaking one's finger at someone means that they have done something wrong. But conventions are established ways of doing things. For a convention to come about, the same thing has to be done in the same way a sufficient number of times. Thus, for a convention to arise, there has to be a first instance of doing things in that way. Although it is true that gestures have conventional meanings, one cannot fully account for their meanings by appealing to convention. For a gesture to conventionally mean x, there must have been a first time that the gesture was used to mean x. A complete explanation of how gestures obtain their meaning must account for how a gesture can be meaningful before any conventions are established.

Merleau-Ponty holds that there is no fundamental difference between the different ways that thought can be expressed. Thus the claims that Merleau-Ponty makes about other forms of expression also apply to gestures. His claims rule out a certain picture of how gestures are produced and how they gain their meanings. Briefly, one might suppose that gestures are brought about by psychological states, which then give those gestures their meanings. On this account, the action of beckoning one's friend is brought about by one's desire to call him over. One has the desire whether or not one performs the gesture, and the desire plays some role in bringing about the movement. The beckoning movement then obtains its meaning in virtue of the desire that led to its performance. Notice that this account presupposes that the desire exists independently of its expression – one desires one's friend to come over regardless of whether one calls him by beckoning. Moreover, it takes the meaning of gestures to be merely associated with them – the hand movement itself has no meaning; it gains its meaning by being associated with a meaningful desire. Since Merleau-Ponty holds that gestures express thought, and thought is not independent from its expression, this account must be rejected. One's desire is not independent of the gesture that expresses it. It is not a pre-existing mental state that can play a role in the production of the hand movement, and it cannot be what gives the gesture its meaning.

Merleau-Ponty also rejects the claim that the meaning of gestures is biologically determined. On this account we are 'hard-wired' to smile when we are happy, stamp our feet when we are impatient, and so on – this behaviour is innate. (The claim that the meaning of gestures is biologically determined is a version of Merleau-Ponty's first proposal, which claims that, given the facts of our embodiment, we cannot help but find certain signs to have certain meanings.) Merleau-Ponty argues that this cannot be a correct account of gestures. If it were, then the meaning of gestures would be the same for all humans, but in fact the meaning of gestures varies from culture to culture. 'The angry Japanese smiles, the westerner goes red and stamps his foot or else goes pale and hisses his words' (Merleau-Ponty 1945: 220; 1962: 189; 2002: 219). Similarly, the hand gesture which means 'go away' in English means 'come here' in Khmer.

Merleau-Ponty's account of absorbed coping explains how gestures are produced. In absorbed coping, the subject's actions are immediately brought about by their perceived environment. They perceive their surroundings as requiring a certain sort of action, and respond to this perception of them by acting. Merleau-Ponty holds that this is how gestures are produced. He writes,

> When I motion my friend to come nearer, my intention is not a thought prepared within me and I do not perceive the signal in my body. I beckon across the world, I beckon over there, where my friend is; the distance between us, his consent or refusal are immediately read in my gesture; there is not a perception followed by a movement, for both form a system which varies as a whole. If, for example, realizing that I am not going to be obeyed, I vary my gesture, we have here, not two distinct acts of consciousness. What happens is that I see my partner's unwillingness, and my gesture of impatience emerges from this situation without any intervening thought.
>
> (Merleau-Ponty 1945: 128–9; 1962: 111; 2002: 127)

I see my friend as 'desirable-near-me' and so as requiring that I call him over. My beckoning gesture arises from this perception of him. If I see that he is not coming over to me, I immediately gesture impatiently. My gesture is produced by my situation, that is, by my perceived environment. It is not the result of thought.

Merleau-Ponty also explains how a gesture first gains its meaning by appealing to the subject's situation. His basic claim is that a gesture is meaningful in virtue of the meaningful situation in which it occurs – it is the context which confers meaning on it. Consider again the example of beckoning to my friend. Imagine that the described case is the first time that anyone has called their friend by using such a gesture. I see my friend as requiring that I call him over, and it is this perception of him which brings about my gesture. The fact that my gesture arises in a context where I am summoning my friend gives it the meaning of calling him over. However, one may be puzzled as to how my perceived environment can call forth my action in this case. Where conventional gestures are concerned, it is easy to see how this could happen. The subject learns to use a certain gesture for a particular purpose and, through practice, they come to see relevant situations as calling for that particular gesture. But one may wonder how my perception initiates a beckoning movement in the case we are considering, where there is no conventional gesture for calling someone over. The answer for Merleau-Ponty is that it is purely by chance that my perception of my friend draws forth a beckoning movement. I could just as easily have performed a kicking action. My situation prompts me to move my body, but it does not determine how my body moves – nothing determines this, although there may be constraints imposed by such things as the mobility of my body, the ease with which a movement can be performed, and so on. The case is analogous in this respect to that of an animated speaker who waves their hands around as they talk. Their enthusiasm for the topic immediately draws forth the movements from them, but there is nothing that determines which hand movements they make. The same is true of my hand movement when I call my friend.

Gestures are often used to communicate with others. A full account of gestures must explain how an audience grasps a gesture's meaning. Where the meaning of a gesture has been established by convention this can be explained on the grounds that both the agent and their audience know the conventional meaning of the gesture. However, it is unclear how a gesture can communicate anything the first time it is used. Especially since Merleau-Ponty appeals to the *agent*'s perception of their environment, and their activity to explain how a gesture obtains its meaning. It is *my* perception of my friend and the fact that *I* am summoning him over to me that confer meaning on my gesture in the case described above. Merleau-Ponty's answer to this problem is simple. He points out it is possible for both the agent *and* their audience to grasp the meaning of the situation in which the gesture occurs. (In fact, this is very common.) Since it is the situation that confers meaning on the gesture, the audience will also grasp the gesture's meaning. Thus, in the example we are considering, my friend grasps the fact that I want him to come over to me and that I am summoning him. His understanding of the situation allows him to immediately perceive my gesture as calling him over. Merleau-Ponty states that this is made possible by our 'taking part in a communal life' (1945: 209; 1962: 179; 2002: 208). It is because we share ways of doing things, ways of looking at the world, and so on, that we both grasp the meaning of the situation and so the meaning of the gesture as it occurs within it. Suppose, for example, that I am looking at an exhibit in a museum. I call my friend over because I think he will find the exhibit interesting. My friend and I are interested in the same things. We both engage in the activity of looking at exhibits in a museum. We both tend to show each other things of interest. My friend will recognise my activity and so grasp that I am looking at something interesting that I want to show him. He will thus understand that I am summoning him and perceive my gesture as calling him over.

Merleau-Ponty extends these claims about physical gestures to language. He refers to utterances as 'linguistic gestures' (1945: 217; 1962: 186; 2002: 216). The parallels are clear. Like physical gestures, utterances have conventional meanings. But, for these conventional meanings to arise, there must have been a first instant when someone used a word or a phrase to express some particular meaning. Merleau-Ponty claims that the meaning is conferred upon the verbal sign by the context in which it is used. The speaker is able to use the sign to communicate with their audience in virtue of their shared grasp of the situation, which comes about through their communal way of life. Once the sign has been used with this meaning, it can be used in this way again. A conventional meaning is thus able to develop as people in that particular linguistic community use the sign in the same way over and over again.

Merleau-Ponty's account construes the relation between an expression and its meaning as internal. By this he means that the meaning of an expression does not exist independently of it. We can see how this is so on the proposal we have just examined. Expressions are drawn forth from the agent by their situation. The situation as a whole has a meaning. The expression is meaningful in virtue of the context in which it occurs. It follows that expressions and their meanings do not come about independently from one another. Instead, a meaningful expression arises spontaneously as part of a situation. Merleau-Ponty's second proposal does not commit him to the claim that an expression could not have any meaning other than the one it actually has. It does not, for example, commit him to the claim that the noise 'dog' could only be used to mean 'canine animal' and could not have been used to mean 'feline creature'. As we saw above, nothing determines which movement or sound is drawn forth from the agent the first time an expression emerges, although this might be constrained by such things as physical ease of production. Thus, the first time an expression meaning 'canine animal' was produced, the speaker could have made a noise other than 'dog'. Merleau-Ponty's second proposal therefore respects the intuition that the link between a verbal sign and its meaning is arbitrary.

THINKING

Merleau-Ponty's claim that thought is performed by its public expression has implications for the nature of thinking. Traditionally, thinking is construed as a mental activity that takes place within the subject and has no essential connection with the subject's body. The subject's body may provide inputs in the form of sensory information. It may also support mental functioning by providing the necessary nutrients to the brain where mental activity is realised. But bodily activity and mental activity are different. In principle, a subject's mental activity could be realised in something other than their brain. In this sense, their brain and body are inessential to their mental life. It is clear that Merleau-Ponty's claims about thought conflict with the traditional picture. If thought is performed by its expression, then thinking is not a process or activity that happens in an inner mental space. It is an activity that takes place in the world and is carried out by an embodied agent – one who can manipulate a pen or brush and produce sounds, who has body parts with which to gesture, and so on.

Merleau-Ponty thus anticipates a thesis, which in the contemporary literature is called 'embodied cognition'. The basic claim is that certain bodily activities are properly classified as a form of thought. Clark and Chalmers (1998) give the example of playing Tetris – a computer game where the player has to organise coloured blocks to form complete rows. Clearly, the computer player's activity is intelligent and 'thoughtful' – they do not move the coloured blocks at random, but do so with the purpose (or intention) of completing rows. Clark and Chalmers (1998) claim that the player should not be viewed as moving the coloured blocks in accordance with a plan they form in advance of moving them. Instead, the best description of their activity construes it as constituting thought about how to move them to complete their objective. A further example is someone who arranges furniture in the back of a van. The subject does not move furniture arbitrarily; they move it with the intention of fitting it all into the van. But the best description of their activity does not view it as guided by prior thought about how to move it. Instead, their arranging furniture itself constitutes thought about how to arrange it. Merleau-Ponty makes a parallel claim about the geometer's drawing (1945: 440; 1962: 384; 2002: 447). He argues that the geometer does not construct their diagram by explicitly following rules telling them how to construct it. As we have seen, there are intractable problems with supposing that following rules is always a matter of explicitly following them. In other words, the geometer does not construct their diagram in accordance with a representation of it that they have formed in advance. Instead, they see what to do as they construct their diagram. Thus the construction of the diagram itself constitutes the reasoning that leads to the proof.

SELF-KNOWLEDGE AND THE TACIT COGITO

It is ordinarily claimed that each of us has a special kind of knowledge of our own mental life. This self-knowledge has two features:

(1) it is first-personal – only the subject can know their own mental life in this way; and
(2) they are epistemically privileged with respect to it.

Descartes takes such knowledge to be indubitable. He then accounts for self-knowledge by claiming that mental states are private inner items, which the subject knows about on the basis of introspection. Only the subject can introspect their mental state, and introspection is infallible. It is possible for others to have knowledge of the subject's mental life, but their knowledge of it will be based on perception of their behaviour, and is not indubitable. Things can go wrong in two ways. First, people sometimes misperceive. I might mishear Belinda say that Elvis is Texan, and so mistakenly come to believe that Belinda thinks Elvis is from Texas. Second, mental states are inner items on Descartes's view and cannot be experienced by anyone apart from their subject. The behaviour that others perceive is at most a sign of the subject's mental life, and may not accurately indicate what occurs within their mind. Merleau-Ponty rejects the idea that one's mental states are inner items that populate a Cartesian inner realm. It follows that they cannot be introspected.

Like Descartes, Merleau-Ponty takes self-knowledge to be based on one's awareness of one's mental life. But the relevant form of awareness is not introspection. There is no such thing as introspection on Merleau-Ponty's account. Notice also that the phrase 'mental life' is something of a misnomer for Merleau-Ponty. On his account, what we ordinarily think of as mental states and activities consist in embodied perception of/interaction with the world. We might say that the subject's mental life manifests in their situation, where their situation is the world as it shows up for them in perception, together with the manner in which they interact with it. One's situation has a temporal dimension – it unfolds over time since perceiving and acting are not instantaneous. It will be easier to grasp these ideas by considering some examples. First, recall Merleau-Ponty's account of emotions and moods. He does not conceive these as inner objects that inhabit a Cartesian interior. Instead, he construes them as ways of engaging with the world – ways of perceiving and interacting with it. My love for someone, for example, manifests in my perception of them as beautiful, lovable, requiring certain forms of tender behaviour, and so on. It also manifests in my loving behaviour towards them, the tolerance with which I deal with others, etc. Emotions and moods can develop and change over time. One might initially be completely captivated by someone, but later become disillusioned and fall out of love with them. Conversely, one's love for someone may only develop gradually, gaining strength as one spends time getting to know them. Similarly, some of what we ordinarily take to be the subject's thoughts play a role in shaping their situation. Their thoughts affect the way they perceive the world and how they interact with it. They influence the decisions they make and the tasks they take on. Linda's belief that dogs are dangerous may shape her situation in these ways. Dogs may appear scary to her. She may interact with them fearfully and avoid them where possible. Linda will be reluctant to visit her aunt who owns a large Doberman, and she will not agree to look after it when her aunt goes on holiday. Just as one's love will be a dimension of one's temporally unfolding situation, so, too, Linda's belief that dogs are dangerous is one aspect of a situation that unfolds over time in accordance with this belief.

Self-knowledge of one's mental life is based on awareness of one's situation. The subject's awareness of their situation has two related components. First, they have an adverbial awareness of their perceptions and actions. As we saw in Chapter 6, one's perceptions and actions are not literally objects *of* which one is aware. The subject is aware *in* perceiving and acting as they engage in them. Second, the subject is aware *of* their environment – they perceive the things and places that comprise their surroundings. Merleau-Ponty argues that the subject's awareness of their situation is a form of *self*-consciousness. It is easy to see why he thinks this. My experience of my situation is awareness of my own existence. It is awareness of *my* actions, *my* perceptions, *my* emotions, *my* thoughts and so on. Furthermore, my awareness of them is first-personal, that is, it is an awareness of them that only I can have. It is clear that only the agent can be adverbially aware of their perceptions and actions – it is the awareness they have in engaging in them. But one's perception of the places and things surrounding one can also provide one with a first-personal awareness of one's mental life. Consider again what is involved in loving someone. My love affects how I perceive the world, so that I see my beloved as beautiful and requiring me to act in loving ways towards them. I perceive them as demanding that *I* act in these ways. Other people cannot experience *my* love as demanding that *they* act lovingly with my beloved. This is an experience of my love which is only available to me. Of course, we saw in the previous chapter that one can have vicarious experiences of love, where one sees the beloved through the eyes of the lover. In such cases, someone else may see *my* beloved as demanding that *they* act in loving ways towards her, in virtue of their perception of me as loving her. But to see my beloved as demanding that *they* act lovingly towards her is for them to experience an aspect of their own mental life. It follows that the perception of the things and places surrounding one can be a first-personal experience of one's mental life.

Two points should be borne in mind here. First, the two components of the subject's awareness are bound up with one another. To see this, consider what is involved in my awareness of my actions. Suppose I pick up a glass and drink from it. I am adverbially aware of my movements as I perform them. But my action is guided by my perception of my surroundings. I see the glass of water as for-drinking and this is what draws forth my action of drinking it. My perception of my surroundings contributes to my awareness of the action I am performing. Second, I have distinguished between the subject's situation and their awareness of it. But in fact this separation is artificial. Merleau-Ponty holds that only a subject can be in a situation. This is because one's situation consists in the way that one perceives and interacts with the world, and only a subject is capable of perceiving and acting. On Merleau-Ponty's account, perception and action essentially involve adverbial awareness of engaging in them. It follows that to be in a situation essentially involves being aware of one's situation.

The subject's awareness of their situation is, as we have seen, a form of self-consciousness. Merleau-Ponty calls it the 'tacit cogito'. It enjoys a kind of 'certainty'. If I perceive my dog as lovable, for example, then he appears to me as lovable, and I am adverbially aware of perceiving him as such. The adverbial awareness I have of my perception is part and parcel of my perception, and although my perception is subject to error – I might misperceive a rock as my dog – it makes no sense to suppose that my adverbial awareness of my perception might be mistaken. To be adverbially aware of one's perceptions just *is* to perceive. It is to be conscious of the world. But the fact that I perceive (and so am adverbially aware of my perception) is not capable of being true or false, mistaken or correct. The notion of error has no application in this context. Consider, for example, the fact that there is a cup of tea on my desk. There being a cup of tea on my desk is not the sort of thing that can be true or false, mistaken or correct. Someone's *belief* about there being a cup of tea on my desk can be true or false. But the belief is different from the mere fact that my desk holds a cup of tea. Similarly, the mere fact that I perceive – and so am conscious of my perceptions – is not the sort of thing that can be true or false. The same holds for my awareness of other aspects of my situation. It is in this sense that my awareness of my situation enjoys a sort of 'certainty'.

However, this 'certainty' does not then translate into infallible *knowledge* of my mental life. Merleau-Ponty describes the subject's experience of their situation as an awareness of their mental life that is not in full possession of itself. It is self-awareness, but it is not yet *knowledge* of oneself. The following example beautifully illustrates this point:

> I make the discovery that I am in love. It may be that none of those facts, which I now recognise as proof of my love, passed unnoticed by me; neither the quickened drive of my present towards my future, nor that emotion which left me speechless, nor my impatience for the arrival of the day we were to meet. Nevertheless I had not seen the thing as a whole, or if I had, I did not realise that it was a matter of so important a feeling, for I now discover that I can no longer conceive my life without this love ... Yet it is always impossible to pretend that I always knew what I now know, and to see as existing, during the months which have elapsed, a self-knowledge which I have only just come by ... I was not unaware of [my love] since it was I who endured the hours of boredom preceding a meeting, and who felt elation when she approached [but] it was lived, not known, from start to finish.
>
> (Merleau-Ponty 1945: 436; 1962: 380–81; 2002: 442–3)

One is aware of one's love as it manifests in one's situation – one lives through the situation. But one has not identified the loving form of one's situation. In other words, one has not thematised one's love; one has not categorised it as love.

One achieves self-knowledge when one correctly thematises or categorises aspects of one's mental life. To do this is to perform an act – it is to *think* about one's mental life. As we have seen, Merleau-Ponty holds that thoughts are constituted by their expression. Self-knowledge must thus be expressed. Like other types of thought, it can be expressed in a number of ways. It is perhaps most commonly expressed in language – talking aloud, writing and silent speech. Merleau-Ponty describes this as 'a consciousness of myself which makes use of language and is humming with words' (1945: 459; 1962: 400; 2002: 466). Merleau-Ponty agrees with Descartes that self-knowledge is first-personal and epistemically privileged – it's not clear that something would count as self-knowledge if it did not satisfy these two conditions. On his account, self-knowledge is first-personal because it is based on the subject's awareness of their situation, and this is an awareness that only they can have. Others can perceive my situation – my friend can observe my behaviour and see the demands for action that my situation makes on me, but he is not aware of my situation in the same ways that I am. The subject's special awareness of their situation gives them a certain amount of privileged insight into it. The lover is the one who perceives their beloved as beautiful and requiring loving behaviour. But the beloved does not show up this way to someone who merely observes the lover. The lover is the one who feels elation when their beloved arrives – the surge of adrenalin, their heart beating faster, their cheeks growing hot as they blush. Another person can see that someone feels elated – they can see the subject's smile, the way their eyes appear shinier, the reddening of their cheeks, and so on – but the subject is better placed than an observer to notice their elation.

But self-knowledge is not indubitable on Merleau-Ponty's account. There are various reasons why this is so. Self-knowledge involves categorising or thematising one's mental life in an act of thought. The subject's thought may go wrong because they simply fail to *notice* aspects of their experience. Just as someone may see a red car parked outside their house, but fail to notice that they have seen it, so too the subject may be, for example, adverbially aware of behaving lovingly towards someone without noticing that they have acted in this way. The subject may also refuse to acknowledge certain aspects of their situation. Imagine, for example, that I am writing a paper and copy a section from someone else's work. I am adverbially aware of copying, but I may not acknowledge that fact when I describe what I am doing because I do not want to acknowledge that I am plagiarising another's work. Similarly, Linda may refuse to acknowledge that she believes that dogs are dangerous. She is adverbially aware of her fearful interactions with them and is conscious of perceiving them as scary, but she refuses to categorise this aspect of her situation as the belief that dogs are dangerous in an act of thought. In some cases, categorising an aspect of one's situation requires one to have a perspective on it, which is difficult to achieve when one is immersed in it. I may, for example, experience an argument with my parents as serious. At the time I am unable to tell whether it is the start of a deep rift or merely a storm in a teacup. Someone else may be better placed than me to judge that it is of little importance. Correctly categorising one's situation may also require one to see how it unfolds over time. Merleau-Ponty's favourite example of love aptly illustrates this. It is only looking back on the course one's life has taken that one is able to see whether or not one is, or has been, in love.

The very fact that one is trying to categorise one's mental life using words may also introduce error and imprecision. The words one has at one's disposal may not accurately capture what one is trying to describe. Consider a swimming student who is preparing to dive into the pool. His action takes time to perform. He lifts his arms above his head, puts his chin down, looks at the water, and pushes off the edge of the pool. He is adverbially aware of his actions as he performs them. He also perceives his surroundings as demanding certain movements from him – for example, the water appears as for-diving-into and this guides his action as he performs it. Although the student's movements are guided by his perception of his surroundings, together with his thoughts about the instructions his teacher has given him, these things do not completely determine which movements he will perform. Nothing determines this. His perception of what he will do may thus be indeterminate – he sees that he will enter the pool head first, but he does not see exactly how his legs will move to enable him to do this. Furthermore, the student's action may or may not be successful. Suppose that the student describes his action on the basis of his awareness of it as it unfolds. He may say that he is diving into the pool. But describing his action in this way anticipates that he will complete it successfully. He may not do so, in which case his thought about his action will turn out to be incorrect. His awareness of his action, in other words, does not provide him with infallible *knowledge* of it. Moreover, another person might be better placed than he to know his actions. His swimming coach, for example, might be able to tell in advance whether the student's attempt to dive into the pool will be successful or whether he will enter the water belly-first.

Similar points apply in the case of thoughts. We can distinguish between episodes of thinking, on the one hand, and the thoughts that result from them, on the other. Merleau-Ponty holds that thinking is constituted by bodily activities. It follows that the subject's awareness of their thinking has an adverbial structure: they are aware in thinking or they consciously think. Their perception of their surroundings will give them a sense of where their action is heading. Suppose, for example, that the subject is constructing a mathematical proof. Their activity is guided by their perception of the situation. They see the proof as requiring them to complete it in a certain way. Their perception of it provides them with a sense of what they will do before they do it. However, their perception of how the proof should be completed may be indeterminate and ambiguous. Thus they may only have a vague sense of how their activity will proceed. Their awareness of constructing the proof will also involve an awareness of the proof constructed. Their awareness of the lines they draw is bound up with their awareness *in* drawing them. If the subject describes what they are doing and its results, their description may go wrong for the same sorts of reasons as those listed above. They may not notice aspects of their activity. They may refuse to acknowledge aspects of what they are doing. Their awareness does not allow them to know exactly what they will do – and what they will produce – in advance. It is only after they have finished that their thinking and their thought will be completely available to them. The words they use to describe them may misrepresent the character of their activity.

Finally, it is worth noting that sometimes the products of one's thinking will be public items – paintings, spoken utterances, written notes, physical gestures and so on. These things can be detected using one's senses, thus one can be perceptually aware of one's thoughts. In cases where one knows one's thoughts on this basis, one's knowledge will not be first-personal. This is because others can be perceptually aware of one's thoughts, and so come to know them in the same way.

CONCLUSION

Descartes conceives of the mind as an inner realm, populated by one's mental states and activities. Merleau-Ponty seeks to provide an alternative by reconceiving the mind as essentially embodied. He sees Descartes's view as linked to a conception of intentionality as representation. Intentional states are of or about the world in virtue of representing it. These mental representations are what populate the Cartesian interior. To overthrow the Cartesian picture, Merleau-Ponty must provide an account of the mind's intentional directedness at the world that does not commit him to inner items. Merleau-Ponty does this in the case of thought by arguing that thought is performed or constituted by its expression, and the expression of thought is a bodily activity. On this account, only embodied beings can think. The results of thought are not inner items. They are public things, such as paintings, books, utterances and so on. Or they are imagined utterances, which must be thought of as subjective elements of the world. Merleau-Ponty's account of thought as expression implies a further thesis concerning how expressions gain their meanings. Expressions are not merely associated with independently existing meanings. Instead, the two are internally related. He offers two ways to cash out this basic claim. His first proposal is that, given the nature of our bodies, we cannot help but find (some) expressions meaningful. His second proposal is that meaningful expressions arise spontaneously out of meaningful situations. The subject's situation draws forth a meaningful expression from them, which others can comprehend in virtue of their sharing a way of life.

Merleau-Ponty then offers an alternative account of self-knowledge. The subject's knowledge of their own mental life consists in thoughts about it. Their self-knowledge is based on their awareness of their mental life, as it is manifest in their situation. Their experience of their situation is first-personal. As the subject of their situation – the one who acts and who perceives the world in the light of their projects, thoughts, emotions and so forth – the subject can know more about it than others. However, self-knowledge is not indubitable. The subject may fail to notice aspects of their situation or refuse to acknowledge them. Their immersion in their situation may stand in the way of gaining a clear perspective on it. The words they use to express their self-knowledge might not accurately capture what they try to describe. It follows that, for Merleau-Ponty, the subject is not transparent to themself.

8

TEMPORALITY

The topic of this chapter is Merleau-Ponty's discussion of temporality, that is, time and temporal existence. He aims to provide an account of time. However, he conceives of time as intimately related to subjectivity, and holds that an account of time will shed light on the nature of consciousness. Merleau-Ponty's views on temporality and its connection with consciousness echo ideas found in the work of Husserl and Heidegger – two of his most important influences. He develops his position through close engagement with their views. Merleau-Ponty employs his usual strategy here. He begins by showing that Objective Thought's conception of time must be rejected. Objective Thought views time as a succession of instants. Merleau-Ponty argues that neither an Empiricist nor an Intellectualist reading of this claim is sustainable. Merleau-Ponty then turns to temporal experience to develop his positive view. The resulting account of time construes it as arising from the interaction between the subject and the world.

OBJECTIVE THOUGHT AND TIME

Merleau-Ponty holds that an essential feature of time is that it goes by. For a conception of time to be adequate, it must preserve this feature.

Before criticising Objective Thinking about time, Merleau-Ponty considers a common-sense view of it. 'Common sense' denotes our mundane ways of thinking about things. Merleau-Ponty takes common sense to tend towards Objective Thought. However, it is not identical with it. Objective Thought encompasses a series of theoretical positions that share the basic presumption that the world is composed of determinate entities that stand in external relations to one another. The theories that share this presumption may conflict with one another – Intellectualist theories are incompatible with Empiricist views – but each theory exhibits a high degree of internal consistency. Common sense, on the other hand, is a ragbag collection of ways of thinking about the world. It includes scientific ideas. But it also incorporates myths and superstitions. Moreover, it sometimes dimly acknowledges aspects of experience that are at odds with Objective Thought. Thus the ideas that comprise common sense do not all cohere.

Common sense takes time to be an objective aspect of the world, that is, an aspect of it that does not depend upon the way that it is experienced. It conceives of time as a river. Rivers flow, thus conceiving of time in this way appears to capture its nature as flux, or going by. But, clearly, this is a metaphor. Time is not literally a rushing body of water. Merleau-Ponty argues that this metaphor is 'extremely confused' (1945: 470; 1962: 411; 2002: 477). The first problem is that whilst it is intended to capture an aspect of the world-in-itself, it presupposes a spectator – someone who witnesses the flowing river. To see this, consider how the metaphor is supposed to work. The past is the portion of the river downstream and the future is the portion of the river upstream, nearer to the river's source. But 'downstream' and 'upstream' must be defined in reference to a static point, e.g. a location on the river bank. The present, of course, will be the portion of the river directly in front of this point. If this is then applied to time, it is natural to assume that the point that defines a certain portion of the time as past, another portion as future, and another as present is the point in time that an observer (or observers) are experiencing. It seems plausible to suppose that these observers are conscious beings such as us. What makes October 2008 past, and October 2012 future is the fact that I am experiencing October 2009. Notice, however, that the point in reference to which the past, future, and present are defined cannot be thought of as analogous to the point on the river bank. The place on the bank which serves to define upstream and downstream is not itself part of the flowing river. If one thinks of the vantage point which defines past, present, and future as a location that time flows past, one thereby places the observer outside time. But conscious beings exist *in* time. Thus Merleau-Ponty suggests that to preserve the metaphor, one must think of the observer as being in a boat on the river, carried along by the flow of time. But now the future is downstream in the direction the boat is travelling, whilst the past is upstream in the direction from which the boat has come. Moreover, the past, future and present can no longer be thought of as portions of the river itself, but the landscape through which the observer is carried by the flowing river (Merleau-Ponty 1945: 471; 1962: 412; 2002: 478). Merleau-Ponty concludes that the metaphor is muddled, and cannot help illuminate the nature of time.

Merleau-Ponty goes on to consider Objective Thought's view of time. Objective Thought conceives of the world as reducible to its basic atoms. Since time is part of the world, it is likewise reducible. An atom of time is an instant. Objective Thought thus conceives of time as a succession of instants. There are Empiricist and Intellectualist versions of this thesis. Merleau-Ponty argues that they both face the same two fundamental problems. They cannot account for the passing of time, and they cannot explain how the instants of time are unified – that is, related to one another – to form a single temporal sequence.

Merleau-Ponty first considers Empiricism. The Empiricist takes the succession of instants to be mind-independent. It is an aspect of the world-in-itself. Merleau-Ponty begins by showing that this conception of time cannot account for the fact that time goes by. He offers two arguments for this conclusion. The first appeals to change. It is generally acknowledged that change in the world (for example, a dog's hair changing colour from black to grey) is intimately bound up with the passage of time, although the exact relation between them is debated.[1] Merleau-Ponty does not say how he takes change to be related to the passage of time. But he clearly thinks that the relation between them is such that, if a model of time can accommodate one, then it can account for the other. His strategy is to show that the Empiricist account of time cannot accommodate change, thereby showing that it cannot capture the passage of time. He writes, 'if I consider the world itself, there is simply one indivisible and changeless being in it' (Merleau-Ponty 1945: 470; 1962: 411; 2002: 477).

We can understand him as thinking something like the following. An object undergoes a change when it gains or loses some property. Suppose that a tree has leaves during the Spring at instant 1, but lacks them during the Autumn at instant 2. One might suppose that the tree has undergone change. However, the succession of instants as a whole does not exist *in* time: it *is* time. Thus the succession of instants as a whole must be thought of as existing eternally. It follows that the tree eternally has leaves at instant 1 and eternally lacks them at instant 2. The tree does not undergo any change. The point can be clarified with the following analogy. Imagine a static landscape. The landscape has different properties at different locations, but the properties at each location never alter. Although the parts of the landscape have different properties, it would be incorrect to say that the landscape thereby undergoes change. Merleau-Ponty holds that to think of time as a succession of instants is to conceive of it as analogous to the static landscape. On this view, the space–time world has different properties at different spatio-temporal locations, but these properties always remain the same. It makes no sense to talk about the space–time world as changing.

Merleau-Ponty goes on to suggest that to accommodate any notion of change on this view requires a witness. He writes, 'change presupposes a certain position which I take up and from which I see things in procession before me' (1945: 470; 1962: 411; 2002: 477). The appeal to an observer is problematic because it conflicts with Empiricism's view that time is a dimension of the world-in-itself and so mind-independent. Moreover, there are other serious problems with explaining change by appealing to a witness. Consider the static landscape. Suppose an observer travels through it. As they travel around, they see different properties. One can sensibly talk of them as observing a changing landscape. Similarly, one might argue that, if an observer 'travels through' the space–time world of instants, they will see different properties, and so we can talk about their seeing the space–time world changing. Notice, however, that in neither case does the landscape *itself* change. The only change consists of alterations in the observer's relation to the world. This notion of change seems inadequate. Many philosophers, for example Geach (1969), have argued that real change must involve alteration in a thing's intrinsic properties, not merely its relational properties. Furthermore, the appeal to an observer who 'travels around' the instants of the space–time world is illegitimate. Who might this observer be? The obvious candidate is a conscious human being, or perhaps a conscious being of a different species such as an ape or dog. But humans, apes and dogs exist in time. This means that such a creature cannot travel around the instants in the same way that they can travel around the static landscape. Instead, the creature will be 'spread across' the instants that fall within their lifespan. For every instant of their life, the time-slice of the world at that instant will contain a time-slice of the creature. For a creature to 'travel through' the instants, they would have to exist outside time. Such a creature would not be bound by the laws of nature. The existence of a supernatural creature like this is ruled out by Empiricism, which considers all that exists to be physical entities that obey the laws of nature.

The second problem that Merleau-Ponty identifies with the Empiricist conception of time as a mind-independent succession of instants is related to the first. On this picture, time's going by involves the successive passage of instants from the future into the present, and then into the past. But there is no way to account for this on the view of time as a mind-independent succession of instants. To account for the passage of instants from the future to the past requires a reference point that moves relative to the instants – a bit like a sliding pointer on a scale. The most plausible candidate for the reference point is the location of a spectator. One naturally assumes that the instant the spectator is experiencing is the present, whilst those that come before it in the sequence are past, and those instants that come after it are the future. As before, introducing a spectator conflicts with Empiricism's view that time is mind-independent. Also, to effect the *passage* of instants from the future to the past requires the spectator to 'move around' the instants. But, as we saw above, conscious beings such as humans exist in time, which means that they are 'spread across' the instants – there is a time-slice of me at every instant of my life – they do not move through them. To explain the passage of time, one would have to posit a supernatural creature, which conflicts with the basic tenets of Empiricism.[2]

Finally, Merleau-Ponty argues that the view of time as a mind-independent succession of instants cannot explain how the instants are unified as a single temporal sequence. The view is thus self-defeating. For the instants to be unified as a succession or sequence, they must stand in certain relations to one another. Each instant must come earlier than certain instants and later than others, and it must have a unique place in the sequence. The problem is that the relations between the instants are temporal. To make sense of temporal relations requires one to make sense of time. Since the notion of time as a succession of instants is inadequate as a conception of time, it provides no way to make sense of temporal relations. A way to flesh out this point is to consider how one might try to make sense of the relations 'earlier than' and 'later than'. One way to do this is to think of the instants as next to each other. Or one might think of some as to the right and some to the left of others. Or one might think of some as in front and some behind others. But all of these are *spatial* notions. To think of the sequence in this way is not to conceive of it as a temporal succession. Without a conception of time, one is unable to make sense of the instants as being temporally related. Thus one is left with a collection of instants that have no temporal order. As Merleau-Ponty remarks, 'these instances of "now", not being present to anybody, have no temporal character and could not occur in sequence' (1945: 471;1962: 412; 2002: 479). One cannot explain how the instants of time are unified as a succession on the Empiricist view.

Merleau-Ponty then considers the Intellectualist view of time. We have seen that Merleau-Ponty takes Intellectualism to recognise and try to remedy the problems faced by Empiricism by appealing to a constituting consciousness. However, Intellectualism is doomed to fail because it presupposes the same conceptual framework as Empiricism and it is this very conceptual framework that generates the problems that Empiricism faces. Intellectualist thinking about time is no exception. The Intellectualist accepts the view of time as a succession of instants, but recognises that the Empiricist cannot account for time's passing by and the unity of the instants as a temporal sequence. Intellectualism then appeals to a constituting consciousness to try and resolve these difficulties. Intellectualism claims that consciousness determines the temporal order of the instants, thus unifying them as a single temporal sequence. If the subject sorts the instants into a sequence, so bringing about a temporal order, then the subject themself must lie outside that temporal order. The subject must exist outside time. If the subject exists outside time, then they will not be 'spread across' the instants. Thus one might suppose that they can 'travel around' them in the way required to make sense of things changing and the passage of instants from the future into the past. But Merleau-Ponty argues that this view of time is ultimately hopeless.

To give temporal order to the instants, the subject must grasp temporal relations. But if they exist outside time, then, Merleau-Ponty claims, they cannot understand them. One way to cash this out is to consider what is involved in understanding what it is for an event to be happening now, yesterday or tomorrow. The subject experiences events as having a different significance, depending on when they happen. If there is a meeting I must attend, and it is happening now, the meeting has a different significance for my actions than if it is happening tomorrow or if it happened yesterday. If it happened yesterday, then it no longer requires me to attend it. If it is happening tomorrow, then it might require me to do some preparation for it. Whilst, if it is happening now, then it requires that I leave whatever I am doing and go to the place where the meeting is happening. The meeting can only have these differing significances for me if I exist in time.

It follows that if I exist outside of time, the meeting cannot differ in significance in this way and so I will be unable to grasp the differences between 'yesterday', 'tomorrow' and 'now'. To put the point more generally, I will be unable to grasp 'past', 'future' and 'present'. In response, one might argue that the subject only needs to grasp the relations 'earlier than' and 'later than' to determine the temporal order of instants. One option available to Merleau-Ponty is to argue that understanding these relations presupposes a grasp of the past, future and present. At the very least, his opponent must provide some reason for thinking that one could grasp 'earlier than' and 'later than' without under-standing the notions of past, present and future. But, even if this could be done, there is a more worrying problem. A fundamental fact about subjectivity is that it has a temporal existence. Thus a theory that accounts for time by placing the subject outside it must be rejected. Merleau-Ponty's conclusion is that Objective Thought's view of time as a succession of instants cannot be endorsed.

Merleau-Ponty has rejected Objective Thought's conception of time. A new account of temporality is thus required. A basic premise of Merleau-Ponty's philosophy is that our conceptions of things should, where appropriate, be based on observation of them. A new conception of time should therefore be based on observation of it. One observes time by experiencing the temporal order of events that happen in time and the objects that persist through it. It follows that our conception of time should be based on the experience of these events and objects. Observation of anything is the experience of an observer. When describing what one observes, one must acknowledge this fact. The failure of Objective Thought means that one cannot take it for granted that what is personal and subjective in experience can be sifted from information about a world-in-itself. As we saw in Chapter 4, Merleau-Ponty argues that the worldly objects we perceive result from the interaction between subject and world that occurs in perception. I suggested that we should read him as reaching this conclusion on the basis of his observations of the world. Merleau-Ponty draws the same conclusion about time: it results from interaction between the subject and the world. However, he does not base this conclusion on his observations of time. He seems to take it for granted throughout his discussion of temporality. Merleau-Ponty's rejection of Empiricism – which holds that time is a dimension of the world-in-itself – provides some support for his view. But it does not establish it. What Merleau-Ponty has shown is that time cannot be a mind-independent succession of instants. His critique of Empiricism does not show that there is *no* defensible conception of time as mind-independent.

The reasoning behind Merleau-Ponty's claim that time is not mind-independent is summarised in the following passage. He writes,

> Past and future exist only too unmistakeably in the world, they exist in the present, and what being itself lacks in order to be of the temporal order is the not-being of elsewhere, formerly and tomorrow. The objective world is too much of a plenum for there to be time. Past and future withdraw of their own accord from being and move over into subjectivity in search, not of some real support, but, on the contrary, of a possibility of not-being which accords with their nature.
>
> (Merleau-Ponty 1945: 471; 1962: 412; 2002: 478–9)

We can understand these claims in the following way. The past and the future are real. They are not fictitious or imaginary. They are contained amongst that which exists. But they have a peculiar sort of existence. Both the past and the future are *absent* from the present – the past is no longer present, and the future is not yet present. To make sense of something being real yet absent, one must appeal to a perspective, and a perspective is manifest in experience. It follows that time must be dependent on the subject's experience of it in some way. The upshot of these considerations is that, to understand time, one must consider the experience of it. It is to this that Merleau-Ponty now turns.

OBJECTIVE THOUGHT AND THE EXPERIENCE OF TIME

Objective Thought does not just offer conceptions of time itself. It also puts forward accounts of temporal experience. Merleau-Ponty considers and rejects these before offering his own view.

Merleau-Ponty begins by considering the Empiricist thesis that memory constitutes awareness of the past, whilst anticipation constitutes awareness of the future. The bulk of Merleau-Ponty's discussion focuses on memory. The Empiricists who put forward this view conceive of memories as past perceptions which are stored in specific parts of the brain. They claim that if the appropriate nerve pathways are stimulated, the past perception will be 'reactivated' and the subject will have an occurrent memory. Bergson (1991) calls this view the 'box theory'; it conceives of the brain (or rather those parts responsible for storing memories) as rather like a filing cabinet. Merleau-Ponty endorses Bergson's critique of this view. The box theory implies that, just as destroying the drawers in a filing cabinet will damage the specific contents of those drawers, so too damage to specific parts of the brain will result in loss of just those memories stored there. The problem, as Bergson points out, is that this is not borne out by empirical evidence. In cases of amnesia, specific chunks of memory are lost – for example, an amnesiac may be unable to remember some part of their past. If the box theory were correct, we should expect amnesia to involve damage to a very specific part of the brain – the part where those memories are allegedly stored. But this is not the case. Whilst specific parts of the brain are damaged, the damage is more widespread than the box theory leads us to expect. Conversely, in cases of aphasia – loss of linguistic abilities – there is damage to very specific areas of the brain. The box theory therefore predicts that people with aphasia should lose very specific memories, such as how to use specific words or specific groups of words. But again this is not the case. People with Broca's aphasia, for example, are able to understand others' speech fairly well, but speaking themselves takes great effort and they can only produce short phrases. Merleau-Ponty accepts Bergson's conclusion that memories cannot be stored in the brain.

Merleau-Ponty considers Bergson's alternative view to be Intellectualist. Bergson conceives of consciousness as related to the brain, but it is not reducible to or determined by the brain's states and processes. In other words, consciousness enjoys a degree of independence from physical matter. For Bergson, memories are stored in the unconscious, which is a part of consciousness. He claims that memories are activated by the body. Brain injuries damage the capacity to activate memories; they do not destroy the memories themselves. Merleau-Ponty thinks that Bergson's view faces an insurmountable difficulty, which also troubles the Empiricist. The problem is that both try to account for consciousness of the past by appealing to a reactivated perception. But a reactivated perception is a *present* experience. Merleau-Ponty claims that, to be aware of the present experience as a trace of the past, one must recognise it as such. But this requires that one already have a sense of the past. To avoid circularity, this sense of the past cannot be based on memory. Merleau-Ponty gives the analogy of marks on a table (1945: 472; 1962: 413; 2002: 479–80). The marks can be thought of as traces of past events – for example, the letters scored on the table top are traces of the day last year that I carved my initials into the table. The ink stains are traces of the day two years ago when I spilled ink on it. However, to think of these marks on the desk as traces of the past, I must already have a grasp of the past. Without that, they are simply marks the desk carries in the present. It follows that awareness of the past cannot be constituted by memory.

Merleau-Ponty takes an analogous point to apply to the claim that awareness of the future consists in anticipation of future events. There are different conceptions of anticipation. Merleau-Ponty's opponents think of it as the projection into the future of what is or has been perceived. Merleau-Ponty points out that a projected perception is a current experience. For it to constitute awareness of the future, one must recognise it as a projection. But to do so requires that one already have a grasp of the future, which cannot be provided by anticipation.

Merleau-Ponty offers a further diagnosis of the problem. The past is what has been, whilst the future is what is yet to come. They are precisely what is not present. It follows that experience of the past and future is awareness of what is currently *absent*. The account we give of time experience must capture this fact. Appealing to memory and anticipation does not allow us to do this. Consider memory. Merleau-Ponty's opponents take memories to be reactivated past perceptions. When I have a perception,

I experience its object(s) as currently within my perceptual reach. When I see my dog, for example, I experience him as being in front of me at the time that I see him. If this perception is later reactivated as an occurrent memory, it has the same content – I once again experience my dog as being in front of me. Similarly, Merleau-Ponty's opponents take anticipations to be the projection into the future of what one perceives or has perceived. If I anticipate my dog sleeping tomorrow, I project my experience of his sleeping form into the future. Just as my perception of him sleeping presents my dog as being in front of me, so too my anticipation shows him as currently present. Merleau-Ponty thus argues that, for memories and anticipations to provide the subject with an awareness of the past and future, the subject needs some way of recognising that, although they appear to be of things that are present, those things are really absent. The worry is that, to recognise this, the subject must already have a sense of the past and future. They must already experience time.

MERLEAU-PONTY'S ACCOUNT OF TEMPORAL EXPERIENCE

For the subject to have an awareness of the past and future, they must experience them *as* absent. Merleau-Ponty points out that we have already encountered the experience of absence in the horizonal structure of perception. As we saw earlier, the horizonal components of perception are implicit experiences of what is not currently present to the subject. They experience the world around them as extended in space from a particular point of view in space. It follows that parts of the things they see at any one time will be hidden from them. But this does not mean that they see a collection of flat, two-dimensional surfaces. The subject literally sees things around them as spatially extended. It follows that their experiences must present them with the parts of things that are hidden from their gaze. The horizons of perception present them with the hidden parts of things, but they do so *implicitly*. Thus, when I look down on the table, I *explicitly* perceive the table top, whilst *implicitly* perceiving the legs, the surface underneath the table, the ground beneath it, and so on. The horizons present what is currently absent from the subject's gaze. The fact that this is presented *implicitly* allows the subject to experience it *as* currently absent.

Merleau-Ponty then argues that awareness of the past and future also consists in implicit presentations of them. It will help us see what is at stake if we consider an example. Suppose that I am watching a duck race. The competitors each write their name on the side of a plastic duck. The ducks are placed on the river behind a barrier. At the sound of a whistle, the barrier is removed and the ducks float downstream. The first duck to pass a certain point on the river bank wins. The duck race is a temporal object which unfolds over time. In this sense, it is like a melody.[3] It is essential to a melody that it does not occur all at once. If its notes are played at the same time, they no longer constitute a melody. Instead, the notes must be played at appropriate temporal intervals. Similarly, the duck race essentially involves the ducks progressing down the river over a period of time. Now suppose that, when the ducks begin floating down the river, I decide I want a cigarette and rummage in my bag. I then realise I have no lighter and walk over to another smoker to ask them for a light. Having lit my cigarette, I walk back to my seat just in time to see the ducks pass the finishing post. Merleau-Ponty holds that certain implicit aspects of this experience account for its temporal character.

Notice that there are two temporal sequences for which we need to account: the temporal unfolding of my experience, and the temporal unfolding of the duck race.[4] My experience unfolds in the following way: I see the duck race start, rummage inside my bag, walk over to someone to borrow their lighter, walk back to my seat, and see the ducks pass the finishing post. The duck race unfolds as follows: the ducks cluster behind the barrier until it is removed. They then float progressively down the river to the finishing post. To account for these two temporal sequences, my experience must have two implicit dimensions: one that presents the temporal unfolding of my experience, and the other that presents the unfolding of the duck race. Consider the experience I have of the ducks just before they pass the finishing post. I explicitly see the ducks loosely clustered at a certain place on the river. For my experience to give me a sense of the ducks as travelling along the river, it must implicitly present them as having been further upstream a moment earlier and as about to move further downstream a moment later. But a moment earlier, when the ducks were further upstream, I did not see them. I was walking back to my seat after lighting my cigarette. Thus my current experience of the ducks as about to pass the finishing post must implicitly present me as walking back to my seat a moment earlier. Likewise my experience of the ducks as they begin the race must involve the explicit experience of the ducks grouped together at a certain point on the river. It must implicitly present both the ducks as about to move further downstream and me as about to rummage in my bag. The implicit presentation of what is to come – both the course of my experience, and the unfolding of a temporal event – may be indeterminate and ambiguous. I may simply experience in broad outline how things will unfold. Similarly, the more remote the past, the more ambiguous its implicit presentation.

The notion of a horizon can be extended to cover the implicit presentation of previous and future stages of an unfolding temporal object. Horizons implicitly present those spatial parts of things that are currently hidden from my gaze. By implicitly presenting me with the hidden parts of the things I see, the horizons of my experience implicitly present me with what the things I see look like from elsewhere. When I look at the table from above, for example, I explicitly see the table top and implicitly see what it looks like from underneath. This horizon therefore presents me with what the table looks like if viewed from below. In this way, the horizons refer to other possible experiences one could have of the things one sees – the experiences one could have of them from other spatial locations. The implicit presentation of previous and future stages of an unfolding temporal object are effectively references to experiences of that object that one could have from a different point in time. The implicit presentation of the ducks as further upstream refers to an explicit experience one could have had of the ducks a moment earlier, whilst the implicit presentation of the ducks as further downstream refers to an explicit experience one can have of the ducks a moment later. Thus one can understand a horizon as implicitly presenting different spatial and temporal views of what one currently sees. *Some* of these views may coincide with the actual course of one's experience, but they need not.

The last sort of implicit content tracks the *actual* course of one's experience. One is implicitly aware what one has experienced and what one is about to experience. Husserl introduces the terms 'retention' and 'protention' respectively, to refer to this sort of implicit content. Retentions are supposed to literally be retentions of previous experiences, and protentions are anticipations of future experiences. But, like the horizons, they are part of the structure of current experience. We can see from this account that the protentions and retentions are a subset of the horizons. Protentions and retentions thus differ from memories and anticipations of the sort discussed earlier. Every perception contains retentions and protentions as part of its very structure. They are components of perception itself. Memories and anticipations, on the other hand, are not components of perceptual experience. They are different kinds of psychological state. The retentions and protentions of experience link one's perceptions together as part of a unified sequence. Consider the experience of an unfolding temporal event such as a marble rolling down a hill. Each momentary perception explicitly presents one stage in the event – the position of the marble. The experience includes protentions, which implicitly present the positions to which the marble will move. It also includes retentions, which implicitly present the marble's previous positions. The next experience will *explicitly* present the marble's new position, thereby satisfying the protention of the previous experience that presented this location *implicitly*. The new experience's retention will include an implicit presentation of what was explicitly presented by the previous experience. In this way, the experiences are linked together as a unified sequence.

Together, the forms of implicit content give me a sense that my temporally unfolding existence – my path through, and interactions with, my surroundings – takes place in a world of things and events that are spatially and temporally extended and temporally unfolding.

Merleau-Ponty then considers an objection to his account. As he has developed it so far, awareness of a temporally unfolding event consists in a succession of experiences. Each experience is of a stage in the event. In other words, the consciousness of an unfolding event takes the form of an unfolding stream of experiences. The stream of experiences is itself an event that unfolds in time. Each momentary experience is a stage in this event – just as each position of the ducks on the river is a stage in the event that is the duck race. Since an unconscious experience is impossible, it follows that to experience the unfolding duck race, one must be aware of one's experience of it. But now there seems to be a problem. Just as the experience of the unfolding duck race consists in an unfolding sequence of experiences, so too, it seems, the awareness of this experience must consist in a *further* sequence of experiences. Moreover, since experience essentially involves awareness of experience, the subject must also be aware of this further sequence of experiences. Again, it is a temporally unfolding event. Thus awareness of it must consist in yet another unfolding succession of experiences. Clearly, this leads to an infinite regress which makes experience of an unfolding event impossible.

Merleau-Ponty's response to this worry is twofold. First, he denies that awareness of a temporally unfolding event consists in a succession of experiences. He writes, 'There is, then, not a multiplicity of linked phenomena, but one single phenomenon of running-off' (1945: 479; 1962: 419; 2002: 487). The experience of an unfolding event such as the duck race is not composed of separate experiences, linked together by their interlocking protentions and retentions. It is a single, continuous experience. The question is how best to capture this. Merleau-Ponty considers a suggestion from Bergson (1991). Bergson claims that, in our experience, the passage from one instant of time to the next is imperceptible. Thus suppose that at one instant the ducks are at location 11 on the river. At the next instant they are at 12. Bergson suggests that when one experiences the duck race, the ducks' movement from 11 to 12 is imperceptible. Merleau-Ponty objects that this 'amounts to denying time altogether' (1945: 481; 1962: 420; 2002: 488). His argument is this. Consider two experienced instants of time – A and B. To claim that the passage from A to B is imperceptible is to claim that A and B are indistinguishable. But if A and B are indistinguishable, then they must be the same experienced instant – call it C. Now consider C and another experienced instant of time – D. If C and D are indistinguishable, then they are the same experienced instant. The same holds for all instants of time. Thus, on this view, there is only one experienced instant. But the experience of time cannot consist in the experience of a single instant. It follows that Bergson's proposal must be rejected. However, it is not clear that this argument goes through. Merleau-Ponty equates the claim that the passage between two experienced instants is *imperceptible* with the claim that the instants are *indistinguishable*. But this is analogous to arguing that since the transition from hairy to bald happens in imperceptible increments (removing a single hair does not render the hairy person bald), being bald and being hairy are indistinguishable. This is clearly false.

Nevertheless, there is another problem with Bergson's view of temporal experience. If the passage from one instant of time to the next is imperceptible, then it will be impossible to experience motion or transition from one state to the next. Consider, for example, the duck race. If the movement of the ducks from 11 to 12 is imperceptible, then it is unclear how one could experience the ducks *moving* down the river. The same holds more generally for any temporal event. If the passage from one stage in the event to the next is imperceptible, then it is not clear how one could perceive the event unfolding. Since we do experience transitions, Bergson's view must be rejected.

Merleau-Ponty then offers an alternative, which deepens the analysis of time-consciousness that he has given. He has so far claimed that it consists in a series of experiences, each of which has protentions and retentions that unify the experiences as a sequence. However, the structure of temporal experience is more complex than this. A retention is literally a retained experience. The experience will thus have its own retentions. Each retention is itself a retained experience with its own retentions, and so on. It follows that each experience contains a nested series of retentions that encapsulate the whole of past experience. The same is true for the protentions. A protention is a projected experience. The experience has its own protentions. Each protention is itself a projected experience with its own protentions, and so on. Thus each experience contains a nested series of protentions that encapsulates the whole of future experience. Merleau-Ponty notes,

> This amounts to saying that each present reasserts the presence of the whole past which it supplants, and anticipates that of all that is to come ... there is one single time which is self-confirmatory, which can bring nothing into existence unless it has already laid that thing's foundations as present and eventual past, and which establishes itself at a stroke.
>
> (Merleau-Ponty 1945: 481; 1962: 421; 2002: 489)

On this analysis, the whole of time is compressed into each experienced instant of it. Merleau-Ponty then suggests that the experience of time, that is, of temporally unfolding events, does not consist in a series of linked experiences. Instead, one has a single experience of an ever-changing present, where what was implicit (the protentions) gradually becomes explicit, and what was explicit gradually becomes implicit (the retentions). This is what Merleau-Ponty, following Husserl, calls 'the living present' (1945: 495; 1962: 433; 2002: 503).

Second, the objection claims that, since the experience of a temporally unfolding event consists in a succession of experiences – which is itself a temporally unfolding event – *awareness* of one's experience must consist in a further sequence of experiences. The objection thus assumes that to be aware of one's experience is for that experience to be the object of a further act of awareness. It assumes, in other words, that awareness of one's own experience conforms to the act-object model. Merleau-Ponty has already rejected that picture. It is bound up with the Cartesian view of the mind as a private, interior realm, populated by one's own mental goings-on. Merleau-Ponty takes this view of the mind to be untenable. His alternative account takes consciousness of one's own experiences to have an adverbial structure. To be conscious of one's own perceptions is to consciously perceive, where 'consciously' denotes the way in which one perceives. It follows on this view that to be aware of one's experience of an unfolding temporal event, such as the duck race, is to consciously perceive that event. Since, for Merleau-Ponty, all perception is essentially conscious perception, to *consciously* perceive the duck race is simply to perceive it. It follows that to be aware of my own temporally unfolding experience is simply to be aware of the temporally unfolding world. Merleau-Ponty writes, 'It is by communicating with the world that we communicate beyond all doubt with ourselves. We hold time in its entirety, and we are present to ourselves because we are present to the world' (1945: 485; 1962: 424; 2002: 493).

Merleau-Ponty has provided an account of the structure of temporal experience. But he is not yet ready to develop a conception of time. His earlier investigation into subjectivity hinted at an intimate connection between time and consciousness. Since time is in some way dependent on the subject, and it is the nature of this dependence that we want to understand, we need to grasp the manner in which it is related to subjectivity. Thus we need to examine the temporal nature of subjectivity.

THE TEMPORAL NATURE OF SUBJECTIVITY

Merleau-Ponty holds that subjectivity is essentially temporal – that is, it essentially exists within time. The basis for his claim is twofold. First, the failure of Intellectualism to account for various phenomena means that its conception of consciousness must be rejected. Intellectualism conceives of consciousness as a Transcendental Ego – a non-physical, atemporal entity that lies outside the world. The difficulties faced by Intellectualism mean that the subject cannot be thought of as a Transcendental Ego, and so it cannot be thought of as atemporal. A new conception of subjectivity must be developed, based on the way that consciousness is revealed to us in experience. Each of us experiences our own existence as temporal. Retentions and protentions of my experience implicitly present me with its past and coming phases. In addition, I remember past events in my life and anticipate future ones. Each of us is born and then, sometime later, dies. Experience thus provides a conception of subjectivity as existing within time. Second, subjectivity is characterised by intentionality, and intentionality is essentially temporal. Intentionality is the feature of 'of-ness' or 'about-ness'. It is the feature of being directed at the world. On Merleau-Ponty's account, the fundamental form of intentionality is motor intentionality. Thus consciousness is intentionally related to the world via *activity*. Activity necessarily takes place over time. There cannot be instantaneous activity. It follows that the most fundamental sort of intentional relation is not one that can happen in an instant. It necessarily has a certain duration. Since subjectivity is characterised by intentionality, and being intentionally related to the world takes time, the subject essentially exists within time.

Subjectivity is essentially temporal. But what is it for consciousness to exist over time? Before considering Merleau-Ponty's response to this question, we need to say a little more about what is at stake. To say that an entity of any sort exists over time is to say that the entity exists at time t1, the same entity exists later at time t2, and it exists at all times between t1 and t2. Clearly, this raises the question of what it is for an entity to be the same at different times. 'The same' has two different meanings. On the one hand, it can mean having the same characteristics or properties. If an entity at time t1 has the same characteristics as an entity at time t2, then they are *qualitatively* identical. On the other hand, 'the same' can mean being one and the same thing. If an entity at time t1 is one and the same as the entity at time t2, then they are *numerically* identical. There can be qualitative identity without numerical identity. Identical twins, for example, have the same properties, but they are not one and the same person – there are two of them. Conversely, the characteristics I have as an adult are very different from those I had as a baby, but the baby and I are one and the same person. It is numerical identity that concerns us here. To say that an entity exists at time t1 and then the same entity exists at time t2 is to say that the first entity is numerically identical with the second. It is to say that one and the same entity exists at both times. To ask what it is for consciousness to exist over time is thus to ask what it is for one and the same subject to exist at different times. It is to ask what determines the subject's identity over time.

We are interested in what it is for consciousness to have a temporal existence. In the case of people, two different senses of 'existence' can be distinguished. In one sense, my existence simply refers to the fact that I am. It is this sense of existence that is at stake in, for example, the claim that Atlantis never existed. To exist in this sense is to be amongst the things that there are in the world. The second sense in which one might talk about a person's existence refers to their life – the events that befall them, the projects they choose to undertake, their relationships with others, etc. It is this sense that is involved in a sentence such as 'he eked out a meagre existence'. The sentence means that his life was impoverished, lacking in comfort, etc. One might suppose that the two senses in which one may talk about my existence can be held apart, so that one can consider what it is for me to exist (that is, for me to be amongst the things contained in the world) without talking about the things that I do and that befall me during the course of my life. The question of what it is for me to retain my identity over time asks what it is for me to be amongst the things contained in the world for a certain length of time. If one thinks that the fact that I exist can be held apart from considerations about the events that make up my life, then one will think that the issue of my identity over time is separate from questions concerning the episodes that make up my life.

Merleau-Ponty denies that the two senses of existence can be pulled apart in this way. On his view, for a person to exist in the first sense is inextricably bound up with their existence in the second sense, that is, with the episodes that constitute their life. Consequently, he takes a person's identity over time to be inextricably linked to the episodes of their life. We can understand him in the following way. What it is for an entity to retain its identity over time is dependent on the sort of entity it is. A parrot at time t1 cannot be numerically identical with a car at time t2, because a parrot is not the sort of thing that can be numerically identical with a car, and vice versa. It follows that any account of what it is for consciousness to exist over time must involve a conception of the sort of thing consciousness is. On Merleau-Ponty's account, consciousness is being-in-the-world. Part of what this means is that the subject is essentially an embodied entity – a conscious body. But this is not all there is to the idea of consciousness as being-in-the-world. On this view of consciousness, the subject is also essentially embedded in their environment. As we have seen, a subject is something that is intentionally related to the world. Intentionality is manifest in activity. Activity essentially takes place in the world – it is impossible to act without a setting in which one's actions take place. It follows that a subject is something that is essentially situated in the world. If we consider the subject as they exist within time, it is clear that their temporal stages must include their situations. Thus the temporal stage of me at 9 o'clock this morning, for example, includes my tea-making situation, since I was making tea at that time. But this means that the subject is to be identified with their existence in the second sense – the life they lead, which is constituted by their activities in their worldly settings.

The upshot of this discussion is that an account of what it is for consciousness to exist within time – that is, to retain its identity over time – will be an account of what it is that unifies the episodes of the subject's life, which we should think of as their temporal stages, as episodes of a single life. Merleau-Ponty considers and rejects two ways in which the episodes of someone's life might be unified. The first option is perhaps the obvious one. One might hold that certain events, activities, and so on, are united as the episodes of a single life by the fact that they all involve the same person. However, the foregoing considerations rule this out. This account presupposes that the subject is distinct from the episodes that constitute their life. It assumes, in other words, that we can consider what it is for the subject to exist in the first sense – to be amongst the things contained in the world – independently from considering the subject's existence, that is, the episodes that constitute their life. But on Merleau-Ponty's account this is not possible. The episodes of the subject's life are the temporal stages of the subject. There is no independent subject whose identity over time can unify certain events, activities and so on as episodes of a single life. The second option is to hold that the episodes of a life are unified in virtue of causal relations obtaining between them. As one might expect,

Merleau-Ponty rejects this option because he holds that the doings of consciousness do not admit of causal explanation.

Merleau-Ponty's alternative view is that the episodes of a life are unified as the life of a single subject by the fact that they cohere. Relations obtain between the phases of a life. We have already seen that the subject's experience over time forms one continuous sequence in virtue of the way that their current experience satisfies previous protentions and contains retentions of their past experience. Experience is not separate from the life of consciousness. It just *is* conscious life. There are other ways in which the episodes of a life cohere. Each stage of a life 'draws together' its past phases. Its character is affected by what has gone before. My past history affects where I am in the world today, and the options available to me. Thus I am in Nottingham working as an academic due (partly) to past choices I made and my past actions. A person's past history encompasses their acquisition of various skills and habits. The skills and habits that they have acquired affect the way the world shows up for them. My repeated interactions with my dog, for example, mean that I perceive him as familiar and lovable. Whether I am jaded and disillusioned or approach my work with enthusiasm may be affected by my past experiences at conferences and as a teacher. Each phase of one's life – the activities one chooses to undertake, the way that one undertakes them, and the manner in which one deals with what the world puts before one – motivates the phases that follow. My perception of my computer as for-finishing-this-chapter motivates my future activity of writing.

But the episodes of a life are not simply related as a series of interlocking phases. They also cohere as parts of a larger whole. Merleau-Ponty holds that one's life has a certain form or, as he often puts it, a 'style'. The shape or style of one's life is manifest by one's past history: it is present in each part of it, and it influences the way that one's life unfolds. To understand this proposal, let us first consider a single activity. An activity does not consist in separate stages that bear no significant relation to one another. Indeed, to call them the stages of an activity already presupposes that they are related as parts of a larger whole – the activity itself. The activity as a whole has a certain form – it is an activity of a certain sort. Let us suppose that it is tea-making activity. The past stages of the activity include filling the kettle, reaching a mug out of the cupboard and placing a teabag in it. These past stages are unified as elements of making tea. The activity's tea-making form is present at each stage of it. It affects the way the world shows up for me, so I perceive the kettle as for-boiling-water, the mug as for-holding-tea, and so on. Finally, the form of my activity influences how it will unfold. The fact that I am engaged in making tea means that I will carry out tea-making actions.

Now consider the activities that I undertake today. They are all related as parts of the larger whole that is my day. My day has a certain shape – it is a certain type of day – a day of work. The fact that it is a work day is manifest in the things I have already done today. The general form of my day is also present in my experience at every moment. It features in the way that my activities appear to me. I experience my morning dog walk as a task to be completed quickly before work begins. I do not experience it as a leisurely activity that I can linger over. I experience my main task – the continued writing of this chapter – as urgent. My lunch with a friend is perceived as a welcome break from work. But I feel the pressure of my urgent work tasks weighing on me over lunch. Once an hour has passed, I feel required to return to writing. The fact that my day is one of work also influences how it will unfold. It affects the activities I undertake and how I undertake them.

Just as my activities are related as parts of the larger whole which is my day, so too my days are related as parts of the larger whole which is my week. My week has a certain form – it is a working week. The shape of my week is manifest by those parts of it that are past. Its shape features in my experience on every day of it. Thus Monday is experienced as the beginning of the week. Tasks are experienced as far more urgent on Monday. Friday, on the other hand, is experienced as almost the weekend. There is a slight air of celebration on Friday. I experience my tasks as less urgent. The form of my week – its character as a working week – influences how it will unfold. It affects what I will do on each day and how I will do it. The fact that it is a working week means that I will work on five days and have the weekend free. My week is also related to other weeks as part of a larger whole – the semester. Again, the shape of the semester influences how the weeks unfold and features in my experience of them. The semester, too, is part of a larger whole: my year. My year is part of a larger whole – my career as an academic, and so forth.

Merleau-Ponty offers a slightly different example, which makes the same point. He uses an example given by Sartre (1958): Proust's (1965) tale of Swann's love for Odette, which he recounts in *Swann's Way*. In this story, Swann falls in love with Odette. But his love later turns to jealousy. Merleau-Ponty reads Proust as suggesting that Swann's love is the *cause* of his jealousy, which then modifies the quality of his love. In his anxiety to ensure that Odette stays true to him, Swann's focus becomes his rival suitors, rather than Odette herself. On Proust's account, Swann's psychological episodes – love, jealousy, modified love – stand in causal relations to one another. Merleau-Ponty rejects this account of their relation. As we have seen, he denies that 'psychic facts' such as these can be explained by appealing to causal laws. Instead, he explains the relation between Swann's love, his jealousy and his modified love in the following way. Swann's love was *always* a jealous sort of love. 'Swann's feeling of pleasure in looking at Odette bore its degeneration within itself, since it was the pleasure of being the only one to do so' (Merleau-Ponty 1945: 486; 1962: 425; 2002: 494). In other words, Swann's love develops in accordance with a form it has right from the outset. Moreover, this is a form that is present to Swann at every stage in his experience of his love, since it is manifest in its character as a jealous sort of love.

Merleau-Ponty proposes that the episodes of one's entire life are related in the same manner. It is important to be clear what Merleau-Ponty is suggesting here. He is *not* claiming that the events of one's life are pre-ordained, so that, from the moment one is born, one is destined to follow a certain path and have certain things befall one. The thought instead is that one's life has a certain flavour or style and unfolds in accordance with it. But a style can be manifest in many different ways, so to claim that the style of one's life guides the way one lives it is not to claim that one's path is set out in detail in advance. Merleau-Ponty writes, 'my world is carried forward by lines of intentionality which trace out in advance at least the style of what is to come' (1945: 476; 1962: 416; 2002: 483). There are many different ways in which, for example, a jealous personality can be expressed. One's jealous nature colours one's engagement with the world and influences the way that one lives one's life, but it does not fully determine in advance the course one's life will take.

Merleau-Ponty's analysis of the temporal existence of subjectivity reveals that the life of consciousness is essentially characterised by the experience of possibilities. He argues that consciousness necessarily exists within time – it necessarily has a temporal existence. For the subject to exist over time is for them to live their life. The episodes of their life should be thought of as their temporal stages. They are unified as a single life – that is, as a single temporal consciousness – by the relations that obtain between them and the way in which they all cohere as parts of a larger whole. Since consciousness is necessarily temporal, the subject must retain their identity over time to be a subject, and they do this in virtue of the manner in which the episodes of their life cohere. The coherence of these episodes involves the experience of possibilities.

We saw earlier that experience has both implicit and explicit aspects. My different experiences cohere in virtue of the relations that obtain between their implicit and explicit aspects. Thus when I hold a stone in my hand, the explicit presentation of the top of the stone is accompanied by an implicit presentation of its hidden surface. If I turn the stone over, I have an explicit perception of its previously hidden surface. The second perception satisfies a horizon of the first, which links my two perceptions. The implicit aspects of perception encompass possibilities. By implicitly presenting what things look like from other places in space or points in time the horizons of perception refer to other possible experiences one could have of those things. Another way in which the episodes of one's life are related to one another is by the relations of motivation that obtain between them. In many cases, for example, my actions are motivated by my perception of my environment as demanding that I perform them. I perceive the kettle as requiring filling, and this initiates and guides my action of filling it. The actions I perceive my environment as demanding are *potential* actions – ones that I *could* perform. The episodes of my life also cohere as parts of a larger whole. My life as a whole has a certain form or style, and its parts cohere by manifesting this style. I experience the general shape of my life in every part of it – the same as Swann's love has a jealous tinge to it at every stage of his relationship with Odette, or the way in which the character of my day is affected by the week of which it is a part. One's life unfolds in accordance with its style or form. Thus one's apprehension of its form is the awareness of the future course of one's life. It is awareness of what has not yet come to pass – what is as yet merely potential.

Merleau-Ponty then claims that living one's life involves converting what is merely potential in one's experience to the actual – for example, by having the experiences referred to by the horizons, by performing the actions one sees one's surroundings as requiring, and by engaging in the behaviour that manifests the form of one's life. He summarises these ideas in the following remark,

> I am not myself a succession of 'psychic' acts, nor for that matter a nuclear I who brings them together into a synthetic unity, but one single experience inseparable from itself, one single 'living cohesion', one single temporality which is engaged, from birth, in making itself progressively explicit, and in confirming that cohesion in each successive present.
>
> (Merleau-Ponty 1945: 466; 1962: 407; 2002: 474)

MERLEAU-PONTY'S ACCOUNT OF TIME

Merleau-Ponty holds that an account of time should explain the special way in which the past and future exist yet are absent. It should also provide a conception of what it is for time to go by. I will consider these in turn.

Merleau-Ponty holds that to make sense of something being real yet absent, one must appeal to a perspective, and a perspective is always manifest in experience. It follows that time, that is, the temporal order of past, present and future, is in some way dependent on the subject's experience of it. As one might expect, Merleau-Ponty identifies the present as what the subject now experiences. In other words, he identifies the present with the experienced present. But some care is needed here. There is an immediate problem with the proposal. The present is picked out by the subject's experience. However, the subject has different experiences at different times – there are many experienced presents, so we need to know which of these is *the* present. The proposal claims that the relevant experience is the one they are having now. In other words, the relevant experience is picked out by the fact that it is present. But since, on this proposal, the present is picked out by an experience of the subject, it follows that it is viciously circular.

The difficulty arises from two assumptions. First, 'the present' and 'now' are synonymous. Second, the subject's experience consists in a succession of experiences. It follows from these assumptions that saying which of these experiences the subject is having *now*, that is, saying which of these experienced presents is *the* present, requires some experience-independent way of identifying the present. Merleau-Ponty rejects both of these assumptions. The second assumption is motivated by the fact that the subject has different experiences at different times. What they experience now varies. One might then infer that there is a series of experienced presents, that is, a succession of experiences. Merleau-Ponty denies the validity of this inference. The fact that what the subject experiences as present is constantly changing does not mean that there is a series of experienced presents or nows. On his account, temporal experience is not constituted by a succession of experiences. It consists in the experience of an ever-changing, living present. There is only one living present. The living present is the now. It follows that there is no problem of picking out one now from many. But the now should be distinguished from the present. The present is the content of the now (that is, of the living present). The content of the now constantly changes, thus what is present constantly changes. Merleau-Ponty can therefore hold that what the subject experiences now is the present, without being faced with the problem of picking out one now from others – there is only one now, so there is no need to identify which now is at stake.

Merleau-Ponty holds that the present is what the subject experiences now. In other words, the present is the content of the living present. However, we need to be more precise about this claim. The living present has a certain structure. Certain things and events are presented explicitly. But the living present also contains a nested series of retentions, which are implicit presentations of what was previously experienced. It also contains a nested series of protentions, which are implicit presentations of what will be experienced. Merleau-Ponty holds that the present is what is experienced explicitly. The nested series of protentions and retentions provide him with a way to account for the manner in which the past and future are both real, yet absent. The implicit presentation of what has been is an experience of it as real, yet absent from the present. The implicit presentation of what is to come is an experience of what is real but absent from the present. Merleau-Ponty thus identifies the past with what is implicitly presented as having been, whilst he identifies the future with what is implicitly presented as what is to come.

One might suppose that this account of the temporal order is too narrow. We intuitively think that there is more to the present than just what one person now experiences. The same is true of the past and future – we think that they encompass more than just what one person previously experienced and will experience. Merleau-Ponty responds to this worry by appealing to the horizonal structure of perception. As we saw in Chapter 4, horizons of my experience implicitly present the world as continuing indefinitely beyond my perceptual reach. In this way, there is a 'world horizon' to my experience. I am implicitly presented with the whole world, although this implicit presentation is so indeterminate and ambiguous that it is simply the presentation of a massive presence. It follows that the present, for Merleau-Ponty, is what is perceived explicitly, together with its horizons that implicitly refer to what is hidden but co-present. My experience does not just contain implicit horizonal references to all that can be experienced at present. My experience has retentions and protentions. The retentions are literally retained experiences. This means that they will likewise have a world horizon. The same is true of the protentions. They are projected experiences, which means that they too will have a world horizon. It follows that my experience contains implicit horizonal references to all that can be experienced in the past and the future.

Merleau-Ponty's analysis now faces a further problem. He claims that the past and future are implicitly presented in my current experience. By experiencing them implicitly, the subject is aware of them as real, yet absent. However, nothing he has said so far explains how some of what one implicitly experiences is experienced as the future, whilst some is experienced as the past. The problem is compounded by the fact that certain implicit aspects of experience present what is spatially distant, but co-present with what the subject explicitly experiences. When I look at my dog lying beside me under a blanket, I explicitly see the top of his head and a little of his back. I am implicitly presented with his hidden parts. But I experience his hidden parts as co-present with the parts of him that I can explicitly see. His hidden parts exist now, even though they are hidden from my gaze. Thus Merleau-Ponty needs to explain how some implicit aspects of experience show what is not present, but either was or will be, whilst other implicit aspects of experience show what is present but hidden.

Merleau-Ponty can explain the difference between the implicit aspects of perception by appealing to what it is to perceive entities as being of certain sorts. Consider first the difference between the implicit aspects of experience that show what is not present and those that show what is present but hidden. It will help us to consider two examples: a dog and a duck-race. A dog is a three-dimensional entity. (Strictly speaking, dogs are four-dimensional because they also exist over time, but we can ignore this for present purposes.) To perceive something as a dog is to perceive it as occupying space in three dimensions. Since one always perceives the world from a particular place, parts of any dog will always be hidden from one's gaze at any one time. To perceive an entity as a dog is thus to perceive it as having parts that are present but hidden. The perception of something as a dog therefore involves apprehending the horizons of one's experience as implicitly presenting parts of the dog that are hidden but co-present. A duck race is a temporal object. It essentially has temporal stages. One cannot experience them all at once. Thus at any one time, certain stages of the duck race will be past and others will be future. To perceive something as a duck race is to perceive it as having different temporal stages that are absent from one's current experience. The perception of something as a duck race therefore involves apprehending the horizons of one's experience as implicitly presenting stages of it that are not present. Now consider the difference between the implicit aspects of experience that present what is past and those that present what is future. The different stages of temporal objects come in a certain order. The order of the temporal stages is integral to the identity of the object. A song such as 'How much is that doggy in the window?' would not be the song it is if its words and notes did not occur in a certain order. Similarly, the duck race would not be a duck race if the ducks did not move in a continuous progression downstream. The perception of something as a certain temporal object – for example, as the song 'How much is that doggy in the window?' – involves the perception of its temporal stages as occurring in a certain order. It thus involves the apprehension of certain horizons as implicitly presenting what has passed and others as implicitly presenting what is yet to come.

One might be puzzled at this point. Earlier, Merleau-Ponty seemed to suggest that one is able to have a perspectival experience of an entity as three-dimensional, rather than seeing it as a collection of flat surfaces, because the horizons of one's experience implicitly present the parts of it that are hidden from one's gaze. Now, however, he seems to be suggesting that one is able to experience the horizons as implicit presentations of parts that are hidden but present because one experiences the entity as a three-dimensional thing seen from a particular point of view. In the former case, the experience of the horizons as implicit presentations of the hidden parts is prior to the experience of the entity as three-dimensional. Whilst in the latter case, the experience of the entity as three-dimensional is prior to the experience of the horizons as implicitly presenting the entity's hidden parts. On this reading, the explanations are inconsistent. In fact, I think the way to read Merleau-Ponty is as holding that neither is prior to the other. Instead, the experience of an entity as three-dimensional and the horizonal presentation of its hidden parts mutually inform one another. We should say the same in the case of a temporal object. Neither the perception of something as a temporal object, nor the implicit presentation of its past and future temporal parts is prior to the other. Instead, they mutually inform each other as part of one's experience as a whole.

An account of time must explain what it is for time to go by. On Merleau-Ponty's account, the present is what is explicitly perceived, with its horizons that refer to other parts of the world that are co-present. The future is what is implicitly perceived as yet to come, whilst the past is what is implicitly perceived as having been. These claims imply a conception of time's going by. What is implicitly presented as the future becomes explicit; what is presented explicitly becomes implicit as it recedes into the past. The passage of time consists in this movement. Merleau-Ponty argues that it is consciousness that effects the passage of time. He writes, 'The passage of one present to the next is not a thing which I conceive, nor do I see it as an onlooker, I effect it' (1945: 481; 1962: 421; 2002: 489). He bases this claim on what he has said about the temporal nature of subjectivity. To be a subject is to exist over time. One retains one's identity over time in virtue of the fact that the episodes of one's life all cohere. Their coherence involves the experience of possibilities. To live one's life is to convert what is potential in one's experience to the actual. One does this by interacting with the world. Some of the possibilities one experiences are horizonal possibilities. One converts these to explicit perceptions through the activity of perceiving, which on Merleau-Ponty's account involves bodily interaction with worldly things. Converting implicit perceptions to explicit ones inevitably goes hand-in-hand with converting explicit perceptions to implicit ones. Thus, through one's activity, the future – what is presented implicitly as yet to come – becomes present and the present becomes past – what is presented implicitly as having been.

Time – the temporal order of past, present and future, and the passage from the future into the past – comes into being through the activity of consciousness. Since to be, for consciousness, is to be engaged in activity, one might say that time is the form taken by conscious existence. The activity of consciousness is essentially interaction with the world. It follows that time comes into being through the interaction between the world and consciousness.

CONCLUSION

Time is not a succession of instants. Nor is it a dimension of being-in-itself. The existence of the past and future as real yet absent can only be explained by appealing to an experiencing consciousness. Merleau-Ponty identifies the present with what the subject now perceives explicitly, together with its horizons that implicitly show what is hidden but co-present. The future is what is implicitly perceived as yet to come, whilst the past is what is implicitly perceived as having been. The passage from the future to the past consists in the conversion of the implicit to the explicit, and the explicit to the implicit. Consciousness effects the passage of time by living its life. Thus time takes shape in the activity of consciousness. It follows that time does not belong to the objective order. (Indeed, Merleau-Ponty denies that there is an in-itself that exists independently from consciousness.) But neither is time fully subjective. Like the world we perceive, time results from the union of subject and world.

Notes

1 Merleau-Ponty's phenomenology

1 Philipse (1995) reads Husserl in this way.
2 The phrase was first coined by Wilson (1959).

2 Traditional prejudices and the return to phenomena

1 For an important early investigation of this phenomenon see Stevens (1935).
2 Köhler (1971) is an English translation of Köhler's (1913) critique of the Constancy Hypothesis, which Merleau-Ponty refers to extensively in this section of PhP.
3 The thesis that single hypotheses cannot be proved or refuted on the basis of evidence, because it is always possible to introduce auxiliary hypotheses to explain recalcitrant data, was put forward by Duhem (1906), and, more recently, by Quine (1951).
4 Quoted by Merleau-Ponty (1945: 16; 1962: 9; 2002: 10).
5 This is, of course, Leibniz's Law.

3 The body

1 There are questions that can be raised about Merleau-Ponty's use of this case, which I do not have space to consider here. Jensen (2009) discusses these issues.
2 Merleau-Ponty attributes the following remark to Schneider, which he takes to be evidence in favour of his interpretation: 'I experience the movements as

being the result of the situation, of the sequence of events themselves; myself and my movements are, so to speak, merely a link in the whole process and I am scarcely aware of my voluntary initiative ... It all happens independently of me' (Merleau-Ponty 1945: 122; 1962: 105; 2002: 120). However, as Jensen (2009) points out, Merleau-Ponty misattributes this remark. It is not Schneider's description of his pathological behaviour, but Goldstein's (1923: 175) description of non-pathological experience. Jensen rightly points out that this misattribution does not affect the conclusions that Merleau-Ponty wants to draw.

3 Noë (2005) also makes this point.

4 The world and its relation to consciousness

1 *Micromégas* is a short story by Voltaire, which describes an alien giant who comes to Earth and is amazed by its apparently minuscule inhabitants. It is sometimes credited with being the first piece of science fiction.

2 The ontological status of universals is debated.

3 He makes this suggestion in an unpublished manuscript.

5 Other selves and the human world

1 See, e.g., Gordon (1995) and Hurley (2005).

6 The mind 1: perception, action and emotion

1 Note that 'intentional' here does not mean 'purposeful'. It means contact that is characterised by intentionality.

2 There is some tension between what Merleau-Ponty says about motor intentionality and the content of perception, and his account of the world's ontological status. This tension may have contributed to his later assessment of the problems he raised in PhP as being 'insoluble' (Merleau-Ponty 1969: 200).

3 My account of this adverbial form of awareness owes much to Moran (2001), who suggests that certain forms of self-knowledge are based on adverbial awareness of the psychological states in question.

4 Of course, Merleau-Ponty allows that action is sometimes brought about by intention. One might wonder whether the intention, in those cases, is an inner item that the agent can introspect. I will address the issue of thought in Chapter 7. For now, I will focus on cases where no intention is involved.

5 Merleau-Ponty uses this term in the detailed table of contents that he included at the end of PhP, but which does not appear in the English translation. The page reference here refers to the French edition.

6 The claim that the Capgras Delusion involves a defective emotional response only partially explains why the subject forms the delusional belief that their relative has been replaced with an imposter. But the rest of the explanation need not concern us here.

7 Plausibly, this is what happens when I grieve for the princess in the film. I see the princess through the eyes of the other characters, and so see her as an object of grief. Seeing her in this way then induces feelings of grief in me.

7 The mind 2: thought

1 See, e.g., Mendes et al. (2008).
2 Merleau-Ponty uses the phrase 'gestural meaning' in two different ways. As well as the use that I have outlined here, he also uses it in connection with his second proposal, which assimilates utterances to physical gestures. Insofar as utterances are gestures, language has a 'gestural meaning'.

8 Temporality

1 For example, Aristotle (2008), Hume (2000) and McTaggart (1927) take this view. Some theorists, e.g. Shoemaker (1969), have tried to show that there can be time without change. I will not discuss this possibility here.
2 These two arguments are reminiscent of McTaggart's (1908) argument for the unreality of time.
3 This example is due to Husserl (1964).
4 This will be the case for experience of all temporal objects.

BIBLIOGRAPHY

Aristotle (2008) *Physics*, trans. R. Waterfield. Oxford: Oxford University Press.

Baldwin, T. (2003) *Maurice Merleau-Ponty: Basic Writings*. London: Routledge.

Bergson, H. (1991) *Matter and Memory*, trans. N. M. Paul and W. S. Palmer. New York: Zone Books.

Berkeley, G. (2004) *An Essay Towards a New Theory of Vision*. Whitefish, MT: Kessinger Publishing Company.

Burnyeat, M. (1982) 'Idealism and Greek philosophy: What Descartes saw and Berkeley missed'. *Philosophical Review* 91, pp. 3–40.

Carman, T. (2008) *Merleau-Ponty*. London: Routledge.

Carroll, L. (2003) *Alice's Adventures in Wonderland and Through the Looking-Glass*. London: Penguin Classics.

Casey, E. (1991) 'The element of voluminousness'. In M. C. Dillon (ed.) *Merleau-Ponty Vivant*. Albany, NY: State University of New York Press, pp. 1–29.

Clark, A. and Chalmers, D. (1998) 'The extended mind'. *Analysis* 58, pp. 10–23.

Cole, J. and Paillard, J. (1995) 'Living without touch and peripheral information about body position and movement: studies with deafferented subjects'. In J. L. Bermúdez, A. Marcel and N. Eilan (eds) *The Body and the Self*. Cambridge, MA: MIT Press, pp. 245–66.

Descartes, R. (1996) *Meditations on First Philosophy*, trans. J. Cottingham. Cambridge: Cambridge University Press.

Dreyfus, H. (2000) 'A Merleau-Pontyian critique of Husserl's and Searle's representationalist accounts of action'. *Proceedings of the Aristotelian Society* 100, 3, pp. 287–302.

Dreyfus, H. and Dreyfus, S. (1999) 'The challenge of Merleau-Ponty's phenomenology of embodiment for cognitive science'. In G. Weiss and H. F. Haber (eds) *Perspectives on Embodiment: The Intersections of Nature and Culture*. New York: Routledge, pp. 103–20.

Duhem, P. (1906) *La théorie physique, son objet et sa structure*. Paris: Chevalier et Rivière.

Ellis, H. and Young, A. (1990) 'Accounting for delusional misidentifications'. *British Journal of Psychiatry* 157, pp. 239–48.

Gardner, S. (2011) 'Merleau-Ponty's transcendental theory of perception'. In M. Sacks, S. Gardner and M. Grist (eds) *The Transcendental Turn*, forthcoming.

Geach, P. (1969) *God and the Problem of the Soul*. London: Routledge.

Goldstein, K. (1923) 'Über die Abhängigkeit der Bewegungen von optischen Vorgängen: Bewegungsstörungen bei Seelenblinden'. *Monatschrift für Psychiatrie und Neurologie*, Festschrift Liepmann.

Goldstein, K. and Gelb, A. (1920) *Psychologische Analysen hirnpathologischer Fälle*. Leipzig: Barth.

Gordon, R. (1995) 'Simulation without introspection or inference from me to you'. In M. Davies and T. Stone (eds) *Mental Simulation*. Oxford: Blackwell, pp. 53–67.

Hamlyn, D. (1957) *The Psychology of Perception*. London: Routledge.

Hammond, M., Howarth, J. and Keat, R. (1991) *Understanding Phenomenology*. Oxford: Blackwell.

Heidegger, M. (1996) *The Principle of Reason*, trans. R. Lilly. Bloomington, IN: Indiana University Press.

Hume, D. (2000) *A Treatise of Human Nature*. Oxford: Oxford University Press.

Hurley, S. (2005) 'Active perception and perceiving action: the shared circuits hypothesis'. In T. Gendler and J. Hawthorne (eds) *Perceptual Experience*. New York: Oxford University Press, pp. 205–59.

Husserl, E. (1964) *The Phenomenology of Internal Time-Consciousness*, trans. J. S. Churchill. Bloomington, IN: Indiana University Press.

——(1970) *Crisis of the European Sciences and Transcendental Phenomenology*, trans. D. Carr. Evanston, IL: Northwestern University Press.

——(1988) *Cartesian Meditations*, trans. D. Cairns. Dordrecht: Kluwer.

Jarvis Thomson, J. (1971) 'A defense of abortion'. *Philosophy and Public Affairs* 1, 1, pp. 47–66.

Jensen, R. T. (2009) 'Motor intentionality and the case of Schneider'. In D. Legrand, T. Grünbaum and J. Krueger (eds) *Dimensions of Bodily Subjectivity*, special edition of *Phenomenology and the Cognitive Sciences* 8, No. 3, pp. 371–88.

Joyce, J. (1939) *Finnegans Wake*. London: Faber and Faber.

Kelly, S. (2001) *The Relevance of Phenomenology to the Philosophy of Language and Mind*. New York: Garland.

Koffka, K. (1928) 'Mental development'. In C. Murchison (ed.) *Psychologies of 1925*. Worcester, MA: Clark University Press, pp. 129–44.

Köhler, W. (1913) 'Über unbermerkte Empfindungen und Urteilstäuschungen'. *Zeitschrift für Psychologie* 66, pp. 51–80.

——(1971) 'On unnoticed sensations and errors in judgement'. In *The Selected Papers of Wolfgang Köhler*. New York: Liverwright Publishing Corporation, pp. 13–39.

Locke, J. (1997) *An Essay Concerning Human Understanding*. London: Penguin Books.

McGinn, M. (1998) 'The real problem of others: Cavell, Merleau-Ponty and Wittgenstein on scepticism about other minds'. *European Journal of Philosophy* 6, pp. 45–58.

McTaggart, J. E. (1908) 'The unreality of time'. *Mind* 17, pp. 457–73.

——(1927) *The Nature of Existence*. Cambridge: Cambridge University Press.

Mendes, J., Ricardo, R., Labidi, S. and Barros, A. (2008) 'Subvocal speech recognition based on EMG signal using independent component analysis and neural network MLP'. *Congress on Image and Signal Processing* 1, pp. 221–4.

Merleau-Ponty, M. (1945) *Phénoménologie de la perception*. Paris: Gallimard.

——(1962) *Phenomenology of Perception*, trans. C. Smith. London: Routledge.

——(1963) *Structure of Behaviour*, trans. A. Fisher. Boston, MA: Beacon Press.

——(1964a) *Signs*, trans. R. McCleary. Evanston, IL: Northwestern University Press.

——(1964b) *Primacy of Perception*, trans. W. Cobb. Evanston, IL: Northwestern University Press.

——(1969) *The Visible and the Invisible*, trans. A. Lingis. Evanston, IL: Northwestern University Press.

——(2002) *Phenomenology of Perception*, trans. C. Smith. London: Routledge.

Moran, R. (2001) *Authority and Estrangement*. Princeton, NJ: Princeton University Press.

Noë, A. (2005) 'Against intellectualism'. *Analysis* 65, 4, pp. 278–90.

Nussbaum, M. C. (1995) 'Objectification'. *Philosophy and Public Affairs* 2, No. 4, pp. 249–91.

Philipse, H. (1995) 'Transcendental Idealism'. In B. Smith and D. W. Smith (eds) *The Cambridge Companion to Husserl*. Cambridge: Cambridge University Press, pp. 239–322.

Priest, S. (2003) *Merleau-Ponty*. London: Routledge.

Proust, M. (1965) *Swann's Way*, trans. C. K. Scott-Moncrieff. London: McGraw-Hill Higher Education.

Quine, W. V. (1951) 'Two dogmas of Empiricism'. *The Philosophical Review* 60, pp. 20–43.

Ramachandran, V. S. and Blakeslee, S. (1998) *Phantoms in the Brain*. London: HarperCollins.

Rizzolatti, G., Fadiga, L., Gallese, L. and Fogassi, L. (1995) 'Premotor cortex and the recognition of motor actions'. *Cognitive Brain Research* 3, pp. 131–41.

Rizzolatti, G., Fadiga, L., Matelli, M., Bettinardi, V., Paulesu, E., Perani, D. and Fazio, F. (1996) 'Localization of grasp representations in humans by positron emission tomography: 1. Observation versus execution'. *Experimental Brain Research* 111, pp. 246–52.

Ryle, G. (1949) *The Concept of Mind*. Chicago, IL: University of Chicago Press.

Sacks, O. (1996) *Awakenings*. London: Gerald Duckworth & Co. Ltd.

Sartre, J. P. (1958) *Being and Nothingness*, trans. H. E. Barnes. London: Routledge.

——(1972) *Psychology of Imagination*. London: Routledge.

Shoemaker, S. (1969) 'Time without change'. *Journal of Philosophy* 66, pp. 363–81.

Stein, E. (1922) 'Beiträge zur philosophischen Begründung der Psychologie und der Geisteswissenschaften, Zweite Abhandlung'. *Jahrbuch für Philosophie und phänomenologische Forschung* 5, pp. 1–283.

Stein, J. (1928) 'Über die Veränderung der Sinnesleistungen und die Entstehung von Trugwahrnehmungen'. In O. Bumke, Bd. I, Allegemeiner Teil I (eds) *Pathologie der Wahrnehmung, Handbuch der Geisteskrankheiten*. Berlin: Springer, pp. 352–426.

Stevens, S. S. (1935) 'The relation of pitch to intensity'. *Journal of the Acoustical Society of America* 6, pp. 150–54.

Wilson, N. (1959) 'Substances without substrata'. *The Review of Metaphysics* XII/4, 48, pp. 521–39.

Wrathall, M. (2007) 'The phenomenology of social rules'. In T. Baldwin (ed.) *Reading Merleau-Ponty*. London: Routledge, pp. 70–86.

INDEX